The Dreaming Way

COURTING THE WISDOM OF DREAMS

TOKO-PA TURNER

HER OWN ROOM PRESS

ISBN: 978-1-7751112-2-1 (Paperback)

ISBN: 978-1-7751112-3-8 (Ebook)

Library and Archives of Canada

Edited by Terri Kempton

Front cover and interior illustrations by Tjitske Kamphuis

Interior book design by Toko-pa Turner

First paperback edition: September 20, 2024

Her Own Room Press, Canada

www.toko-pa.com

Praise for Toko-pa Turner

"**This is a truly wonderful, wisdom-filled book.** Toko-pa Turner has fulfilled her mission of bringing dreaming back to the people who, in our rational culture, have been deprived of its blessing. She puts us in touch with a forgotten friend and teacher called Wisdom, once known to shamans of every culture. The book is exquisitely written, illustrated by remarkable and revelatory dreams. I cannot recommend it more highly for its beauty, its poetry, and its many gifts." — **Anne Baring** Ph.D., author of *The Dream of the Cosmos*

"**In Toko-pa Turner's brilliant new map to animist dreamwork, metaphor is the mythic mycorrhizal system linking us to the more-than-human Wisdom.** Toko-pa upends the idea that dreams are possessions intended for our personal optimization. She repaints dreaming as an ecology of psyches spanning species and ideologies. In a time of division and collapse, our ability to dream is vital to our survival. With intellectual rigor and spiritual generosity, Toko-pa shows us that this new dreamwork will not be solitary work. It will be ecological and profoundly relational. " — **Sophie Strand**, author of *The Body Is a Doorway*

"Toko-pa Turner takes us into the living landscape of our dreaming self. **She reconnects us to our nighttime twin, which has the guidance and wisdom we so desperately need if we are to heal our broken world.** Allow her words to return you to this numinous, symbolic realm and its patterns of connection that can nourish us in hidden ways, where the Earth and our own body sing together." — **Llewellyn Vaughan-Lee**, Ph.D., author of *Sufism: The Transformation of the Heart.*

"This gentle and lovely book is so necessary in our increasingly frantic culture. It offers a vision of reality that is far deeper and more enlivening than what we find in popular culture, and gives us practical methods to bring that vision to bear on our immediate experience. Beautifully presented and explained as the common birthright of every person on the planet, Toko-pa shows us that imagining and dreaming are fundamentally communal, social and transpersonal events. *The Dreaming Way* **is the groundwork for a social theory of imagination that can be practiced by all of us. It's an utterly essential lesson for the rebirth of societies everywhere.**" — **Tom Cheetham**, author of *Imaginal Love*

"*The Dreaming Way* is about so much more than our dreams—it is about restoring our belonging, connecting to unseen wisdom, and letting nature guide us so we can move through the world more awake, more *alive*. Toko-pa stunningly weaves her depth of understanding with her reverence for the Mystery to guide readers in cultivating a living, breathing relationship with *The Dreaming Way*. Blending the mythical with the tangible, the ineffable with the practical, *The Dreaming Way* **is the most profound, illuminating, and supportive book on dreaming I've ever come across.**"— **Lisa Oliviera**, author of *Already Enough*

"**Toko-pa is a great gift to this beleaguered world.** I've often had tremendous difficulty interpreting my dreams and nightmares. I intuitively knew there was something there for me, but they felt too symbolic, too other-worldly. Never the twain shall meet. This book is shifting that. I feel seen, invited and emboldened to find the bridge between worlds. **I'm not sure I have ever read a book with this much wisdom.** Read it, sit with it, allow it to bring you home to all that is."— **Jeff Brown**, author of *Grounded Spirituality*

"Life is difficult but do we know that we are provided by nature with autonomous systems of guidance? Among them are our feeling function, our energy flow, and, ironically, our symptoms. But perhaps most of all, our dreams continue to monitor our lives, and offer the perspective of what Jung called the two million year old soul within us. ***The Dreaming Way* explores the gift of dreaming in a helpful and articulate way which proves instructive toward a more thoughtful conduct of life."** — **James Hollis,** PhD, Jungian Analyst and author of *The Middle Passage: From Misery to Meaning in Midlife*

For my dear grandparents
Irena and Tadeusz
whose dreams gave rise to mine

Table of Contents

Preface

People sometimes ask how I came to devote my life to dreams, but I can't remember a time when it wasn't so. I was raised in the Inayati Sufi Order, which was founded on the teachings of Hazrat Inayat Khan. Inayat Khan was a poet, philosopher, and musicologist from India who brought a mystical version of Sufism to the West in the early 1900s. He emphasized the underlying harmony between all the world's religions and taught that there was only one holy book, the manuscript of nature. One moral, love that springs from deeds of kindness. One thing to praise, beauty that uplifts the heart. And one truth, the wisdom found within and around each of us.

My family lived in a Sufi *khanqah*, which is the Persian word for a commune and centre for mystical practice and gathering. At any time, we lived with ten to fifteen individuals, nine cats, and a constant flow of community events in our sprawling but run-down tenement in the red-light district of Montreal. We ate our meals together, practised meditation and yoga, and sang *zikr*, which is a form of devotional chanting and dancing. We also shared our dreams in the morning.

Sufi pilgrims passed through every day, sometimes staying for weeks, other times disappearing the next day. They would arrive to study with visiting teachers, check out our jumble sales, or sit in on an evening of music and recitation of poetry. Unlike a nuclear family, my brother and I don't really remember being looked after —our parents just blended into our bustling, hippie existence.

There weren't any other children in the khanqah, so I spent a lot of time reading, which my mother says I taught myself to do at the age of three. I must have devoured all the children's books on the shelves of our home, because by the age of nine or ten, I was reading the poetry of Hafiz, Gibran, and Rumi, Carlos Castaneda on *The Art of Dreaming*, and other books on altered states of consciousness.

At that age, I was already participating in meditation, ecstatic dance, and entering trance states through chanting. As far back as I can remember, I was in awe of my dreams, and had some of the most mystical experiences of my life before puberty. One of my earliest memories was of meditating with a double-terminated quartz crystal I had chosen at a gem show. Though I was awake, I was able to enter a vivid dream state and found myself inside the crystal itself, which was as tall as a skyscraper. I entered an elevator that took me to the topmost floor and exited into an infinitely long hallway with doors on either side.

Each of the closed doors had a title of a discipline on it, like mathematics, art, and philosophy. I don't remember which door I chose, but when I entered I saw a classroom of empty desks and chairs. At the front of the room stood a teacher who barked at me, "Finally. I've been waiting for you—you're late!" I rushed to the front row of desks and took what I assumed was my seat. The teacher said nothing more to me, but placed a large, illuminated book in my hands. It had an ornately embroidered cover and the parchment pages were handwritten in calligraphy, and adorned with gold-leaf-and-floral borders.

The moment the book's weight landed in my hands, I felt a transmission take place, as if the entire contents of this book's wisdom travelled into my body by osmosis. Startled, I broke the spell and found myself sitting cross-legged in my bedroom holding my crystal.

It took several minutes for my heart to stop pounding, and I knew my life had been altered by this experience. Looking back on it now, I can see how it was my first calling into a life of devotion to dreaming. The dream seemed to say that there was a different way of learning, one that didn't require reading or the collection of orthodox credentials. There was an invisible library that was waiting for me within, granting me access to endless wisdom. All I had to do was keep travelling there, availing myself of the teacher within.

In my book *Belonging*, I tell the story of how I left home at the age of fifteen. When my mother and stepfather moved out of the Sufi khanqah and into the suburbs, my brother and I were suddenly confronted with how deeply dysfunctional our family was. My stepfather was a spiritual leader in the Sufi community, but behind closed doors he was a violent and dissociated man. My mother was a yoga teacher, but living with undiagnosed mental illness. She volleyed between severe depression and episodes of unbridled rage. We all felt the impacts of her illness—but I was most often the target.

The day I was committed into the System, I became an orphan. That was also the day I started a dream journal. My dreams became a lifeline for me, because I had no other meaningful source of guidance. I rarely understood what they meant, but there were times when their symbols would appear in the world the morning after having dreamt them. In those moments of synchronicity, I would feel the same electricity I felt holding that illuminated manuscript in my hands. I knew there was more to life than the one I was living in shelters and group homes, and paying attention to my dreams kept me connected to that greater wisdom. Looking back now, I can say that my dreams parented me.

When I was nineteen, I found myself in a second-hand bookshop and picked up a dog-eared copy of *Man and His Symbols* by C.G. Jung.* I devoured it in one sitting. I felt as if I'd discovered my long-lost lineage in this thriving subculture of folks who were interested in the psyche and dreams—people who had devoted their lives to the study of mythology and symbolism. As I read, mystical experiences from my childhood came rushing back to me. I remembered the vivid dreams I received that taught me things adults couldn't explain.

Over the next decade, I read everything Jungian I could get my hands on and volunteered for a years-long internship at the Jung Foundation of Ontario. In those precious years, I met and studied with some of the greatest living, second-generation Jungian analysts like Marion Woodman, James Hollis, J. Gary Sparks, and many others.

I often considered becoming an analyst myself, but I was about ten years too young to be considered for the program and could not afford the exorbitant tuition. So I read the same books as the curriculum, audited the same lectures and workshops, and was also in analysis for years with a Jungian psychotherapist. But despite everything I knew I could offer the field, it began to dawn on me that I would never be on the inside of this exclusive group.

The Jungian public was often reminded by those in positions of authority of the "dangers" of relating to one's own unconscious without supervision. In discouraging (even frightening) people like me from having an independent relationship with our own dreams —lest we experience a psychotic break—it positioned Jungians as "experts" of the psyche who, like medical professionals, took the place of folk healers. But as I began to practise dreamwork in my community, I could see how the analytical approach to dreamwork had significant limitations. The language of psychology is inherently alienating because it does not connect with the soul of

---

* Carl Gustav Jung (1875–1961) was a Swiss psychoanalyst and the founder of Analytical/Jungian Psychology.

dreamers. As the poet John O'Donohue once said, it has "a neon kind of clarity to it," while the soul is always more at home in poetry, the language of candlelight, "which has a hospitality to shadow."[1]

Though I'd gotten skilled at it, I also began to see how useless it was for me to interpret anyone else's dreams. In order for the work to be meaningful, dreamers needed to arrive at their own realizations. This meant that, more than any other skill, I needed to embody the archetypal feminine (a principle called *yin* in Chinese). Among other things, yin is that which holds the kind of deep presence that allows another to connect to their inherent wisdom. Though I'd learned a great deal of theory about "the feminine principle," I longed for someone to speak *from* the feminine, and to draw it out in my own character. I longed for the mysticism of my youth, which sought the divine directly through beauty, music, and connection with nature. I longed for dreaming to be retrieved from those ivory towers and the academic gaze—to be returned to everyday people.

One weekend, in the middle of a workshop with a visiting analyst, I had a life-changing dream that catapulted me onto the wayward path that underpins this book.

The Witch's Grave
I dream some of the male analysts from the Jung Foundation are deep in a forest building a platform out of wood. Thinking she was long-dead, they are building it on the grave of a powerful witch, who is now awakening in a rage. In what feels like an instant, she leaps from her grave and unleashes her fury, slaughtering everyone in sight. It is a terrifying bloodbath.

I remember going to class the next morning feeling like I had a wicked hangover. The dream shook me so deeply that when I left the workshop that day, I never returned to the Foundation again. I knew the dream was showing me how the Jungians I so dearly loved had built their educational and business enterprise on an older, feminine way that had been left for dead. And she was furious. Dreams and magic were the domain of a greater authority than the one I'd been following. And I was determined to find her.

Over the next few years, I unlearned a great deal of the theory I had been taught as I worked to have a more embodied relationship with my dreams.

It was one of the scariest and most rewarding times of my life. Every night I went to sleep excited to find answers to my questions, and woke up having had remarkable encounters and lessons taught to me by my dreams. But I was also assailed by inner tyrants who, one after the other, threatened and harassed me. I dreamed of landlords who invaded my apartment, lovers who cheated on me, violent predators who chased and attacked me, domineering bosses, and perpetual dreams of searching for footwear in unsafe places. It was clear that the destructive energy I was meeting had deep roots and many permutations. I needed to unpack the internalized patriarchy that dismissed my value, invalidated my inner knowing, invaded my peace, and harangued me to prove my worth. I would never be able to stand in my own creativity so long as all my energy was being drained by these unconscious forces within.

The work I needed to do was to confront those foes, both in my dreams and in waking life, until I was able to defend my own values and abilities. These weren't easy dreams because they raised to the surface the real-life wounds of my history. Every time I had one of these nightmares, I wrote it down. I journaled about my feelings and experiences, tugging on the underlying beliefs and destructive thoughts that were keeping me from expressing my true nature until they gave way. It was as if my dreams were pulling me through the dark tunnels of my limited thinking into a brighter world where I could inhabit my purpose.

When I was brave enough, I began to share my passion for dreamwork with others. I gave talks at local libraries and hosted small workshops. I built my first website for the Dream School in 2001. I began to write a weekly dream column called "Dreamspeak" for newspapers and magazines. None of these things were easy and I had to fight through my anxieties to share myself with the world. I cycled in and out of depression and discouragement. But the more I came out as the creative person I was meant to be, the less plagued I was by shadowy dreams.

Every time I made a small triumph against those internal and external tyrannies, I was rewarded with a gorgeous dream. I would find myself breathing underwater, following a vulva-pink manta ray into the depths of the sea. I would discover hidden rooms in my house or hear ancient spells whispered in my ears. I would find jewels in the body of a turtle, or an amaryllis would bloom into a gorgeous woman and speak wisdom to me. Owls landed on the branches where I walked and eagles flew into my third eye, awakening me into a lucid dream. I discovered my ability to shapeshift and travel through hyperdimensional space. It was a powerful time that was as challenging as it was inspiring. But as my dreams became richer and more beautiful, I knew that I was being led into my life's vocation. It is my deep wish that everyone in the world could have an exhilarating and poignant relationship with their dreams as I have found for myself.

Whether you are curious about getting to know your dreams, have some experience already, or want to facilitate dreamwork for others, my hope is that *The Dreaming Way* has something to offer you. In conceiving this book, I imagined the teacher I longed to have at the many points along my own journey and wrote in the spirit of that mentorship. It is equal parts poetry and technique because we need both a sense of the sacred to guide our practice, as well as tools to anchor our work.

The first four chapters offer a radically different lens through which to begin thinking of the imagination as another *reality*, and Wisdom as the animating force behind our dreams. We'll explore some core tenets for navigating this Otherworld, and metaphor as the biological language of connection. Chapters 5 through 10 delve into the tools and techniques of dreamwork. You will learn how to spot the broader patterns in your dreams, understand their universal elements, and improve your dream recall. In Courting the Dream, you will receive five essential Keys to guide your dreamwork practice, followed by a deep dive into shadow work in Poison is the Medicine. The last four chapters of the book are devoted to an exploration of how Wisdom manifests in the material world. We will look at some of the many ways we can engage with dreaming while awake, including dreaming together in families or tribes, and facilitating dream groups.

The dreams throughout this book have been shared with permission, using pseudonyms to ensure the dreamers' privacy. Each dream contains guidance, not only for the individual, but for all of us who are (or will be) crossing similar thresholds. It has been an honour to have walked a distance with each of these remarkable people and I am grateful for how they have contributed to this field guide of the soul.

As you follow *The Dreaming Way*, may your life open to a multiplicity of benevolent relations both in your imaginal and material worlds, creating a broader sense of belonging in your life. Even as you practise on your own, you are never alone on this path. We are a gentle multitude, mounting a revolution from within. May it be through our shared devotion and passion that dreaming, one day, returns as a practice shared in families and communities, guiding us toward our mutual wellbeing.

Introduction

I DREAM *I am alone in an unfamiliar house. The walls and floors are a warm cypress wood. The interior is understated, with minimalist decor and natural textures everywhere. As I descend a set of steps into a sunken living room, I am stunned by what I see through the floor-to-ceiling windows. Instead of looking out onto a landscape, there is an underwater world beyond the glass! Schools of neon yellow fish go gliding by, shy crustaceans scuttle in and out of coral reefs, and blades of kelp undulate in the currents, revealing and concealing a path leading deeper into this sea world.*

Suddenly I see a mermaid swim out from the kelp forest! With flashing silver scales, and a sinewy green tail fin, she slows to a hover so she can peer at me through the glass. I catch my breath as we both become aware of the other, our eyes locking in what I can only call an exchange.

As we gaze at each other, I feel a tug on an ancient part of myself that I recognize in her. I long to live as she does: in an ocean garden filled with the wonders and dangers of being truly alive. Though all that separates us is a pane of glass, she is free of the inhibitions of humanity. She can just be as she is, in her wild and magical animal body. But in our exchange, she also sees me in my world of things. I am weirdly aware of my aridity and all the inanimate objects around me. Seen through her worldview of flux and fluid symbiosis, I wonder who between us must seem like they are captured in an exhibit. She disappears then, with a declarative thrust of her tail, deep into a fathomless world.

When I awoke from this dream, I knew I'd been given a glimpse into the great wilderness of psyche. I ached to return to the dream, so I could follow my new friend. I wanted to swim by her side, and explore the undersea world. But the day-world was already pestering me with its to-do lists and responsibilities.

Every night, we fall asleep, dropping our allegiances to the physical world, and an alternate version of ourselves awakens on the other side. We step into a dreaming body, the only vessel that can move in the mercurial dimension of symbols and story. It is a kind of nightly death to leave behind the weight of bones and flesh, abandoning the storylines of our lives.

Here, where there is no continuity or physical laws, we rely on a different set of abilities. Our accumulations of strength, status, and appearance mean nothing in the dreamtime. Instead, presence, curiosity, and flexibility are our greatest powers. We wade into the wild and fathomless depths from which all the world's myths were born, and from which every invention takes its origins.

We become someone entirely new who may have a different lover, live in a different country, or find ourselves on an unexpected mission. We may possess the ability to fly, breathe underwater, or read books by osmosis. We may even be a different species altogether as we undertake our mythic adventures in a world that is fluid, imminent, and responsive to our presence.

But when the time comes to cross back into the day-world, we forget everything we saw and did. Or if we remember, it is in fragments that we dismiss, laugh about, or try to outrun for the haunting traces they leave behind. We go back to thinking there is nothing real beyond our waking world. Instead, we live these two distinct versions of ourselves, each forgetting the other, like two halves separated by a pane of glass.

There is a world of magic hidden behind this one. It occasionally breaks through ordinary reality in moments of uncanny grace, or in an enchanting dream, as a flash of insight brought about by poetry, music, or through the wonder of nature. We are given these glimpses behind the heavy curtain of rationalism to see how all of life really moves as one. These wisdom-events bring us a sense of meaning and orientation in our lives, confirming that we are on the right path and everything is unfolding as it should. A friend of mine calls this "seeing through magic eyes."

These glimpses are fleeting, and they fade as quickly as they come into view. Sometimes, in the distance between these moments, we are given to wonder if we made it all up. As life begins to fill with losses and disappointments, missed yardsticks of progress, and endless responsibilities, years and even decades can evaporate without so much as a peek behind the veil. Slowly, we begin to feel disoriented and alienated, wondering where or who to turn to for guidance—and if meaning really exists.

One day, a scary dream jolts us awake, or an event that can't be written off as coincidence forces us to question what we think of as reality. Maybe a recurring dream stalks us to distraction, or we may be overwhelmed with tides of emotion that we can't name. It feels like something is trying to get our attention. Yet, even with the otherworld pushing into waking-life, attempting to be remembered, the outlines of our dreams seem written in disappearing ink despite our best efforts to capture them. We always seem to resume our problem of forgetting, even wilfully so.

We moderns are unique in our dismissal of dreams. Indigenous cultures around the world have historically valued dreams as fundamental to daily life. On every continent, somewhere in every sacred text, in many of the creation stories, we find great dreams have always guided people to understand their place in the larger web of relations. In fact, it's hard to find any ancient culture that didn't, in some way, revere and value the wisdom of dreams. But we have inherited a legacy of dismissal. Every time we tell ourselves or our children, "it was just a dream"; every time we push our dreams away because they are scary, repulsive, weird, or embarrassing; every time we say, "I don't dream," we are re-enacting that legacy in our own lives.

The result is that, as a culture, we are living only half a life. We have backed ourselves into an evolutionary cul-de-sac. We take our cues for living not from a greater organizing intelligence, but from our own siloed and immature consciousness. Now we find ourselves on a dangerous precipice as a species, experiencing epidemic alienation, mass species extinction, climate crises, and many other forms of collapse.

At the most fundamental level, it is our disconnection from the rest of nature—from our own wild, dreaming self—that has set this collapse in motion. So how do we come back into connection? Where can we start in our own small lives to find a sense of purpose in relation to the larger whole? How do we find meaning in these difficult times, so that our lives feel necessary to the world?

We can begin by reuniting our estranged worlds, seen and unseen, by tending to their equivalence in our lives. Reversing the culture's materialist approach to life would be like turning a mighty ship around in a powerful current, but at the individual level it's a much more manageable shift. Every one of us can learn to take our cues from the imagination. And if enough people pivot to follow the way of their dreams, we become like a murmuration that can reorient on a dime. There is a new world waiting to be realized through each of our lives, one individual at a time. To set this in motion, we must be willing to question the assumptions of our inherited thinking about psyche and dreaming.

We need to chip away at the enculturated notion that we need an expert to interpret our dreams. The truth is, people have always gathered around a fire to share their dreams. This is how the world's greatest myths and stories were born. It is how wisdom was transmitted across the generations, about how to live relation to the rest of nature. Dreams have always been the wellspring from which humans have drawn a sense of purpose, meaning, and connection.

One of the greatest skills honed in dreamwork is your symbolic capacity, which is part of your natural heritage. You do not have to amass a storehouse of symbol systems, or a library of mythological knowledge. You don't need any outside authority to tell you what your dreams mean. Understanding their language is as natural as grasping the moral of a story, or finding beauty in an artwork. You already contain everything you need to remember, understand, and embody the inextinguishable wisdom of your dreams.

But we need to debunk some of the pervasive myths that keep us from having a meaningful relationship with our dreams. The first is that psyche and brain are synonymous. Though we tend to equate them, the brain is a complex physical organ housed in our bodies, while psyche is a sacred dimension of reality. In other words, the physical world isn't the only *real* reality.

So many of the world's cultures can trace their origins back to animism: the recognition of an animating life-force, or soul behind the physical world. Psyche is more like a field that includes our own bodies and reaches into the animate world around us. It extends into every aspect of the cosmos. Though being in a body allows us to access a gateway into this larger network, psyche is without any definite barriers. Like autumn giving way to winter, we cannot say where "our" psyche ends and another's begins. But dreams are a living bridge to this otherworld and, like connective tissue to the wisdom of nature, are meant to shape us as individuals and as a species.

It has been the mission of my life to help bring dreaming back to the people. To retrieve the power of dreams from a psychology rooted in rationalism, so we can reclaim our own dreaming authority. To revive an ancient yet radical idea that there is a friend who lives within and around us, called Wisdom, who patterns our dreams with intent to pull us toward our unique destiny. That destiny is a smaller pattern that fits into the larger pattern of nature itself. In other words, dreams are nature, *naturing* through us.

More than interpreting our nightly visions, I view dreamwork as a reciprocal dialogue between our two worlds, seen and unseen. By engaging in that conversation, we are restoring belonging to our own lives and to the world. As our dreams nudge us in step with the larger intent of nature, we grow to see how necessary we are to these troubled times. Our shared future depends on each of us rekindling this connection between psyche and nature. Only when we learn to follow this broader Wisdom can we meet with the social, psychological, and ecological challenges of our time.

CHAPTER 1

The Imaginal World

BEHIND THIS WORLD lies another hidden realm, too vast to fully comprehend—and more real than the world of our senses. It is the origin of all creativity, the wellspring of dreams, and a timeless source of wisdom. Every innovation throughout human history originated here. All the world's languages, every technological advancement, and every poem ever written first took shape in the Imaginal World.

In a culture that values productivity above all else, it is almost heretical to advocate for dreams and the imagination. We live in a climate of urgency, where many of us feel a need to attend to the world "before it's too late." But there is a paradox in that rushing anxiously ahead, without introspection, gets us into the same trouble we are trying to resolve. When we attempt to create change from a place of anxiety or outrage, we often replicate the very conflicts we are protesting.

I believe there is a more intimate form of protest—a rebellion before the rebellion—that needs to happen at the deepest level of the Self before any meaningful change can be made in the world. That rebellion is against the tyrannical forces of oppression within each of us that restrict us from accessing our own originality.

Consider that the word "originality" comes from the root *origin*, which is derived from the Latin *oriri* and means "the place where something begins or arises." From this perspective, originality is not something you invent so much as an utterance through you by your origins.

Imagination is not a thing. It is not a muscle we have to strengthen or a part of the brain that we need to unlock. It is not bestowed on a chosen few "gifted" creatives. It is a place where something begins. Inherent to us all, the imagination is a reality—quite unlike this one—where visionaries have always travelled to harvest new images and ideas from this sacred ground to guide, propel, and inspire.

In modern society, we have very little respect for the imagination. The word "imaginary" is often used derogatorily, synonymous with "fantasy" and "make-believe." For many, the word "myth" has come to mean a lie. If a grown person spends time in the world of imagination, they may be called dreamy or seen as having their head in the clouds. But the truth is that a person of imagination who values their dreaming life, and makes time for contemplation, or reads myths and listens to stories, is more deeply connected to and considerate of the world, because they are tapping into the eternal patterns of Wisdom.

The ancient Greeks called this otherworld the *anima mundi*— the world soul. Much like the human soul is attached to the physical body, the world is believed to have a soul. If humans are the plants or fruiting bodies of a rhizome, then the *anima mundi* is that subterranean network that connects all living beings.

Variations on this worldview appear in cultures around the globe. For example, the Indigenous religion of Japan, Shinto, is the belief in an unseen realm full of nature spirits and ancestors called the *kami*. The kami are not visible in the human realm, but they are alive and aware, and inhabit every aspect of nature. The Indigenous Nations of Australia also recognize another dimension to reality. Though they call it by different names, like *Jukurrpa* or *Everywhen*; it is often translated into English as "the Dreaming." Inseparable from the natural landscape, the Dreaming are the beliefs, teachings, and stories of how things came to be as they are, and how one should behave in relation to those ancestors. Just about every culture in the world can trace its origins back to the recognition of an animating life-force or soul behind the physical world.

The Taoists of ancient China refer to a hidden world called the Tao. Also known as The Way, the Tao is the natural flow of energy that runs below the visible surface of life. Living in harmony with the Tao is referred to as *wu wei*. In the Chinese language, wu means "effortless" and wei means "action." So a person who practises wu wei is in a constant conversation with those elemental forces of nature that shift and move within and around us. Like water seeks to flow with life's changes rather than forcing its will, Taoism is about learning how to move in harmony with these hidden forces.

I chose the title for this book as homage to the ancient Taoist perspective that, like a changing stream, our dreams have an inclination—a Way—that comes directly out of nature. It is what nudges us from behind, and pulls us from ahead. Different from pursuing goals that are shaped by the values of the culture, following the Dreaming Way is about moving from this deeper inner life force—living in accordance with the rhythms of nature itself. As you learn to track the curves and bends of your dreams, you begin to see how they have an intrinsic purpose. They are moving your life in a meaningful direction. When you follow this Wisdom, you grow to understand that it's a tributary of a far greater knowing. The Way is pulling us into harmony with ourselves, each other, and the greater ecosystem.

For the Sufis, this otherworld is as real as the world of our senses. It was the great Islamic theologian, Henry Corbin, who coined the term Imaginal World to convey the Sufi concept of *'ālam al-mithāl.* * Though it roughly translates into "the world of the imagination," Corbin chose the term "imaginal" to distinguish it from the word "imaginary" which has grown pejorative in the modern mind. Think of how often it's used to convey contempt or dismissal, like "That didn't happen—you're imagining things." or "She has a vivid imagination, so you have to take what she says with a pinch of salt."

To properly conceptualize the Imaginal World, we have to subdue what Corbin calls our "agnostic reflex." This is the deeply ingrained habit of mistrusting or being sceptical about that which is mysterious or unseen. Because we have learned to view everything through the lens of rationalism, our culture largely dismisses dreams as nonsense, treats visionary states as hallucinatory, and considers myth and symbols as little more than fanciful fiction. We treat the imagination as less real—and therefore less valuable—than physical matter. But the Sufis see through a different lens; the figures and symbols of the Imaginal World are *more* real because they precede the world of form.

From the Sufi perspective, we do not exist in a one-dimensional reality. To understand this very different worldview, we have to imagine a threefold layered cosmos. The first layer is the immediate world of our senses. But just beyond this lies the Imaginal—a hidden realm of angelic beings, symbols, and patterns. This symbolic dimension transcends our concept of psychology, because although humans can experience and interact with it, we do not invent it. It is alive and aware and possesses its own autonomy. The imaginal is a middle realm, and lies between our world and a third dimension. The Sufis call this third layer the Beloved,

---

* Throughout his work, Henry Corbin (1903–1978) used the Latin term *Mundus Imaginalis* (Imaginal World) as synonymous with the Persian and Arabic terms 'ālam al-mithāl (the world of images) and Malakut (the world of souls). Arguably the greatest scholar of Sufi philosophy of the twentieth century, Corbin made a lifelong commitment to bringing ancient Sufi wisdom to the Western world.

but it is known by many names—the Creator, God, Nature: the divine love that connects us all.

Sometimes called the "country of nowhere" because it cannot be located with the physical senses, the Imaginal World is where we travel when we dream.* It can also be reached through contemplation of nature, sacred imagery, and scriptures. The Sufi dervishes also *whirl*, like orbiting planets, as a form of meditation to connect with the Beloved.

Though it is nearer to us than our own blood, we cannot enter the Divine realm directly because it is formless—and we are not. But when we slip into our dreaming bodies, we can meet its emissaries in this middle realm. Dreams are the act and evidence of reciprocity between our sacred and physical realities. They are the fruits of our exchange, carrying the seeds of novelty and healing within them. When these seeds are planted, they have the power to alter the nature of physical reality. If we have the presence to see it, signs of the sacred are written into every inch of the phenomenal world.

Mystics, shamans, and artists have always travelled to and from this "country of nowhere" to retrieve healing images, songs, and visions to guide and inspire others. But as rationalism took hold of our collective imagination, fewer and fewer made this challenging voyage. We gradually started forgetting how or why to make the journey, and our own world grew fractured and exhausted. In times of isolation, loneliness, and hardship, we can still hear the Imaginal World calling us back, luring us through dreams to the living edge of discovery, meaning, and purpose.

We typically think of dreams as the imagery that unfolds in our brains while we sleep. But while the brain is certainly involved in dreaming, to think that dreams originate there is like believing the wardrobe itself is Narnia. We've inherited this narrow conviction

---

* The Persian term *Nâ-Kojâ-Abâd* literally translates as *Land* or *Country of Nowhere* to designate a place outside of place.

from the scientific world, who consider dreaming a purely neuro-
logical phenomenon. The prevailing theories say that dreams are
the brain's way of consolidating memory and rehearsing possible
futures. Some schools of psychology give them a bit more
credence, yet still regard dreams as a tool for self-analysis—representations of the individual's thoughts and emotions that, when
deciphered by experts, can promote personal growth. But long
before rationalism became the fundamental ideology of our time,
the wisdom traditions understood dreaming as a portal into
another world.

Though we tend to think of dreamwork as interpreting our
nocturnal visions, I'd like us to hold a broader definition: Dreamwork is the practice of a dynamic reciprocity between matter and
spirit. In this way, our concept of dreaming extends beyond
personal psychology into the animate, unseen world behind this
one. I emphasize practice in this definition because dreamwork is
a devotional artform. There will always be more to learn (and
unlearn). But as we reach out to the mystery, it is amazing to
discover that it reaches back! Whether that reply comes in the
form of a new dream building upon our last understanding,
synchronicities that affirm our direction, or signs from nature that
we are onto something, we can feel that a momentum is underway.
Like any good conversation, that dynamism is only kept alive by a
reciprocity of attentiveness.

It is this dynamic exchange that enables us to remake ourselves
and the world. The Imaginal is the origin of myths and stories,
songs, and all human ingenuity. But you can go even further to say
that humankind itself is an expression of a larger creativity—just
one of the infinite conceptions of nature. What we call "nature" is
actually the visible expression of this great art-making impulse of
the universe.

We have these experiences of dreams feeling important,
coming true, or spilling their magic into ordinary reality, but when
we share those dream-stories with others, they rarely land well.

We may be mocked or dismissed, or just see the other's eyes glazing over with disinterest. We may avoid sharing our dreams with others because we can't get past our own inner denial. We all, to some degree, carry the dismissive attitude of the culture that views dreams as nonsense. This isn't anyone's fault. It's because we are stuck in a centuries-long phase of worshipping rationality and materialism. Whether we like it or not, our lives are governed by reason, logic, and profitability. The culture is set up to keep us constantly managing practical concerns so there isn't any room left to imagine a different way of being.

The real reason we forget our dreams is that the bridge between our worlds has fallen into disrepair. The way has grown unfamiliar to us. Out of our need to belong, we learn to hide what's magical in us to survive in the modern world. We set up camp on the side of materialism and eventually we begin to believe there is nothing beyond our clocks and calendars, careers and capitalism. There's nothing inherently wrong with these pursuits but when materialism becomes our fundamental ideology, it atrophies the imagination. Seen through this lens, forgetting is a choice. It is a passive choice, but a choice nonetheless.

The price of forgetting, however, is steep. As the materialist worldview hardens like concrete, you begin to experience life as dull and flat, lacking in meaning. You may find yourself going through the motions without any passion or sense of purpose. Exhaustion seems not to be relieved by any amount of rest.

But the otherworld will never stop trying to get your attention; to be remembered by you. Sometimes its call comes in inexplicable waves of sadness welling to the surface. You may feel a longing for a connection you can't quite name, as if something has gone missing from you. Or you may find yourself nostalgic for a joyful era in your past when you felt harmoniously involved with the rest of life. Sometimes the call comes in the form of an uncanny event, like an image from your dreams appearing in the waking world. Or you might have unsettling or recurring dreams. Unfortunately, the call can also look like a physical crisis or an event that splays your life apart like a bolt of lightning. It's often in these low moments that we finally turn toward the Imaginal World for guidance.

In the ancient *Nag Hammadi Scriptures* found in Egypt it is written, "Truth did not come into the world naked but in symbols and images. The world cannot receive truth in any other way."[1] Have you ever noticed how, after leaving an hour-long lecture on any subject, it is the telling of a story that you remember most? This is because stories awaken our dreaming faculty, which is visual, emotional, and intelligent, all at once. Story engages the full spectrum of who we are. Before words, before sensation, and even before thought, the body's first language is one of symbols. Dreaming is as biologically essential as breathing, having a heartbeat, and blood circulating through our veins. Like all our automatic processes, the spontaneous creation of images keeps us alive. Stitched together in meaningful patterns, the dream is a conduit of information, wisdom, and values by which we can forge our lives.

Unlike the images of modern media that refract the values of the culture back to us, dreams draw upon an ageless intelligence that is rooted in wholeness. Similarly, the art and myth of traditional cultures contain archetypal symbols that evoke such deep resonance for us because they carry the essential patterns and truths of Wisdom itself. Like a poem being recited for our ears only, our dreams contain ancient spells meant to move us into our next becoming.

In order to follow the Dreaming Way, rational thinking can no longer be our primary lens of understanding. We need this highly developed part of our consciousness to progress and function in society, but we have let it grow monstrously strong. Like an overdeveloped muscle ruling every aspect of culture and psyche, its counterpart has been dangerously weakened. Rationalism has prevailed for 400 years, impairing our imaginal capacity in a time when wisdom and creativity have never been so desperately needed.

PSYCHOLOGY: SCIENCE OF THE MIND

Over the last century, psychology has been extremely valuable in giving us a shared language and framework for the dynamics of the human psyche. But with roots in rationalism, it has also contributed to our disconnection from other ways of knowing.

While the word "psyche" literally means soul, the field of *psychology* is defined as the "science of the mind." Largely influenced by seventeenth-century philosopher René Descartes, Western psychology was born as a scientific quest to investigate the objective logic behind human behaviour and mental processes. This meant that in an effort to be legitimized by the scientific community, psychology focused only on observable and quantifiable phenomena. Dreams were left out of the equation. Even though we spend over a third of our lives sleeping, dreams are still rarely explored in mainstream psychology programs. In its campaign for validity in a science-focused culture, the study of psyche has become largely dissociated from its mystical roots. Science imparted the belief that dreams are products of the mind, which is studied in isolation from the body, culture, and larger ecosystem in which we are embedded.

It wasn't until the late 1800s that psychoanalysis, the field pioneered by Sigmund Freud and Carl Gustav Jung, began to lend credence back to dreams—albeit still through a rationalistic lens. Dreaming remains an insignificant footnote in the field of psychology and is presided over by analysts and psychiatrists. Even with respectful treatment, dreams in the abstracted context and language of academia are considered puzzles to be analyzed and interpreted. This is what I call the "acquisitional approach" to dreamwork. Not unlike treating nature as a resource to be exploited for profit, the underlying question is typically "What does it mean for *me*?" as if in analyzing a dream correctly we should get a payoff in the form of advice or answers. Rather than treating the Imaginal World like an ATM machine or fortune cookie, I believe we need to consider that our dreams possess their own aliveness. We need to start asking what they want and need *from us.*

Like anyone raised in the dominant culture, I wrestle with the supremacy of rationalism in my own psyche every day. I think of decentring rationalism as a recovery process. After being so steeped in the language and conceptual frameworks of psychology, there have been times when I've been scolded by my dreams for slipping into an objectifying mindset. I remember when I was first learning about dreams, I became obsessed with the idea that I could meet my "dreammaker" face to face. In a practice you'll learn later in this book, I did a dream incubation to ask, "Can I meet the one who makes dreams?"

Meeting the Dreammaker

I dream I am in an outdoor animal sanctuary, which is more like a wooded zoo. Turning a corner, I come suddenly upon a majestic bald eagle who is chained at the ankle to a post. He is beautiful and huge, but visibly angry, pulling helplessly at his steel restraints which clatter with the weight of futility. I feel ashamed and complicit for being there.

When I woke up from this dream, I felt chastised. Having incubated the request to essentially "meet Mystery," I instantly recognized the imprisonment of the eagle as symbolic of my ego's desire to know things that should remain out of reach. An eagle is only an eagle because it flies free and rarely descends into the world of two-leggeds. I was given the answer to my question, but not the one I expected. I made a vow to never objectify my dreams like this, capturing them for my own amusement. I knew that if I wanted to have a respectful relationship with these wild creatures, I would need to humble my acquisitional drive and learn how to move in the dream's own landscape, follow the rules of *its* nature, and focus instead on making myself approachable to the mystery. In an effort to unhinder my dreaming practice from rational thinking, I began to learn what I could about the dreaming practices of older cultures. What I discovered was that dreaming has been at the heart of community life throughout history on every continent.

Ancient cultures around the world always centred their relationship with dreams as a matter of sacred practice fundamental to daily living. Important dreams are found throughout the Bible, the Upanishads, Greek philosophy, and in ancient Chinese, Yogic, and Islamic traditions. In fact, it's hard to find any people in antiquity that didn't, in some way, revere and value dreaming. Especially in the mystical and Indigenous traditions around the world, wisdom was always sought through dreaming practice, even when it was considered heretical to do so.

We tend to think of mysticism as the exclusive domain of saints and medicine people, but a mystic is any person who involves themselves directly with this symbolic dimension, who goes looking for the divine within. What we call the imagination is our ability to relate to symbols in their own environment. Unlike pulling a symbol into our world and subjecting it to analysis, a mystic meets it on its own ground.

Rather than acquiring letters from institutions to validate their knowledge, the aspiration of a Sufi is to open the "eye of the heart."[2] This eye of the heart is not the physical one: it is the mystical capacity in every human being to perceive and engage with the inherent wisdom of the world. This wisdom speaks in a language of symbols and metaphor. While the rational mind focuses on individual parts, the eye of the heart perceives an ecology of energy and meaning. Unlike analysis, which pulls things apart to gain knowledge about their workings, the eye of the heart holds a contemplative curiosity in which life's inherent meaning is invited to reveal itself.

Rationalism aims to observe the world with as much passivity and neutrality as a camera lens, but the eye of the heart is relational. While the rational mind distances itself from what it sees, the eye of the heart recognizes the connection between things. One is imminent and temporal; the other rooted in eternal wisdom. Both of these capacities are essential to being human, and necessary to dreamwork itself. To strengthen the imagination, we must favour and engage what I call the aptitudes of the soul—receptivity, the body's wisdom, intuition, relationality—qualities typically associated with women and "the feminine."

When I reflected on my dream of the wrathful witch, upon whose grave the Jungians were building their platform, I understood her as the embodiment of that feminine way that has been buried and disavowed in psychology—and in my own life. By nature she is not evil, but she has had to become that way to get our attention. Like Medusa who transforms into a Gorgon after being raped by Poseidon, or Kali who goes on a rampage when her devotees are dishonest or harm others, the witch has endured thousands of years of slander and denial. As we'll explore in Chapter 10, when we reject or hide a part of ourselves (or at the collective level) it doesn't just disappear—it lives on in the shadows. It grows increasingly dangerous until we learn to invite it forward in its authentic expression.

Up until the twentieth century, women's contributions to the study and practice of dreamwork were largely unrecognized. Of course this is true of women's achievements throughout history in every field. Despite making up half the world's population, women only occupy 0.5 percent of recorded history.[3] While there are a huge number of archaeological artefacts from prehistory depicting women as spiritual authorities, men's accomplishments have been disproportionately represented in written history—a phenomenon

that continues to perpetuate gender stereotyping and its consequences for us all.

Women have always been midwifing the dreams of their families and communities. They gathered then as we do now, in sacred
spaces to speak the secret things of our inner lives, share the
dreams we've been having, and wrestle with how to bring their
medicine to fruition. Whether consoling their children when they
awoke from nightmares, minding the thresholds at birth, illness,
and death, or tending to the visionary states accompanying big life
transitions, women have always been at the centre of magic-
making.

But around the fifteenth-century, a violent split took place in
the European mindset between so-called good and evil. With the
rise of puritanical Christianity, a massive shadow formed and a
deep grave was dug. Those who practised moon rituals, midwifery,
the healing arts, divination, and dreamsharing, were labeled as
witches by the Church—and hundreds of thousands of these
women were burned, jailed, and persecuted over the following
centuries.

It is important for us to talk about this exclusion of women's
authority in relation to magic and dreams because it is an ancestral
trauma that inhibits all genders from empowering our archety-
pally feminine gifts. Consider how we have been taught that we
need to consult experts who hold the intellectual keys to
unlocking our dream's mysterious language. To give our authority
to these experts also means accepting the complicated legacy of
psychology and psychiatry itself, which has traditionally centred
white men and ignored or pathologized all other bodies and identities. In my early twenties, I experienced one of the most powerful
dreams of my life.

The Sleeping Lady
I dream I am being initiated by a sombre tribe of medicine people.

The final test of my initiation is taking place in an underground labyrinth of caves. The caves contain chambers just large enough to fit a single person. I understand that I am meant to enter one of these body-sized chambers in the pitch dark to complete my initiation. I can smell the earth in this dark, cool space, and feel a combination of fear and brave willingness to enter it alone. After a few moments, I suddenly perceive a large spider in the cave with me. I instinctively know that I have to reach out to hold it between my fingers. When I do, it floods the entire cave with light! In that same moment, I receive a transmission: that this light is the cure for an ailment of someone in the above-ground world. I know then that my initiation is successful.

This turned out to be a life-changing initiatory dream, setting me on my path as a dreamworker. I woke up feeling like those caves were somehow familiar so I began to research the internet for the word pairings "dream + caves" and "initiation + caves." That's when I first discovered the Hypogeum.

The Hypogeum is an enormous subterranean temple built on the island of Malta around 3000 BC. It is an impressive architectural feat of interconnected chambers, spanning several blocks and running ten metres under the earth. It's estimated that 7,000 individual remains are buried in this necropolis, but it is also believed to have been used as a dreaming temple. Archaeologists found many pottery vessels, votives, and other sacred artwork in the chambers, but most notably, a sculpture known as "The Sleeping Lady" was found in the main chamber of the temple. Depicted as a large-hipped woman sleeping on her right side, the Sleeping Lady was a clue that led many to believe the Hypogeum was used for dreaming rituals.

In ancient Greece, these famous Asclepion temples were used for dream incubation.* After fasting and purification rites, patients

---

* These temples were dedicated to Asclepius, the first physician-demigod in Greek mythology. He was said to have great healing powers, so pilgrims would

would go into the dream caves to sleep overnight in the hopes of receiving divine guidance from their dreams to cure what ailed them. When they awoke they would recount their dreams to the attendant priest or priestess who would give them a prescription, usually involving herbal medicine and other regimes guided by the dream.

I was amazed to discover that, without ever being exposed to the ancient dreaming temples of Malta, I dreamed myself in them. Five thousand years after the Hypogeum was built, I was initiated in this subterranean temple, entrusted with a new responsibility: to grasp the healing light in the dark to cure "above-ground" ailments. Looking back on it now, I believe I was being inducted into this vocation by the Dreaming itself, or perhaps by the ancestral tradition of priestesses who tended to the dreams of others.

It is said that women dominated the spiritual professions of antiquity. Over recent decades, feminist archivists have worked tirelessly to restore depictions of powerful women into cultural esteem. This vast and scattered archive of sacred feminine depictions are often interpreted as symbols of fertility and sexuality, embodied aspects of the feminine that were rejected by the Church. But at one time women also held the highest positions of spiritual authority as shamans, medicine healers, oracles, and dream priestesses.

As women were allowed into academic institutions, the twentieth century was blessed with the likes of Marie-Louise von Franz, Marion Woodman, Clarissa Pinkola Estes, Jean Shinoda Bolen, Sylvia Brinton Perera, Anne Baring, and Ann Belford Ulanov—Jungian analysts who were particularly interested in the feminine dimension of the divine. While they were steeped in the structure and lexicon of psychoanalysis, they were also breaking new ground, elevating the primacy of the body, feminine arche-

---

travel to temples built in his honour in order to seek spiritual and physical healing through dreams.

types in the psyche and fairy tales, and reinvoking traditional knowledge into the field.

As a culture, we are slowly restoring this lost lineage into cultural esteem, yet the real damage has been waged in our psyches. We have largely accepted the split between the imaginal and material worlds. We are taught to discount the inner life and take our sense of direction from the external world when it should be the other way around. This inversion only reinforces an already lopsided culture. The unfortunate result of not being guided by deeper wisdom is personal and collective disorientation.

It's not difficult to see how humanity is careening toward its own demise, taking much of the other-than-human life on earth along with it, but this disorientation is also felt by each of us personally. It expresses itself as anxiety, illness, alienation, and meaninglessness. We are more connected through technology than we've ever been in history, and have derived great benefits from these advances. But without the guiding influence of soul-and-body oriented wisdom, a one-eyed approach to life always leads to instability and crisis. I'm not suggesting we should discard science or rationality, but as William Blake suggested, we should develop a twofold vision—the ability to not only look at things as they are, but see *through* them to their relational ecosystems.*

So how do we, living in the context of the all-pervasive rationality of the culture, rekindle our symbolic intelligence? How do we locate ourselves in our mythic unfolding when we're constantly navigating worldly demands? How do we find orientation and a sense of purpose in a culture that discourages imagination?

---

* William Blake first used the term "twofold vision" in his *Letters*, to Thomas Butts, (Nov. 22,1802). As the writer Philip Pullman interpreted, "Twofold vision is seeing not only with the eye, but through it, seeing contexts, associations, emotional meanings, connections. Single vision is the literal, rational, dissociated, uninflected view of the world." (from the article "William Blake and me," in *The Guardian* (Nov 28, 2014)

In my experience, people become prolific dreamers by learning to treat their dreams as sacred, tending to the equivalence between our twin lives. I'd like to help you weave the living bridge into this otherworld so that together we can recover what has been lost. I'd like to show you that, despite what you've been told, it is deeply necessary to walk in both worlds. I'd like to explore with you how to move in the Dreaming Way with curiosity and respect. And I'd like to help you dismantle the obstacles that keep you from befriending and enacting your imagination.

You must begin with remembering. This isn't a matter of learning something new so much as remembering what you've always known. Perhaps you knew it in childhood, or even further back in your ancestral memory. Or maybe you've always been aware that the world of myth, dreams, and imagination is what gives meaning and direction to our lives.

Scientists have attempted to explain why we forget our dreams in multiple ways. There's one theory that dreams are short-term memories, so we have no need to store them in the hippocampus, which is the part of the brain connected to long-term memory formation and retrieval. Another speculates that dreaming is merely a consolidation process, so the brain considers them otherwise inessential. I am inclined to think of the brain, which is indivisible from the rest of the body, more like a tree in a forest, drawing on symbol-nutrients fed to it by the imaginal network.

Imagination isn't just isolated in our brains, it is connected to a shared psyche—what Carl Jung called the collective unconscious or the archetypal realm. This is why we see the same motifs and patterns in myths and fairy tales from vastly different cultures and geographies. For example, the Tree of Life is a widespread symbol. In the Abrahamic religions, a tree of knowledge grows in the Garden of Eden. In Jewish mysticism, the kabbalistic tree of life is a kind of symbolic map of creation. In Norse mythology there is a sacred ash tree supporting the world known as *Yggdrasill*. In ancient Assyria, there was a great tree symbolizing the divine order of life. And in Chinese Taoist mythology there is a peach tree called *pántáo* that puts forth a fruit every 3,000 years and grants immortality to the one who consumes it. Though their properties vary from culture to culture, these venerable trees are a universal archetype of connection—channels of wisdom—between the earthly realm and the heavenly world of the gods.

Delivered in myths, stories, dreams, and even in waking-life events, archetypes carry the patterns of human nature and the world. When we consciously interact with them, they can show us how to transition across critical thresholds, as our ancestors have done for millennia before us. It's amazing to consider that this dynamic exchange is biological. Nature communicates in images, through our own bodies. We are image-producing organisms. What are these images for? How do they serve us? How can we serve them?

We can think of the symbols in our dreams as visiting ambassadors representing other realities. They may be portraying outer dynamics in a way that is tailored for our own growth and understanding. Like the man who dreams of being unable to run around the bases after hitting a homerun, the symbols represent his difficulty following through in the workplace. They offer him an analogy so he can draw upon the new context for ideas on how to resolve his issue. Sometimes our dream symbols are glimpses into different parts of the time cycle, representations of a probable future or distant past. Other times they are timeless, expressing the immutable shapes and stories of the universe. Once in a while, they are divine transmissions.

From this perspective, imagination isn't a thing, or even a faculty, it's a field of collaboration—a place of exchange between what you know and something that knows much more than you. It's the resonance or reverberation between those two things that produces creativity. What comes out of this exchange is not something you are making up, nor is it something given to you. It is a participatory exchange, a collaboration that generates wisdom and meaning in our lives.

Like the humble acorn holds the potential for the mighty oak tree, so too is our intrinsic pattern concealed within. But not even the acorn can become an oak without the right conditions: the nutrients of the soil, warmth and light of the sun, and space to spread its crown. We too must collaborate with Wisdom in order to draw our story into the open. Here are some ways to begin awakening the eye of the heart:

Expose yourself to more stories. Myths and fairy tales are born from the collective's dreaming. They contain the patterns of human nature and the world. When you listen to a story, it awakens your own dreaming because it speaks in living images. It also acts as connective tissue between us, joining us in the places we have something in common. *Women Who Run with the Wolves* by Dr. Clarissa Pinkola Estes is an inspiring collection of myths and stories exploring the wild feminine archetypes.[4] I also love the work of Madeline Miller, who reimagines the figures of Greek Mythology in her intriguing and accessible novels.[5]

Rethink your allegiances to the outside world. Where might the invisible algorithms of culture be driving your imagination for you? Notice your addictions to substances and activities that fill up every sacred pause. These pauses are essential for magic to gather.

Consciously strengthen negative capability. The Romantic poet John Keats described negative capability as "being in uncertainties, mysteries, doubts, without any irritable reaching after fact and reason."[6] It takes great courage to be alone in this way, not knowing what you will find, entering into the inevitable discomforts of solitude to meet your wild self. Only you can keep faith alive in that darkness that eventually your path will lead somewhere fertile. Create a sacred room in your life, a physical space of any size in your home. Most importantly, make it a place of intent, where you can practise summoning your courage to withstand the irritations and doubt that lie between you and your originality. Adorn it with sacred talismans and tools (like a journal, zafu, tarot cards, *I-Ching*, paints, altar, etc.) so that you can reach for steadying support if you need it.

Listen to your body. It is the place of intersection between inner and outer worlds, and it is on this ground where we give presence to their reconciliation.* Throughout this book, I will remind you to listen to the communications of your own body as you practise dreamwork. Since body and psyche are indivisible, we can consult with both to know about either. Your physical sensations often alert you to how you feel, and your thoughts and emotions tend to manifest physically. The relationship between matter and spirit will be the focus of Chapter 11: Wisdom in Matter.

Somatic awareness is foundational to dreamwork, because the Imaginal World is physical to your dream-body. If you dream of being in an out-of-control car, do you not fear for your own safety? When you wake up from that dream, those dream-body sensations are what anchor you in the dreamwork process. But yours isn't the only body in that dream—maybe there is a panicked passenger who is begging you to slow down, or the car itself is failing from neglect. As the dreamer, you can inhabit multiple bodily perspectives. Instead of being the one who is driving, you can try inhabiting the experience of the car, the body that is being driven. Is it parched from being too low on oil, or in disrepair from being too aggressively driven? Our dreams help us to shift out of our habitual perspective so we can tend those unacknowl-edged bodies-in-psyche. Every gesture of inclusion you make to the needs of these inner others will forge a deeper and more nuanced relationship with your inner knowing. Developing bodily awareness in waking life will also help you attune to subtle energy

---

* Sufis occasionally refer to the imagination as the *World of Similitudes*, because everything in the heavens and on the earth has its counterpart in the Imaginal Realm and it is through the body that we access this between world.

fields, notice shifts in mood, hear what's not being said, intuit what's coming, and communicate without words.

Acknowledge the ways you are supported. In a time of great hardship in my own life, I met an intuitive who told me that instead of wishing for a torrent of support, I should honour the trickle. She told me that the very practice of appreciation is what grows the trickle into a rivulet, a rivulet into a stream, the stream into a river, and finally the torrent I'd been wishing for. In cultivating a relationship with the Imaginal, there is no gesture more powerful than to acknowledge in tangible ways how your questions are being answered. Even if that answer comes in the form of a small affirmation, do something to celebrate and recognize this magic. In Chapter 12: Rituals and Enactments, we'll explore rituals and practices for following our dream breadcrumbs, but remember that any conversation of depth needs responsiveness from both sides to stay engaged. It is this reciprocity that strengthens magic, so try not to drop this thread. Or if you do, just pick it back up again.

Write down your dreams. Dreamwork stretches the imagination because it requires us to suspend rational thinking, engage the inner senses, and hone our symbolic language skills. The living images in our dreams are the connective tissue to the rest of the animate world. When we are in communion with our dreams, not only do they restore a sense of magic and meaning to our personal lives, we regain a sense of relational purpose in the ecosystem.

Spend time in nature often. This is the earth's body, which is also our body, and it serves to support, nourish, and connect us. When you wander through a forest, it's as if the boundaries of time seem to stretch into eternity. As your lungs fill with the scent of pine needles and sap, your mind begins to clear. Ideas begin to find you as easily as your steps land between roots and rocks in the path. The sound of applause in the rustling canopy above your head reminds you to be nothing more than your lovely self. There is little more nourishing to the imaginal than to be in a wild, untrammeled place in nature. As Pir Zia Inayat Khan writes, "A tree has no itinerary or destination. What better guide could there be on the pathless path – which leads not from here to there, but from nowhere to everywhere."[7]

To open the eye of the heart is to cultivate an intimacy with this imaginal reality. It can be engaged through contemplation, music, whirling, drumming, prayer, ritual, play, and other practices we'll explore in later chapters. Keeping our expanded definition in mind, dreaming is also not limited to our nocturnal travels. It can also take the form of waking-life metaphors, symbolic events, revelations, and encounters with grace.

Developing your imaginal faculties often results in a quickening of magic, clairvoyance, precognition, synchronicity, and other mysterious abilities. While reason allows you to organize thoughts and senses in the physical world, the imagination allows you to perceive and engage with the sacred. To look beyond the literality of existence to its symbolic essence. As you do, you begin to descend into the roots of nature's power and wisdom. The purpose in making this descent is not to escape the world, but to fall deeper in love with it. Contrary to what we've been taught, the effect of engaging with our dreams is profoundly grounding. Not only does it give you a sense of location in your own mythic unfolding, it brings you into a deeper intimacy with the world and puts you in rhythm of The Way.

When you tend to the equivalency of the inner and outer worlds, you begin to walk with the awareness that earth and all its inhabitants have their own souls. You no longer see a tree as an object, but as a being with whom you are in a relationship. As you do with any relation, you witness the tree witnessing you—and you are both changed by the intimacy. You notice that the way a single arbutus is shaped, different from its neighbour, is a form of self-expression. The tree leans all the way back over an ocean bank, leaves like hair dipping into the water. It is a prayer of its own essence in form. You realize that it has habits, gestures, and a song that is particular to its upbringing. Like a flexible dancer, it bares its thighs out from the red skirts of its bark as if to say, "I am strong and daringly vulnerable." The arbutus has a personal history and an ancestral wisdom carried in its dreaming. It also has its own community in relationship with the soil where it roots down, the wind that crackles through its leaves, the changing sky it stretches for, and the creatures who make its curly, cool branches a home. Just as two people who live together sometimes share dreams, over time you and that tree become inhabitants of each other's imaginal reality.

The Dreaming Way means living in a practice of reciprocity between the two worlds. In actuality, they are inseparable. For this reason, I've been playing with the word "soulbody" to get myself in the habit of collapsing that dualism we've inherited. While our "first attention" draws upon the information we receive through our physical senses, the "second attention" uses our inner senses.[8] The soulbody unifies these two attentions into one, becoming a wholistic lens through which we perceive and walk in two worlds. We begin to live as a pianist plays, with the right hand asking the question, the left hand answering, the left hand asking, the right hand answering. Eventually, our sides move as one, in a reciprocal layering of harmonies and counterpoints.

Following the Dreaming Way, you will encounter both internal and external tyrants who are threatened by the new attitude. It's important to remember that nothing about modern culture is conducive to dreaming. The collective view is that dreaming is unproductive, ungrounded nonsense. Marc Ian Barasch explains the danger of that fallacy: "There is a part of us that has contempt for the psyche and, in a sense, for the truth, because the truth is often disturbing. When we say a dream is just a trifle or a fantasy, we insulate ourselves from reality. We are actually defending ourselves from the wisdom of dreams and their tendency to chal-lenge our beliefs."[9]

Even if we spend our lives "defending ourselves," the world

behind this world hums and chatters, prompts, and nudges. It tirelessly attempts to engage us in conversation, until finally, it has to raise its voice to be heard. It wakes us with fright, our hearts pounding with the threatening images that burst through the nadir of night into our consciousness. Our instinct is to distance ourselves as quickly as we can from the weird, invasive, repulsive, and sometimes terrifying images. But they keep returning, often with a serial quality, until we are brave enough to turn toward the unknown with a small measure of curiosity. In a society that discourages kinship with the sacred, to extend this privilege to yourself is an act of bravery—and even rebellion. By redirecting even a measure of your devotion from external life to the imaginal, you are contributing to the shifting of power in the world. You are enacting a revolution from within.

The Dreaming Way is not for everyone. It will almost certainly put you on a path that moves against the grain, away from mainstream values. This isn't to say we can't strike a balance between the needs of the soul and the demands of the culture, but to do so requires a good amount of courage and endurance. By choosing to enter into kinship with your dreams, you will come to recognize a deeper authority than the ones of the dominant culture. As a result, you will likely experience erosion in your ability to tolerate hierarchical structures of power. And you will have to navigate their mighty and tenacious counterparts *within* you that try to keep you from realizing your origins. You will encounter the ways in which your life force has been inhibited, thwarted, co-opted, or neglected. As you unlearn the habits and conditions that led to these losses, so too will you receive guidance, synchronicity, and inspiration as your rewards.

When I first started out in earnest on this path and began to speak in public about the value of dreams, I dreamed of riding my bicycle up a steep hill into oncoming traffic. Another person might have taken this as a sign to turn around and go with the flow. But anyone who creates a soulful life knows that this is a living image of wisdom: to go against the grain, like salmon swimming upstream as they follow a powerful inborn impulse to get home against all odds. Wisdom requires us to risk what's familiar and comfortable for the chance at finding true belonging.

Following wisdom needn't be as risky as this dream suggests, though any amount of daring can feel like this when we've been trained to comply, to fit in, to fly under the social radar. However, dreaming is the path of life-force. To follow it is to connect to the implicit vitality of creativity itself. Like in all of nature, the living edge of renewal requires us to shed anything that hinders life. Once, after making it through a hinterland of shadow work, I received an extremely moving dream that became the basis of my understanding of dreamwork.

Spiral Garden

I dream of a monk who is working with careful devotion in a garden. Dressed in wine and saffron-coloured robes, he is quietly weeding and planting small starters in the morning light. I see his nimble fingers working in the soil as if they are my own. When the dream oculus pans outwards, I am in awe to see that the garden itself is in the shape of an ever-widening spiral.

I awoke brimming with the warmth of understanding that the shape and value of dreamwork was contained in this simple scene. To engage with dreams is to be like this monk—working with spiritual devotion at the living edge of the unknown, following the curve of our growth spiral. Each weed he pulled was an unhelpful attitude I was uprooting, each plantling an embryonic sprout in my psychic growth. Planting the seeds nature itself has provided, and tending to their mysterious potential. The spiral would take me many more years to understand: how healing is not linear but more like orbiting core wounds, looking at them from shifting perspectives, gaining distance and discernment on each turn of the circle.

All creatures have an instinctive nature that guides them in their particular way of being. Like the elephants who travel vast deserts and know in their ancestral bones where to find a watering hole, or the birds who are born knowing how to build a perfect nest, we too have nature moving through us. I believe dreams are working tirelessly to reconnect us with that inexhaustible well of wisdom and originality. The living images in our dreams are the connective tissue to the rest of the animate world. And when we are in communion with our dreams, not only do they restore a sense of magic and meaning to our personal lives, we regain a sense of relational purpose in that ecosystem.

Thinking relationally is the great aptitude needed in our times. One of the skills that comes directly out of dreamwork is our ability to find cohesion in seemingly disparate narratives, or between contrary symbols. With enough practice, we start looking for symbiosis in all matters—seeing through the lens of mutualism. We discover that what is needed by the other is essential to our own well-being, and vice versa. Soul doesn't end with the perimeters of your own body, it is attached by invisible arteries to the world's soul.

We can think of the personal psyche like a node in a vast ecology of interconnected psyches. The figures we meet in our dreams are the inhabitants of this world, giving shape to the unseen forces thrumming behind the visible surface of all life. Those symbols are the counterparts of the experiences we have in waking-life, and they are also representations of ancient patterns, and emergent phenomena from the cooperative sums and differences of that ecopsyche. Understood properly, our dreams are meant to guide not only our personal growth, but the evolution of planetary consciousness.

CHAPTER 2

Wisdom of Sophia

I, the fiery life of divine wisdom,
I ignite the beauty of the plains,
I sparkle the waters,
I burn in the sun,
and the moon,
and the stars.
With wisdom I order all rightly.
Above all, I determine truth.[1]

HILDEGARD VON BINGEN

BEFORE I DO DREAMWORK, I always say a prayer to help us
remember that our conversation takes place in a sacred context. I
begin by acknowledging the body's enduring support—it is, after
all, the home where soul and world meet. I promise to listen to its
communications. Then I offer gratitude for the opportunity to
practise. What an exquisite privilege it is to be in communion with
others who value their dreams! I give thanks to the dreams who, in

their infinite intelligence, are so miraculously designed to heal. And I acknowledge our holy helpers, those benevolent beings who guide our lives with invisible hands. Whether that guidance takes the form of our dream symbols, bodily instincts, intuitive senses, or other kinds of ancestral magic. I finish with the intent to open the eye of the heart, to perceive that wisdom that is pulling us into right rhythm with the rest of nature.

Though we use a thousand different names for that which gathers and governs us in an invisible web of relationships, those names are often embedded in religious ideologies that divide us. But as Hazrat Inayat Khan so poignantly teaches, there is an underlying harmony that connects them all called Wisdom. Everything in the physical world has its roots in this hidden dimension. As we open the eye of the heart, we become able to see below the surface of things into their internal world—how Wisdom burns "in the moon and in the stars," as the mystic Hildegard von Bingen poetically puts it, and "ignites the beauty of the plains." I practise in devotion to that divine Wisdom that animates the world who, throughout the ages, has been known as Sophia.

Sophia is an ancient Greek word that means *wisdom* and is the central image of Greek philosophy. You can find it in the root of the word "philosophy" (philo-sophia), which literally translates into "love of wisdom." In modern language, wisdom has become a noun, describing a noble human attribute, however when we trace Sophia back to her origins, we find an ancient feminine divinity who is instrumental in the creation and upkeep of the world, and is the true source of human revelation.

"Wisdom is a knower in you," says my old friend and Jungian analyst, J. Gary Sparks. "Not something that you know, something that knows you. There's a reversal of centrality."[2] Wisdom isn't arrived at through an accumulation of outside knowledge. It is our intrinsic ability to recognize eternal truths without having been taught what to look for. As the word implies, re-cognition is to know something *again*. This means that before we realized it, the truth already existed. So while we normally credit someone as a wise person when they offer sage advice, what we really mean is that they are exceptionally attuned to the inherent wisdom of nature. Sophia is the name for that force behind life, and within our own bodies, that is pulling us into coordination and cohesion with the rest of nature.

In this chapter, we are going to explore some of the ways Sophia appears in various sacred scriptures dating back thousands of years. While not exhaustively tracing her history, it is important that we touch on some of her key appearances to contextualize how and why she is central to dreamwork. Just as we would with any symbol, it's valuable to look at Sophia through various perspectives, since each holds an aspect of her layered complexity. But we don't need mediation by religion or its ambassadors to relate to Sophia. In fact, it is only in seeking her directly in the Imaginal World that she reveals herself.

Throughout this book, we'll look at the ways in which Sophia manifests for us in our dreams, in synchronicity, and in nature. I will refer to her alternately as Wisdom and Sophia, because both names are accurate, and each evokes different associations. That Sophia is feminine is one of her most compelling qualities. Her gender is revolutionary in that it challenges us, after 2,000 years of abolition by biblical patriarchy, to associate the feminine with the divine. Keep in mind that I am speaking from a revisioned Jungian lineage that identifies the feminine principle as a broad set of attributes present and available in all genders.[3] Wisdom, on the other hand, is a word that lives beyond the gender binary, and is only truly understood as that which reconciles paradox.

SOPHIA THROUGH HISTORY

The written history of Sophia dates back at least 2,500 years, though scholars believe we can find her by many names revered in much older cultures, such as the ancient Egyptian Goddess Isis,

Ruha d'Qudsha, the Goddess of the Iraqi Mandaeans, and the Hindu Goddess of Wisdom, Saraswati. Appearing in early Judaism, Christianity, Gnosticism, and Alchemy, Sophia is one of the most powerful figures in divinity. But over the centuries, her name and image have been so actively suppressed that she is also the least known.

The Oxford English Dictionary defines wisdom as, "the ability to make sensible decisions and give good advice because of the experience and knowledge that you have." This modern concept of wisdom is the one most of us recognize, and more or less echoes the Sophia of Greek Philosophy (600–300 BC). The Greeks equated the search for wisdom with the quest for the meaning of life, which Aristotle believed could be achieved through reason and scientific knowledge.[4,5] He emphasized, as the dictionary still does, practicality as an aspect of wisdom—to make one's "beliefs and values cohere with one's actions."[6] Yet in the Wisdom writings of the ancient Hebrews, this quest for meaning wasn't an intellectual pursuit so much as a spiritual effort.* The goal of wisdom was to come into communion with the "divine order of things, written into the nature of life."[7]

This idea of a divine order in nature was central to Jung's understanding of the psyche. He discovered that when you understand one dream, the next dream is an evolution upon the image you just integrated. And when you don't understand a dream, its message will keep repeating in recurring dreams or motifs until you do. This is a simple observation, but the implications are profound: it means there is something within us that knows where we're going, and wants us to fulfil that intrinsic potential.

You could say that Sophia is the architect behind the narrative unfolding of our dreams, leading us into our next becoming. When

---

* The three Wisdom writings in the Hebrew Bible are Proverbs, Ecclesiastes, and Job. Included in the Apocrypha are two more books, Ecclesiasticus (or Wisdom of Ben Sira), and the Wisdom of Solomon.

we say we are following our calling, it is Sophia's voice we are hearing. Wisdom is "that factor that creates images in the inner field of vision and organizes them into meaningful order."[8] If we learn to follow her patterns, she leads us—through dreams, synchronicity, and other symbolic events in our lives—to fulfil a unique destiny. Destiny, as I interpret the word, is the idea that all of nature—ourselves included—follows an implicit order, a set of divine instructions. We each have an inborn story to fulfil that is reflected back to us in our dreams.

It's thrilling to experience the progression of images across a series of dreams. The first dream begins by giving form to the intangible, often an obstacle you are being asked to overcome in your life. That may be an image of a mountain to climb, an authority figure who bullies you, or an intruder who invades your privacy. Without this image, the issue would still be intangible, expressing itself indistinctly in symptoms of anxiety or depression. Now that you have an image, you can correlate it to analogous dynamics in your waking-life: the mountain speaks of a huge project you're about to scale, the bully embodies a dynamic confronting you in the workplace, and the intruder gives shape to your inner critic.

These correlations help to affirm the "realness" of your situation, showing you how psyche experiences the unseen dimension of events. The difficulty of your project can no longer be dismissed as something inconsequential, because it really is a mountain in the Imaginal World. This is Wisdom at work: knowing that what's unseen is still substantial gives you a foothold from which to enact change. Maybe it helps you to remember to take one slow step at a time with your mountainous project, or recognize when you're feeling bullied so you can summon your inner authority. Maybe it helps you exercise stronger boundaries against intrusive thoughts. When you successfully shift your orientation, you will receive new dreams such as seeing vistas from a higher ground, making an ally of an adversary, or visitors knocking before they come in. Somewhere down the line, these new perspectives become essential to the person you are meant to become in order to give what you have to offer the world.

With enough experience, you learn to trust the dream's prompting, even without knowing how the story will resolve itself. Sophia holds a coherent and meaningful map for our lives, giving us one step at a time with occasional glimpses into the whole picture. Different from fate, which is a pre-arranged future, she is that which holds the *potential* for our becoming. Like the humble acorn holds the potential for the mighty oak tree, so too is our pattern written into the nature of life. When we participate with Wisdom, we are drawing that story into the open.

In the Hebrew scriptures, Sophia is called *Chokhmah,* which also translates into "wisdom" in English. This Hebrew word has a broader range of meaning than its counterpart in English. While Chokhmah does refer to intellectual prowess and sagacity, it can also apply to a craftsperson with refined skills, or anyone demonstrating a unique talent for diplomacy or eloquence. Most intriguingly, Chokhmah is also said to be found in persons with a mastery of dream interpretation.[9] So a person who does anything exceptionally well, often after a lifetime of devotion, is said to be given wisdom. In the Arabic version of the word, *Hikmah* (also Wisdom), is understood as a refinement of the human soul, in which one becomes like a mirror, reflecting the divine.

WIFE OF GOD

Sophia is a paradox in that it refers to both a hidden quality in some humans, but it is also the name of a divine feminine figure, most notably in the Book of Proverbs in the Hebrew Bible, and other Jewish and Christian texts. She was a divinity that existed alongside God as his feminine partner in creation. In her personified form, she appears 149 times in the Bible and tells us exactly who she is. Through her own declarative statements in Proverbs

(8:22–31), Sophia tells us that she existed before the world was made, and dwelt with God in the acts of creation:

> *The Lord created me at the beginning of his work, the first of his acts of long ago. Ages ago I was set up, at the first, before the beginning of the earth. When there were no depths I was brought forth, when there were no springs abounding with water. Before the mountains had been shaped, before the hills, I was brought forth—when he had not yet made earth and fields, or the world's first bits of soil. When he established the heavens, I was there, when he drew a circle on the face of the deep, when he made firm the skies above, when he established the fountains of the deep, when he assigned to the sea its limit, so that the waters might not transgress his command, when he marked out the foundations of the earth, then I was beside him, like a master worker—and I was daily his delight, rejoicing before him always, rejoicing in his inhabited world and delighting in the human race.*[10]

When I first learned about Sophia, I was incredulous that such an important feminine figure existed in the scriptures. There, in the foundation of all Abrahamic religions, is evidence of the divine feminine. God had a female partner and was drawing on Sophia's guidance and collaboration in creation, yet very few of us were ever taught her name.

I found myself driven to learn of her origins, and how she'd been stricken from the official doctrine. The more I discovered, the clearer her image became inside me, like something I'd always known but had never heard named. I couldn't help wondering how different civilization would look—how different my own life would be—had the Wisdom teachings been venerated. Even for those of us who weren't raised with traditional religion, the influence of Christianity extends far and wide in the dominant culture; we have all been shaped vicariously through its institutional and social constructs. I remember looking at Michaelangelo's fresco on the ceiling of the Sistine Chapel, as if for the first time, to see Sophia tucked under God's left arm as *they* created Adam together.

There are seven books in the Wisdom literature, sometimes called Poetic Books or Sapiential Books: Proverbs, Psalms, Job, Song of Songs, Ecclesiastes, Wisdom of Solomon, and Wisdom of Ben Sira. These seven books were excluded from the New Testament by the Protestant Church, who rendered them apocryphal texts. The word "apocryphal" originally meant secret or hidden, because its content was too esoteric or sacred to be read by the uninitiated, but over the centuries, as the Church distanced itself from these writings, the word came to mean *spurious* or *heretical*. Fascinatingly, in the New Testament, many of Sophia's characteristics and teachings were subsumed in the figure of Jesus, who was sometimes referred to directly as the Wisdom of God.[11]

Though in ancient times, she was recognised as a Goddess by other names, the biblical scholars of today do not consider Sophia a deity but rather a *hypostasis*. From the ancient Greek word, *hupóstasis*, meaning "foundation, substance, essence," she is understood to be the underlying substance of reality—the holy foundation supporting all of nature, and the cosmos. As an animist, I recognize this "holy in nature" as the unnameable Way that I've been courting throughout my life. This is perhaps what the philosophers were also searching for in their quest for the meaning of life. They were attempting to come into communion with Sophia's patterns in the material world. This is a topic we will explore in much greater depth in future chapters.

What Christians now refer to as the Holy Spirit is a concept widely believed to have been abstracted from this ancient feminine personification of Wisdom.[12] In the Wisdom of Solomon (7:22–8:1) it is written, *"For wisdom is more mobile than any motion; because of her pureness she pervades and penetrates all things. For she is a breath of the power of God, and a pure emanation of the glory of the Almighty .... For she is a reflection of eternal light, a spotless mirror of the working*

of God, and an image of his goodness. Though she is but one, she can do
all things, and while remaining in herself, she renews all things."[13]

QUEEN OF HEAVEN DETHRONED

To understand how such a powerful figure could be erased, we
need to travel back to ancient Jerusalem to a time period called the
First Temple (1200–586 BCE). It refers to the great temple built by
King Solomon in the tenth century when ancient Israel still
observed polytheism, worshipping a pantheon of gods and
goddesses in a religion called *Yahwism*. The temple was dedicated
to Yaweh but there was also a statue for the Goddess Asherah, who
was regarded as his divine partner. In 621 BCE, King Josiah of
Judah led a powerful group of priests, called the Deuteronomists,
to take control of the temple. They banned all pagan altars and
idols, slew any "idolatrous" priests, destroyed rural sanctuaries and
fertility cults, and consolidated power in the monotheistic religion
that came to be known as Judaism. As Jungian therapist and
biblical scholar Anne Baring writes, "They removed every trace of
the Queen of Heaven, who was worshipped as the Holy Spirit and
Divine Wisdom."[14]

But this wasn't the first time the world turned its back on the
divine feminine. Having devoted decades of her life to the study of
the historical developments of religion, Baring set out to understand the erasure of feminine archetypes in religion by going back
even further in history. She explains how during the Palaeolithic
and Neolithic eras, the Great Mother was the principal deity
worshipped around the world.

One of Her oldest representations is the voluptuous Venus of
Willendorf discovered in Austria, believed to be over 25,000 years
old. She was also found in different forms in Mesopotamia,
Western Asia, and Northern Africa. She represented the understanding that all of life was connected and interdependent. The
multitudes of species, and the cosmos itself, were in sacred rela-

tionship with each other within Her body. There was no separation between creator and created, or spirit and matter.[15] But around 2000 BCE in the Middle East, "there was a change so great that its repercussions are still felt today because it has been the major influence on Western civilization. This change was the replacement of the Great Mother by the Great Father ... As the monotheistic Father God brought creation into being as something separate and distant from himself, so Nature gradually became split off from Spirit and was no longer sacred."[16]

As Erich Neumann writes in *The Great Mother,* "In the patriarchal development of the Judeo-Christian West, with its masculine, monotheistic trend toward abstraction the goddess, as a feminine figure of wisdom, was disenthroned and repressed. She survived only secretly, for the most part on heretical and revolutionary bypaths."[17]

One of those heretical bypaths was Gnosticism, a mystical offshoot of Christianity originating around 100–300 CE. In the Gnostic creation story, Sophia, a cherished aeon (angel) of God, makes a fateful error that casts her out of the Pleroma (Heaven). This fall from grace is what results in creation as we know it, with Sophia becoming trapped in matter.

The Gnostic story of Sophia echoes the Christian myth of a split between human and divine. This familiar motif of the feminine "fall" into sin and disgrace, like that of Eve's original sin, was by express design. The Deuteronomists created this official doctrine for the New Testament in a time when women were forbidden to hold any priestly office or even speak in the church. Christianity's enmity between the "higher" and "lower" aspects of human nature, between mind and body, was naturally projected onto women. The repression of what they associated with "the feminine," including the body, sexuality, nature, and sinfulness changed the course of Christian civilization.

WISDOM IS PARTICIPATORY

Unlike traditional religion, the Gnostics believed the purpose of incarnation was to redeem Sophia from bondage by seeking the divine within ourselves. Symbolically speaking, this reiterates the idea that the divine is hidden in the natural world—in the substance of our own bodies—and that the redemption of Wisdom is a participatory process.

How we redeem Sophia is a complex question. Our first clue, which occurs again and again in texts relating to Sophia, is that wisdom can only be found through reflection and searching. In Ecclesiasticus 6:26 it is written, "court her with all your soul, and with all your might keep in her ways / go after her and seek her; she will reveal herself to you; once you hold her, do not let her go / For in the end you will find rest in her and she will take the form of joy for you."[18]

In other words, wisdom is not divinely bestowed on some and held back from others. Nor is it something that we invent or cultivate as individuals. It is the outcome of a reciprocal process that requires devotion on our part, and the benevolence of grace. As Old Testament scholar Bernard Anderson echoes of the ancients, "They believed that written into the very nature of things is a divine order which can be found through human searching and reflection."[19] So rather than seeking an intermediary to guide you spiritually, you can have a personal relationship with holy wisdom by turning toward the natural world, your own body, and dreams. Sophia reaches out to us in symbols and synchronicity, and we reach back to her through dreamwork and contemplation.

* * *

With each of these reflections, a more complete picture of Sophia starts to emerge. We know that she originates in a far older polytheistic worldview which is pluralistic by nature. Likely from

Egypt, and patterned after the Goddess Isis, she is known by many names in many cultures. From the ancient Hebrews, we learn that Sophia existed before the world and plays a definite role in its creation. In ways we'll continue to explore, she behaves as an intermediary between God and the world (or spirit and matter). She holds a map of our potential, or what the great Jungian analyst Marie Louise von Franz calls the, "timeless, pre-existent, cosmic plan."[20] The Greeks equated that plan with "the meaning of life," but when we consider that Sophia is found not only in the symbolic realm, but in the "substance of reality," we begin to see the striking similarities between the Wisdom teachings and the beliefs of animistic cultures.

You can imagine how disruptive Sophia would be to mainstream religion—and why she was stricken from official canons or depersonalized into an attribute of Jesus or God. As a feminine divinity, her gender is of course unacceptable to patriarchal religions that only deify a masculine God. But as "one who contains multitudes" she also runs contrary to monotheism itself. Sophia's teachings are rooted in nature and the body, encouraging the marriage of opposites. By contrast, the major religions advocate for dominion over nature (and our animal instincts), and maintain a split between good and evil, divine and material. While the patriarchal model of spirituality is hierarchical and demands obedience and deference to priests and intermediaries, Sophia invites us to seek her privately; she is "attainable to everyone."[21]

UNION OF OPPOSITES

One of Sophia's most formidable characteristics is that she embodies paradox. There is a wonderful poem in the Gnostic manuscripts found at the Nag Hammadi library in Egypt called "The Thunder, Perfect Mind" in which Sophia declares herself as present in every aspect of life, from the sordid to the holy. Here are a few key passages from this much longer translation:

For I am the first and the last.
I am the honoured one and the scorned one.
I am the whore and the holy one.
I am the wife and the virgin.

I am the mother and the daughter.
I am the members of my mother.
I am the barren one
and many are her sons.

I am she whose wedding is great,
and I have not taken a husband.
I am the midwife and she who does not bear.
I am the solace of my labour pains.
I am the bride and the bridegroom
and it is my husband who begot me.

[...] I am control and the uncontrollable.
I am the union and the dissolution.
I am the abiding and the dissolution.
I am the one below,
and they come up to me.

I am the judgement and the acquittal.
I, I am sinless,
and the root of sin derives from me.
I am lust in outward appearance
and interior self-control exists within me.
I am the hearing which is attainable to everyone
and the speech which cannot be grasped.
I am a mute who does not speak,
and great is my multitude of words.[22]

From this gorgeous poem in the Gnostic Gospels, we begin to understand Sophia as a figure who reconciles the opposites. She embodies what philosophers call dual-aspect monism, which holds spirit and matter as distinct but undivided aspects of one reality. Similar to the Sufi concept of a threefold cosmos, Sophia offers us a conception of spirituality *unsplit-off* from our earthly experiences.* She is above and below, divine and corporeal, holy and whore, honoured and scorned. In a theme we will return to, reconciling paradox in this way is foundational to the kind of dreamwork I will invite you to practise.

Jung once wrote, "The meeting of two personalities is like the contact of two chemical substances: if there is any reaction, both are transformed."[23] Meeting Sophia is like an alchemical encounter, because she leaves us altered for having met her. Nowhere is this more vividly depicted than in the alchemical treatise known as *Aurora Consurgens*, "Rising Dawn" in Latin, which is an 800-year-old mediaeval text illuminated with vibrant symbols. Through the author's visions and dreams, we see the stages in this internal alchemy as Sophia intervenes in the psyche of this one man's life. Jung and von Franz believed that because of who Aquinas was, and what he stood for, *Aurora* gives us a powerful glimpse into the reconciliation of opposites that is being asked of our cultural epoch.

This rare text was rediscovered by Jung in the course of his research on alchemy as metaphor for the inner transformation. But it was Marie-Louise von Franz, Jung's esteemed colleague, who painstakingly translated and interpreted *Aurora Consurgens* line by line in what is broadly considered one of her finest works. What's particularly fascinating is that though the text is unattrib-

---

* I love this language (coined by Alice Walker) because it implies an intactness that includes our faults, aberrations, or oddities, and that splitting them off is a disservice to love. Alice Walker, *The Temple of My Familiar*, Harcourt (1989), p 287–289.

uted, many believe it to be the last work of Saint Thomas Aquinas.[24, *]

Aurora Consurgens is the story, told in seven parables, of an orthodox Catholic man who is challenged by Sophia at the end of his life to restore the divine feminine in his psyche and work. Filled with quotes from the Wisdom literature, the central theme in *Aurora* is the reunion of opposites: between a man and God, lover and beloved, matter and spirit. The author's visions catapult him through a series of life-altering transformations as he attempts to reconcile the paradox of divinity living in his own body and desires. He volleys from awe to depression as he tries to resist the gradual disintegration of his one-sided patriarchal worldview.[25]

In his artworks, we see the allegorical sun and moon in a jousting match as his two sides battle it out within his own psyche until, after much hardship, the opposites are joined as one. Beheld finally as an androgynous figure, a conjoining of feminine and masculine, the author is forced to reconsider his hierarchical conception of a God who denies the feminine, the body, and nature. Instead he is shown that creator and created are, and always have been, one, or as von Franz frames it, a "psychophysical unitary reality."[26]

Generally when we think of unity, we imagine an indistinct oneness. However, one of the most important teachings of Sophia is that in uniting opposites we are not erasing their differences, but holding a third perspective that contains both. Similarly, the word "soulbody" brings two distinct worlds, psyche and physical,

---

* Aquinas (1225–1274) was a mediaeval scholastic philosopher and theologian, considered one of the greatest thinkers in the history of Christendom. To give you a sense of his importance, his system of thought called "Thomism" was declared the official philosophy of the Roman Catholic Church. As the father of Scholasticism, (the systemized education of theology) Aquinas' *raison d'etre* was to bring intellectual reason to the support of faith. But because psyche works to bring balance to one-sided attitudes, these mystical visions of Sophia would have gone against everything he'd been teaching his entire life.

into one wholeness, making it paradoxically not two, and not one, but two-in-one.

The Canadian philosopher Jan Zwicky says wisdom is the ability to grasp wholes that occupy the same space, yet are different. Like two melodies whose intervals are identical, but sit on different scales. A harmony is struck between the two to create a third combined sound yet neither melody ceases to exist. Wisdom is generated by one's ability to grasp both forms without abandoning either. As Hildegard wrote in *Antiphon for Divine Wisdom*, "One wing soars in heaven/one wing sweeps the earth/and the third flies all around us."[27]

You can see why Jung and von Franz were fascinated with this text. They believed it not only contained the author's call to integrate Wisdom, it revealed the suppressed (and repressed) material of Western Christendom at the time. A worldview that still surrounds us today, characterized by a rationalistic, anti-feminine, disembodied spirituality.

This is why Sophia is so relevant to us today. We remain affected by that dualistic split between spirit and matter. The result of creating a culture that doesn't believe in the sacredness of matter is collective disembodiment. When we don't experience the holy in nature, we are unable to feel kinship with the very body that animates and sustains us. The result is a catastrophic power drive for human growth and progress at any cost to the ecosystem. Just as we over-extract resources from the earth, we demand our own exhausted bodies perform with the same machine-like utility. This is why so many of us are being called into our own alchemical transformation by Sophia in our dreams.

It is the basis of Jungian psychology that we come into this world with an intrinsic plan for our lives. We fall into psychological suffering when we become someone other than who we're meant to be. When we stray too far from that plan, the eventual result is heartbreak, suffering, anguish, or even catastrophe in our material lives. This is when Sophia appears, often in the form of synchronicity or dreams to lead us back to ourselves, one step at a time. When our ego is in conflict with our true nature, she is that twinkle of Wisdom in the depth of darkness showing us the way out. The choice is ours. We can follow that pattern of purpose or pretend it doesn't exist. But as Aquinas discovered, and as we are discovering collectively, it has a "nasty way of arranging actualities" when ignored.[28]

FINDING WISDOM IN CHAOS

Sometimes called the "dark night of the soul," there are inevitable periods in one's life when the conversation with Sophia runs eerily quiet, leaving us alone on an empty tundra, questioning whether meaning exists at all. Sometimes this happens after we've sustained a shock of some kind, causing us to lose faith in the thread of purpose we've been following. It can also be the result of taking a path not in alignment with our true nature. Sometimes a dark night sets in after a prolonged exhaustion or disappointment. But even in the loneliest of times, Wisdom is summoning us toward our next becoming. It just may require us to fall to pieces first, before we can rearrange them.

No matter how adept you are at following the Dreaming Way, it won't inoculate you against suffering. In dark times people sometimes say, "everything happens for a reason." But the difficulty with this philosophy is that it disintegrates in the presence of real violence, grief, and profound loss. One cannot make a tidy sum of "everything" when these factors are involved. The phrase is rarely used by someone who has met with mortality squarely, and endured it, because life is more complex and roundabout than what "reason" can account for. While the saying does contain a germ of wisdom, it tends to be used as shorthand for, "I am uncomfortable with this level of suffering ... can we please end the conversation?" When we try to force reason on a difficult experience, it can be felt as a tyranny both enacted by others and from within. Especially in a circumstance we cannot escape, such as illness, war, poverty, or oppression, the idea that suffering is necessary in some way is a very bitter pill to swallow. In the dark night of the soul, it's not a *reason* we are looking for, it is *meaning*.

In his moving memoir on surviving the Holocaust, *Man's Search for Meaning*, Viktor Frankl wrote, "In some way, suffering ceases to be suffering at the moment it finds a meaning."[29] Meaning, in this sense, is the value and purpose retrieved in hardship. Like carving a bowl, suffering can shape a unique capacity in us that can be used for good. Like the mother whose son is killed by a drunk driver, who goes on to raise global awareness about the dangers of driving and drinking. Or the woman who survives domestic violence to open a sanctuary for other women who need help. Meaning can also be as simple as being kind, making beauty, or helping others in your community. Even the smallest purpose can keep you alive, one day at a time. Without hope for redemption, or something to live for, we lose the source of vitality we need to persevere through hardship.

For as long as someone is struggling for the basic necessities of staying alive, it's impossible to find meaning in devastating circumstances. In having to attend to survival, one loses the "range of motion" of the imagination. The privilege of imagination is out of reach of the person whose every ounce of energy goes toward escaping oppression. But as Toni Morrison says, "I know the world is bruised and bleeding, and though it is important not to ignore its pain, it is also critical to refuse to succumb to its malevolence. Like failure, chaos contains information that can lead to knowledge—even wisdom."[30]

It is the word "chaos" that strikes me as the jewel of this quote, because the patterns of nature always contain phases of dissolution, disorganization, disease, and decline. There is a branch of mathematics called chaos theory that looks at how dynamic systems like weather, the stock market, even road traffic—systems that appear to be full of irregularities and disorder—are actually governed by underlying order. A system can spontaneously evolve from chaos into order under the right circumstances. We can see this in our own lives. When you look back on your greatest opportunities and achievements, didn't they always follow a time of doubt, confusion, and discomfort?

In ancient Greek and in many Indigenous cultures, chaos was the mythological state that preceded the creation of the cosmos. Chaos, or what is often described as an infinite void or abyss, was the first thing to exist. And it was from this primordial state that a new order emerged. I think what's really being asked of us in moments of crisis is to discover what wants to be given a good death. To acknowledge, grieve, and find a way to say goodbye to the old landscape of your life. To move forward and discover its new shape. To find what new things, however tiny and fragile, want to live in its wake.

This was the task put to Aquinas. He underwent a chemical reaction, as we all do when confronted by Sophia—between what we thought we knew, and what something that knows better than us. This is why she appears to us in times of anguish, as one thing recedes to make room for something new to exist.

Nobody goes willingly into initiation. By its very nature, initiation is a humbling of the will; it shatters us on all levels. And though every part of us may mount resistance to being changed, we are not meant to emerge intact. We are not meant to *re*-cover what has been revealed. Rather, we are meant to be *dis*-illusioned, *dis*-solved, *dis*-appointed before any thought of rebuilding or declaring reason.

So the question becomes what, if anything, can you do to bring about order in times of chaos in your life? Where can you find guidance when you feel abandoned by life? When Sophia goes quiet, what can steady you in the absence of your own knowing? When even your dreams have disappeared, and you are utterly disoriented, how can you find or create purpose to carry you through hardship?

In the non-dualistic frame of Sophia, we hold the paradox of good and evil as different faces of the same divinity. It means that somehow we have to live with both suffering and joy and see them as necessary to our being human. It is so much the habit inherited by the dominant culture to split these things off from one another. When I was diagnosed with a degenerative illness, I was shocked to discover that I carried the underlying Christian belief that I was being punished for something I'd either done wrong or hadn't done well enough. Indeed, this was echoed in my progressive community as well. I can't tell you the number of well-meaning people who suggested that I was sick because I needed to heal an unaddressed emotional wound in my life.

While it is convenient to blame sin, or a malevolent entity for creating death and chaos in our lives, the paradox of life and death is *the* central condition of any earth dweller. Like all of nature, we are constantly moving through cycles of flow and hindrance, life and death. In fact, if we learn anything from the forest floor, death is one the most active and fertile states of the life cycle. So how did we come to favour life over death?

The idea arose in Late Antiquity (c. 3–8 CE), when Plato declared that the body and soul were separate entities. This led to a hierarchical paradigm of flesh-versus-spirit, in which the body (and all its desires) were considered lowly, and the soul was aligned with all that was good and holy. Before that, for a huge swath of recorded history, the Great Mother (c. 25000 BCE—5000 BCE) was worshipped in many forms as a symbol of the "unity of all life in Nature."[31] Not only were body and soul unified in the Neolithic Goddess, as Lithuanian archaeologist Marija Gimbutas writes, she, "personified every phase of life, death, and regeneration. She was the Creator from whom all life—human, plant, and animal—arose, and to whom everything returned." [32]

In the second-century Roman classic novel *Metamorphoses* by

Lucius Apuleius, the protagonist has a vision of Isis, upon whom Sophia was patterned. She says, "I am nature, the universal mother, mistress of all the elements, primordial child of time, sovereign of all things spiritual, queen of the dead, queen of the immortals, My nod governs the shining heights of heaven, the wholesome sea breezes, the lamentable silences of the world below. I know the cycles of growth and decay."[33]

Our task in dreamwork is to unite these paradoxes by descending into the underworld, deep into the unconscious, down in the body to find and redeem the soul that lives there. As the authors of *Wisdom's Feast* wrote, "It is not the incarnate Sophia's role to bind or connect us to the earth, but to help us recognize that our understanding of ourselves as separate from the earth is a delusion."[34]

If you are lucky enough to have a person in your life who knows you so well they can hand you back the shattered pieces of yourself in good order after a disaster, you will always find some comfort in love. But in my experience, no other person or people can provide the deep palliative medicine of the soul. A dear friend can be a brief surrogate; but in hard times, we need a near constant source of connection and guidance. We need to tap the wellspring of vitality deep within the core of our own bodies to rematriate us to our own patterns. That relationship can only be struck in solitude, so it is often in anguish that we finally turn toward Wisdom.

To show you how vividly Sophia appeared in the psyche of one woman in the depths of isolation and heartbreak, I want to share the following dream and discussion with you. As you read her story, notice how many of the attributes and teachings of Sophia that we've covered appear in her symbols and revelations. This was the first dream Virginia brought to our work together.

The Black Madonna: Virginia's Dream

I am leaving an opulent cathedral through a crowd of people who are milling about in its square. I must cross through a ceme-

tery. Beyond that, I discover a door with stone steps descending into an ancient temple. I am afraid of going down the steps, but when I do, I am astonished to find an altar to the Black Madonna. When I emerge from this place, I hear singing, so I follow it. I peek behind a door to find a congregation raising their voices in worship. I long for this kind of belonging.

Knowing nothing about what was going on in her life, I recognized this as a big dream and asked Virginia if she was in the process of making a huge spiritual transition. "Absolutely, yes!" she replied without hesitation, and began to share some of her story.

She started by telling me how she recently lost a child. Unable to withstand the aftershocks of that loss, her partner left the relationship, heaping heartbreak upon heartbreak. Not wanting to suffer alone with the compound nature of this grief, she sought support from her spiritual community of ten years. On the surface, their practice revolved around the value of shadow work. But when she shared her story with the group, they were visibly uncomfortable, and her tragedy was swept awkwardly aside. As they distanced themselves from her, Virginia was left feeling painfully exiled from her community, adding again to her already doubled grief. "I knew I had to leave that group," she concluded, "but after everything that's happened, I have no idea where I belong."

We took a moment together to fathom the magnitude of her losses that seemed to be pushing her life into transition on several fronts. Then we turned toward the dream that, appropriately, begins with leaving. At first the Catholic cathedral seemed like an ill-fitting symbol for her spirituality, which was decidedly alternative, but then I asked for Virginia's associations to Catholicism. She described the religion as hierarchical, rigid, and patriarchal. When I reflected those words back to her, she recognized with some surprise how closely the two forms of worship resembled each other. She said, "The leaders of my spiritual group are all men and their rigidity shows in how others are rarely given a voice in the community, especially if we disagree. Also, I was given the sense that my grief was inappropriate and made things messy."

Even in the world of alternative spirituality, it is common to find these institutional hallmarks of oppression. The drive to power—whether for money, influence, or dominion over others— is at the core of every vertical model of religion. And the goal is always ascension: to transcend suffering to remain in light, purity, and wellness. As Virginia was discovering, this way of thinking manifests as a rejection of life itself. There is no such thing as life free from suffering, confusion, illness, and death. Any grounded spirituality will not only value the dark end of the living spectrum, but treat our passages through it as the holy undertakings they are.

In a group without this understanding, Virginia's suffering was treated as intolerable, and it became clear that she would have to leave her long-standing community. It would fall to Virginia to make a terrifying encounter with the shadow that nobody else was willing to touch. The dream was a foretelling of the passages she would have to make alone if she was going to emerge from this hardship.

Her first passage in the dream, upon leaving the cathedral, was through a cemetery. We took this as symbolic of having to traverse the ground of loss, as Virginia was grieving the death of her child, her ex's inability to support her through that loss, and her break with the community who were unable to hold her in hard times. In the dreams that followed, we went deeper into these heartbreaks, each of which needed to be witnessed and grieved well. And as we neared the heart of her grief, Virginia encountered the fear that she might not be able to survive the passage.

This fear was epitomized in another dream when she came face to face with a terrifying black snake that had come uncoiled from the earth and was the size of a river. In that dream, her ex had left the door open to this snake, and it had pushed its way into the kitchen to encircle Virginia. As we worked with this powerful image, we discovered that she felt terrified of being overtaken by the grief, bitterness, and anger of her losses. Like the snake that threatened to swallow her whole, her deepest fear was not being able to live or love again. She described her dream-ex as, "completely useless, with no idea how to handle the snake." Like his literal inability with her grief, he also represented of the part of Virginia that wasn't sure she could handle this dark encounter. However, just before waking up from this dream, Virginia called out for help from her friend Javier who, in waking-life, is the caretaker of her land. She described Javier as capable, nurturing, and dependable—"a real angel in my life." We explored him as symbolic of an emergent masculine archetype that was coming to life in her own maturity. As she reflected on Javier's qualities, she began to play with the idea that they were attributes she herself possessed, traits that were being summoned in this difficult time. And of course the snake is also an ancient symbol of transformation, which was encircling Virginia with its alchemical inevitability.

In her original dream, there was a door beyond the cemetery that led down into the temple of the Black Madonna. The dream seemed to say that Virginia needed to descend into an older, earthier, feminine form of worship. Her dreams over the next six months entailed that descent, containing many images of wisdom found in the earth. In one dream, she was given a half-finished necklace of stones harvested from the sea that, when polished, shone like emeralds. In another, she had to plant real hearts in the earth to fertilize the growth of trees. It was as if her embodied experience of grief and hardship was asking to be valued, polished, planted, and cared for.

After tending to her soul through dreamwork, ritual, and actual tree planting, Virginia was rewarded with a dream that took place in another cathedral. This time, the gathering was vivacious and informal, filled with musicians singing South American medicine songs. There was no sense of hierarchy in the church, only the warm relatedness of the medicine music. She came upon a mandala amulet that she knew was meant for her. It was green with life and looked like a peyote crown. Virginia felt the mandala was symbolic of the unity she was now living that was both spiritual and earthy. As she learned to value and give relevance to her own suffering, she had discovered a more mature spirituality that was inclusive of her suffering, unsplit-off from hardship. She went on to record an album of music that emerged from her experience, and grew a new community around herself.

From the very first dream, Virginia saw her path laid out before her, but only in retrospect could it be entirely understood. She needed to go through the alchemical process of leaving the cathedral of spiritual hierarchy and bypass, crossing through the cemetery to confront her fears and grieve her losses, making the descent into Sophia's realm where her vulnerability could be valued and cradled. Once she retrieved those split-off parts of herself, Virginia was able to live in a more embodied and intact relationship with her grief. Just as the Gnostics imagined Sophia like shards of divinity trapped in matter, we are redeeming her in our lives and in the world when we find wisdom in life's most difficult experiences.

Understanding our suffering as part of Sophia's plan takes the sting out of our pain because, as Sparks puts it, "what really causes despair is not misery, but meaninglessness."[35] This happens when we believe what we are going through has no relationship to anything else. When the way is completely lost and we lose sight of the horizon, this is when Sophia appears as starlight does, shining an ancient cosmic knowing onto our path as if to say, "This isn't the end. This moment is connected to a chain of moments, leading somewhere. There is life beyond the deathing field, but you must let it hone you before you can live it."

There is a wonderful quote from Jung that begins, "Tears, sorrow, and disappointment are bitter, but wisdom is the comforter in all psychic suffering."[36] Virginia followed this pattern of wisdom in her dreams, which helped her from succumbing to the anguish of her losses. This is the comfort Wisdom offers. She says, keep going. Not only is there more to your story beyond this anguish, but one day your story will be the starlight for another to follow out of their own darkness.

In disorienting times, when our horizon is obscured, our goals often shrink to more humble efforts like staying alive, getting through the night, or just walking on solid ground again. When we've dropped the thread of our own story and our pattern has become broken and disorganized, what we're really experiencing is a loss of Wisdom. As Jung continues, "bitterness and wisdom form a pair of alternatives: where there is bitterness wisdom is lacking, and where wisdom is there can be no bitterness."[37]

I think of the magicicada who lives as a nymph underground for up to seventeen years before becoming its future self, with wings that carry it up into the airy light after knowing nothing but legs and dark and wet earth. Fascinating that "imaginal" is the word entomologists use to describe this final version of itself—the realized form that always existed in the potential of the nymph. The root of the word comes from "imitate," as if there was a pre-existing image that it was compelled to become.

The person suffering from meaninglessness must find that imaginal version of themselves, but like the magicicada that dissolves into goo before taking its final shape, so much of trans-formation is about loss. Only a shell of its former self is left—and even that must be abandoned on the branch where it lifts off. To become its next self, first it must dis-integrate, dis-orient, and dis-solve. It must unencumber itself by shedding, sloughing off, and releasing old solutions and orientations. The imaginal version of ourselves is lightweight, airborne, as yet unanchored by form. The transformative process may be so gradual that we don't even perceive it as radical change. It may not be as dramatic as a butterfly emerging, shimmering its fresh, powdery pigments in the sun. It may just feel like who you've always been but without the weight of the expectations you'd been carrying.

Life before the chaos of transformation is usually safe in its own way, but also distant. Rather than observing life from the vantage point of a perch overlooking the sea, you are now immersed in its wild waves. And there is no alternative but to be tossed and changed and polished by the sea. What can you do but surrender to the absence of order, participating more deeply with Sophia? After all, trying to maintain a view of the horizon is impossible when the ocean abducts you. It is much calmer below the surface, where the currents of her nature can be felt as closely as the breath in your own lungs.

Not long ago, I had an intriguing dream. An elder gifted me a first-edition novel from his collection of antiquities. Written in the Middle Ages, the book was extremely rare and rich with history. As I held it for the first time, I understood its value was not just who the author was, or how it was sewn and bound in the materials of its time, but for how it had also been ruined. As we flipped through the pages, my mentor pointed out special places where wax had been spilled, pages folded or torn. Like fossils in stones, I understood these injuries were, in and of themselves, what gave the book value. Toward the back, I found a set of pages that had a hole bored right through them, shredded into confetti by some destructive force. There, deep in the gash left behind, I suddenly saw green and exclaimed, "I can almost see the trees this paper was made from!"

The heart of this dream is about the value of decomposition. All of nature is in a continuous cycle of creation and destruction. At any given time we are either composing or dismantling the forms and stories that make up our lives—sometimes both at once. Whether it's the end of an era and we are closing off a project or grieving a relationship, or the start of a new idea or attitude, we are always in some stage of generativity and decay. This is true of psyche as well. When a story we tell about who we are gets old, we feel a growing sense of ennui about its repetitiveness. We may hear ourselves telling the story to someone new and feel as if we're speaking from a script that's lost its meaning. This is how we know that something is ready to be composted, sent back to the primordial soil to fertilize our new story sprouts.

This dream was, for me, a mirror into the value of experience; how the ways in which I have been injured and improperly cared for are of intrinsic worth. Like fossils, the experiences of my history have shaped who I am, and have drawn out the wisdom I have been able to share in my story.

There is also a powerful reminder in this dream about the creative energy that's made available in the death of an old story. The green in the gash was a living portal into the story's origin. Like the ouroboros, the beginning is embedded in the end. As we come around to where the tail meets the mouth, it's like a new chapter wants to be written from the muck of what's been lost. Once the trees were shredded into pulp to make the paper on which the story was written—now the story decomposes and we can see the early green of vitality again.

This is why Sophia appears in times of anguish. It is in these turning points when she is most visible. Like a rending between the worlds, she is that face that appears in the chaos of lines. She may show up in your dreams as starlight—that pre-existent, cosmic light in the dark—an illumination of knowing beyond your personal unconscious. Occasionally she appears personified, like the Black Madonna in Virginia's dream, or as one of the many pre-Christian figures of the divine feminine. Sometimes she takes the shape of a huge snake of transformative power that reminds you to shed your comfortable old skin, freeing you to become the imaginal version of yourself.

She may also appear in various images of paradox, or *two-in-one* forms, like Virginia's sacred and earthy amulet, or Indigenous music in a cathedral. She may show up as interacting opposites, like two circles, androgyny, or a double-helix. Sophia is found along that living seam between polarities, where the opposites crackle with electricity. Sometimes Sophia is in the image of going against the grain, like a salmon swimming upstream, or someone cycling against the direction of traffic, because she calls us to brave against the norms—so we can improve upon them.

Wisdom cannot be seen or proven, like knowledge can. We don't arrive at it through a chain of logic, so we can't explain the route for someone else to follow. Wisdom appears of her own accord and can only be substantiated in our embodied resonance. Through a delicate alchemy of focus and receptiveness, Wisdom delivers us from the roiling of opposites into paradox. She gives us the ability to embrace *bothness*, releasing the need for a duel between contraries, so we can rest in their symmetry. From this relational ground comes a surge of energy, like picking up a scent to better track the way of the world.

Seeking Sophia is a lifelong practice of tracking the cycles and patterns of nature in our dreams. We are always making adjustments as we strengthen our symbolic perspective. We listen for the way, like a river that runs below the earth. We never know where it is leading, but we feel its power and meaning pulling our lives forward. Following Wisdom can be disruptive and arduous at times, especially when it takes us down unconventional paths. Bushwhacking through the brambles of the unorthodox way, one can lose faith in the unseen, especially when the route grows painful, exhausting, or lonely. But as we cut the path, it is also shaping us into the kind of person who is called wise.

Wisdom is synonymous with the Way. It is that which is pulling our lives toward purpose. We always have a choice to walk that path, or not. We are never punished for leaving it behind for a time, or prevented from renewing our commitment to it. We may meet Wisdom in the heart of crisis, or when we are most distant from ourselves, but at any given moment, we can deepen our kinship with Sophia—by following our dreams and the enigmatic clues she leaves for us in waking-life. She is the *anima mundi*, working tirelessly to bring us in sync with our own life force, and the rest of nature. Throughout this book, we will keep circling our inquiry on Wisdom, attempting to learn her symbolic tongue, and even court her favour through ritual and imaginal practices. After all, it's only when we pick up the thread of our own story and have a hand in the weaving that we can ever know intimacy with Sophia.

CHAPTER 3

Orientation in the Otherworld

WHEN A PERSON about to undertake a sacred quest in fairy tales, they are given magical objects or enchantments to take with them. These spells and talismans may not make sense to the protagonist at the outset of their journey, but when the time comes to cross a gnarly threshold or face an intimidating foe, they remember their sacred bundle and use a spell to solve a riddle, a key to gain entry into a secret realm, or draw upon the wisdom of an ally at just the right moment. This chapter is like a magic bundle, containing important pieces of wisdom to prepare you for the journey ahead and shore you up in times of doubt on your Dreaming Way.

THE MAGIC OF NOT-KNOWING

When you enter the Imaginal World, you must approach it as you would any foreign-to-you culture: with respect for its native ways and perspectives. You must be prepared to leave behind your waking ways of moving—strategies that may be useless and even harmful here. As you fumble through the dark, you may feel a rising discomfort as you search for something substantial to grasp on to. But with experience, you will learn that discomfort is like oxygen in the otherworld. It is precisely this not-knowing that is the way to the Way. Disorientation is the initiatory substance that prepares you to be astonished by Wisdom's approach. Like allowing your eyes to adjust on a dark moon, synthetic lights must be extinguished before constellations will appear.

In the day-world, you use the clock to tell you what time it is, a calendar to organize your events, a GPS to locate and direct you. You depend on the continuity of life which is roughly the same from day to day. People and places retain their shape or, mercifully, only change gradually. Words remain stable on pages. And while there are certainly confusing and disorienting events in ordinary reality, logic can usually be applied to help you untangle them.

None of these laws apply in the dreaming. Time and space are flexible. Ancient relations turn up in modern milieus and forests are behind bedroom doors. Everything and everyone is mercurial and ambiguous, subject to change and even overlap. Logic is ineffectual here, and even counterproductive, like trying to call for help on a dream phone whose numbers keep scurrying away. However, being disoriented can deliver you to the place you didn't know you were meant to find.

If we really want to know ourselves in relation to the cosmos, we must be willing to challenge some of our inherited ideas about psyche. We need an open mind to discover where it is located, what dreaming is really for, and what counts as strength in the subtle realm. We must be willing to step out of our familiar world and into the unknown, where we aren't always comfortable but where we feel most alive. As the great psychonaut Terence McKenna once said, "Nature loves courage. You make the commitment and nature will respond to that commitment by removing impossible obstacles. This is how magic is done. By hurling yourself into the abyss and discovering it's a feather bed."[1]

It takes courage to enter the dreaming wildlands because you must ultimately go there alone. Not just in the sense of being unaccompanied, but without the comforts and crutches of your certainty, those mental structures that keep us company on the most intimate level. The word "courage" comes from the Latin root *cor*, for "heart," suggesting your heart is needed to lead. So much of life can be an elaborate project to hide and protect our hearts from injury, but if we want to access the most courageous part of ourselves, we need vulnerabravery.* We need to unhinder our sensitivity to come back into connection. Only then can we perceive and attend to the needs of the world around us.

In dreams, you are reconnecting to the very matrix of existence. The first task you are given is to interrupt the doggedness of your own rationalism. The dominant attitude toward dreams is so banal and dismissive, yet we rarely consider challenging those inherited beliefs. In large part this is because capitalism is set up to keep us distracted and scrambling to survive. On another level, I think we know that if we valued the imaginal life even half as much as the physical one, the whole structure of our world would tremble, because upon those materialist foundations a million other ideas are built. In fact, whole civilizations are constructed upon these mundane cornerstones, and we live in stacked compartments along their paved roadways.

But far out of town, beyond the outskirts of development, wild things grow and thrive in the absence of intervention: hearty, woody wildflowers, robust rivers, sturdy old trees, and boulders who know things. The Dreaming Way is a living ecology of ideas and forms that are in a constant flux of exchange, erosion, emergence, and decline. In this place of seeming disorder, this country of nowhere—with no roads, no cities, no rules—we have a chance

---

* "Instead of putting up our defences when we meet with conflict, vulnerabravery is the conscious choice to keep our heart open so that we might discover what's hidden within it. It is a great paradox that when we let ourselves be undefended we find our true strength." Toko-pa Turner, *Belonging: Remembering Ourselves Home*, Her Own Room Press (2018)

to discover the true source of power and originality. In this unconstrained wilderness, dreams unfold in a slow-motion music of cosmic cycles, leaving glacial striations in the bedrock of who we are. Like original instructions from a greater intelligence, we can follow those patterns of wisdom to bring our lives into harmony with the Way. To orient ourselves by this deeper set of impulses, we have to cultivate an appreciation for ambiguity and grow our tolerance for uncertainty.

As part of the larger project of planetary transformation, it's incumbent on each of us to contend with the ways in which we've fallen out of sync with the guidance of nature. This is a different kind of activism than most of us are used to: it requires us to confront the most ferocious adversaries within. We all have internal bullies who are invested in keeping our materialist cornerstones exactly where they are. But as old attitudes crumble, the wild self thrives—and a whole new set of capabilities begins to sprout from within. You develop skills that allow you to move deeper into hidden realms of wonder and wisdom, giving you access to the creativity our world so desperately needs.

RELATIONALITY: SEEING THROUGH MANY EYES

There is an inherent order to the Dreaming Way that can't be discovered with linear thinking. Instead, what is needed is an aptitude for imagination, whose central skill is relationality. Relationality is our ability to zoom out from the ego's perspective to perceive the whole living system around us. To see how things are connected in a web of kinship and mutual influence, and to care for its well-being. It's a very old idea that Indigenous peoples have always observed: we exist in an intricate entanglement of relations. In dreamwork we are challenged to dispel the lonely perspective of the "I" to grow considerate of the whole ecopsyche.

We normally think of relations as the ones belonging to our families and social circles. But in the animistic way of understanding the world, our relations extend far beyond the human community. As professor of Religious Studies and author Graham Harvey writes, "The world is full of persons, only some of them are human."[2] Our species lives in a complex and symbiotic ecology with many other species. In biology, this mutualistic existence is called a holobiont. Another great example of a holobiont is the coral reef, a community of coral animals, algal symbionts, microbes, and bacteria, who have co-evolved and depend on each other to survive. Just like them, we are living in a long-term community with all the fungal, bacterial, and viral cells that live within or upon us.

It's more accurate to call ourselves a "we" than an "I." If we accept the idea of ourselves as a holobiont, then it follows that we can approach our psychic ecosystem in much the same way. Reality doesn't just stop at the physical realm—it extends into the Imaginal World. Psyche is an ecology full of beings who possess their own aliveness and exist in degrees of kinship with us and each other.

Relationality is the skill of seeing that web of connections and not just its constituent parts. Instead of only identifying with the protagonist in a dream, we can inhabit the perspectives of other characters and elements. When we understand the domino effect of behaviours in a system, we can better perceive its emergent wisdom. We see this kind of "systems thinking" throughout nature, like shoaling fish who coordinate as one body. They aggregate as a community to gain strength in numbers, resulting in a better defence against predators. Schooling also gives them the advantage of "many eyes" to perceive threats and opportunities.

This ability to see through many eyes is one of the great gifts and requirements of dreamwork. Relationality is what enables us to connect with the living symbols in our dreams, to learn what uniqueness they possess, what drives them to act, and what they long for. But it also helps us to see how individual parts are influencing the larger symbiosis. Shoaling fish have an innate democracy; if an individual makes a different decision—say to swim toward a delicious snack, or away from a potential threat—others can decide whether or not to follow him. If enough members of the school also decide to follow, the whole group will change direction. Similarly, when we see through the eyes of a fellow dream figure, we may decide to follow their impulse instead of our own, in service to the greater good of the psychic ecosystem.

Thinking relationally is what enables you to discover the invisible link of meaning that connects you to your imaginal others. For instance, perhaps you dream of being a passenger in a car with someone who is driving too fast. You urge them to slow down, but they veer off onto a dirt road, almost driving you over a cliff. Every aspect of this dream is related to every other part. That you are a passenger suggests you are not in "the driver's seat" of this situation ... but who is? Like puzzle pieces, there is a relationship between the "passengerial" attitude and the reckless energy of the driver who is speeding. One part gives up control while the other "takes the wheel," neither consulting the other's needs. We sometimes find ourselves driven by a frenzy while another part of us suffers. The dream encourages us to see the less embodied aspects of our psychic experience. We could also explore the car, the veering, the dirt road, and the cliff, all of which would add dimension to our predicament.

Not only are all these symbols connected to each other, but they have links to waking-life. Following the Sufi belief that all subtle bodies have their analogue in the material world, relationality is the skill of spotting those natural sympathies. The reckless driver might be the part of yourself that is "driven" by ambition but ignores the needs of your body which, like the passenger, needs to slow down. This relational link isn't one you forge yourself. It already exists in Sophia's field of meaning, clothed in metaphor. Once you establish these relational connections, ways of knowing are exchanged between the two worlds, and both you and the dreaming are enhanced by your relationship.

DREAMWORK IS RECIPROCAL

Mysticism is the devotion to living in reciprocity with the sacred dimension beyond the physical world. Derived from the Greek *mystikos*, meaning "initiate," a mystic doesn't believe something because they've been told it exists, but endeavours to experience it for themselves.[3] Unlike other "transcendent" forms of spirituality, the mystic doesn't chase ecstasy and deny suffering. Nor do they look for a teacher outside of themselves. All mystics are dreamers, and all dreamers are mystics. We reach for the divine—often through our own grief and despair, anger and longing—to encounter the holy within. This is how we heal our own hearts, and how beauty and wisdom are restored to the world.

As Sophia reminds us, "I have come to those who reflect upon me, and I have been found among those who seek after me."[4] Reciprocity begins with our willingness to enter the dark thicket of our own dreaming to find a true sense of direction and purpose. This is a complete reversal of the way we tend to organize our lives in Western culture, where we take our direction from the world of form and (only occasionally) engage in reflection as a form of recovery. Many people ask themselves why they feel so depressed or unwell, disconnected and lonely. It is because this closed system slowly drains us of well-being, like a potted plant that is never given any fertilizer. In the Dreaming Way, the soul informs our choices, and we move into life from that soulfulness. Then new dreams respond, prompting us to make the next adjustments, pulling us deeper toward our path.

Too rarely do humans participate in this mystical conversation. Our lives are left to languish, uninformed by the soul's inclinations. On a collective scale, this indifference is visible in all the ways civilization abuses its connection to nature for profit, power, and prestige. On a personal level, it is evident in our feelings of alienation, anxiety, and meaninglessness. We long to feel connected to something greater than ourselves alone, to know that our lives are ennobled by a sense of purpose, but we leave the feast of wisdom uneaten.

We tend to think of imagination as an "inner" experience, but in Sufism it is considered a psychic reality where a reciprocal exchange takes place. As Henry Corbin writes, the Imaginal World is "the place of the encounter between God's descent toward the creature and the creature's ascent toward God."[5] We find a remarkably similar description of Sophia in J. Gary Sparks' interpretation of *Aurora Consurgens* where he explains, "We ascend to Sophia in dreamwork. She descends to us in synchronicity."[6]

When we equate the psyche only with the mind, it renders dreamwork a purely mental enterprise. I'd like to encourage you to think of psyche as a place, accessible to each of us, where we can travel to be in communion with the sacred. There is a constant exchange taking place between the imaginal and material worlds. We are in conversation with soul, and soul is in conversation with its source, by whatever name you call it—nature, *anima mundi*, God, the sacred, Brahman, Great Spirit, or the Divine. It is ultimately from that source that we derive our ethics—not in the sense of religious ideologies, but those core values that arise from the earth and the cosmos. Engaging in this exchange has a calibrating effect on the way we live. It puts us in step with what I like to call relational purpose. Every individual has a unique calling, but that calling is intimately tied to the intent of nature, upon which we are dependent and obliged.

Like the analogy of the acorn containing the unrealized oak, every being has a set of original instructions to grow into. The images that populate our dreams behave as structured clues to that fate. But the growing oak tree depends on a community. The biggest, oldest standing ones in the forest are called mother trees, and they send extra nutrients across mycorrhizal networks running through the soil to the young saplings that need it most.[7] Trees also work together to regulate their microclimate. Even in falling to one's demise, a nurse log offers its body as rich ground for new seedlings. Like the oaks, none of us exists in isolation. We live in a complex ecosystem of other beings, all of whom have purposes of their own. Different from the new age idea that "we create our own reality," a more mature understanding of purpose is one of collaboration. We certainly participate in shaping our lives, but so does everything around you. Though we can't possibly grasp this level of complexity, dreamwork is that middle ground where you can attend to the reciprocal and dynamic exchange between your soul and the soul of the world. And as we do this, we are led in a meaningful direction in symbiosis with a larger plan. The soul is the guiding friend in each of us that tirelessly works to align us with that broader, relational purpose.

Though we might hope for catalytic dreams that change our lives in one chiropractic jolt, this process is more like constant tiny adjustments to keep our two worlds in sync. Often what we experience as a mundane event in waking-life has important symbolic significance to psyche. This is because the soulbody has its own experience of events, and the dreamtime is where that symbolic reality appears. Sometimes these two ways of seeing are so distant from each other that we have a hard time relating between them.

To give you an example, let's say you have a friend who keeps interrupting you. You tolerate them because they have other qualities you appreciate. After spending time with them one afternoon, you feel a bit annoyed that they didn't listen to what you had to say, but you brush it off. That night, you dream the same person drives a giant SUV right up onto the sidewalk and over your toes. Though you might not be conscious of any damage done in your daytime exchanges, psyche experiences real harm and describes the enormity of that harm in images. You've heard the idiom "step on someone's toes" to describe a bully or domineering intent, so the dream communicates this metaphor to draw your attention to that dynamic. However, because it is an SUV, we can say that there is an escalation of scale, a power differential, between human feet and a motorized vehicle.

With this understanding of the dream, you may have more compassion for your soulbody's experience of events. You might decide to follow through by asking the friend to be more considerate of your input and boundaries. Maybe they are able to make this change with you. Or maybe it remains intolerable, but your self-awareness allows you to turn toward more reciprocal relationships.

As the old Hermetic phrase "as above; so below" reminds us, things that happen on the outside often reflect internal dynamics, and those patterns may even repeat again at larger scales. We'll return to this idea of the fractal nature of dreams in depth in Chapter 14: The Ocean in the Drop, but consider that the dream may also be pointing to a way in which you relate to yourself. Maybe something in you *overrides* your own sense of authority in the world. Are you invalidating yourself before you even speak? You then carry this possibility into your day and notice how automatically you override your own *standpoint* before even having a chance to express it. To integrate this learning into your waking-life, you decide to practise valuing your own voice, finding opportunities to be heard. While it's impossible to say how this calibration will bring you closer to your destiny, imagine how a thousand shifts of this kind could reorient your whole way of being in the world.

Once you respond to a dream by adjusting how you move in waking-life, psyche responds with an evolving image. Like following clues on a path meant just for you, there is a sense of momentum that grows out of your conversation with the imaginal that is exciting, empowering, and affirming. And there is no bottom to the depths of this intimacy. The dialogue matures indefinitely. As you remember Sophia, she remembers you … and a momentum of reciprocity grows between you.

BENDING THE DREAM

Everything you need to know about the symbols you encounter is contained within your understanding of the world around and within you. And it isn't just a one-way broadcast; you also have the power to bend or alter that reality with your intent. There is a wonderful word for this in German, *umwelt*, which describes the unique way in which an individual organism perceives and shapes their environment.*

Nowhere is this perceptual uniqueness more obvious than in dreams. One person may dream of a church and describe it as a refuge, while another may dream of the same church and call it a place of oppression. The differences in their *umwelten* are the result of countless influences including history, biology, culture, personality, and soul. The way we perceive the world is the result of having been shaped by it, but we are, in turn, dynamically shaping it through those constructs. As Richard Tarnas wrote, "Our world view is not simply the way we look at the world. It reaches inward to constitute our innermost being, and outward to constitute the world .... World views create worlds."[8] Though reciprocity between psyche and the world happens mostly invisibly, it is laid bare in our dreams. In the Imaginal World, because it is unconstrained by continuity, we have a chance to behold and experiment with the plasticity of our *umwelt*.

At best, "I" is a temporary congealing of the ego's perception, a bundle of ideas that can be scattered and rearranged by significant events and relationships. But there are many more parts at work in the unconscious. Like living in a diverse village, psyche is inhabited by a multiplicity of needs and beliefs that are constantly changing form. Some of these we inherited from our families and cultures, some are much older than that, some are brand new, and some are just passing through like inclement weather. In dreams,

---

* In the biological sense, first used by Jakob Johann von Uexküll (1909)

we see this web of mutual psychic influence very clearly in the diversity of characters we interact with. The "I" in the dream is really only one player among many.

Instead of being swept along in this stream of unconscious experience, it's possible to choose how you inhabit your dream reality. If you practise lucid dreaming, which is the art of becoming awake within your dream, you can make different choices and develop mystical skills like flying, teleporting, breathing underwater, and telepathic communication. You can even learn to shapeshift, or invoke an ally at will.

Lucidity is just another word for awareness. Whether asleep or awake, it occurs on a spectrum. When we are under-resourced, we tend to be less lucid, and when we have space and quiet around us, we bring more presence to both worlds. Through dreamwork we can find a sweet spot between allowing the dream to naturally unfold and moving through it with a depth of awareness. Instead of using lucid dreaming to become a ninja to fight off an intruder, or fly away when trouble appears, you discover the meaning of the intruder so that you can stop him before he takes shape. The real magic of lucidity is becoming conscious of our own *umwelt* so we can begin to bend it in both worlds. Only when we see the shape and form of our perceptions and assumptions can we alter them at the root.

While "dream control" is a fascinating and exciting undertaking, it can also be dangerous if not grounded in intention and stable mental health. If someone is using lucidity to avoid difficulty, or for entertainment—treating dreaming like a video game— it can be addictive or even harmful. Without the proper foundations in place, lucid dreaming can cause dissociation from reality, and exacerbate anti-social behaviour. In the ancient traditions, lucid dreaming (called Yoga Nidra in the Upanishads, and Dream Yoga in Tibetan Buddhism) was always a spiritual practice. It was used in combination with meditation to overcome fears, attain mystical states, and realize the illusory nature of self and reality.[9]

The tricky part is learning to see the ecology of our *umwelt* through symbolic eyes. We have difficulty perceiving the implicit dimension of reality due to our bias for a literalist worldview. This is especially true because our dreams are made up of familiar images and people we know in waking-life.

For example, you may dream of a friend of yours getting into a plane accident, and think, "Oh I better warn them not to take any flights." However, if you were to spend some time exploring your friend's traits and characteristics, you may discover they hold symbolic resonance with your own life. Let's say you describe them as ambitious and impulsive; qualities you admire. That may connect you to having recently taken some big risks yourself. Maybe you're even seeing those ventures "take off" into new heights of your career. The plane crash can now be seen through a symbolic lens; it may express how you've been feeling a crash from that initial high or, perhaps, a painful disappointment.

What's often needed in dreamwork is a telescoping ability to alternate between narrow and broad ways of seeing. In moving back and forth between the literal and the figurative, you can strengthen your symbolic capacity—zooming out from what you *literally know* about a thing so you can perceive its subtle body and *how it means*.* Only from this meaning can you locate yourself in relation to that symbol to discover its influence in your life.

When we take a dream image at its surface presentation (a pregnancy is a pregnancy), we are unable to see its metaphoric meaning (a pregnancy is the growth of new life within). But when we sound a symbol's depth for nuance and dimensionality, we begin to see how its shapes and gestures echo analogous situations in our waking-life. This is the discovery of meaning. A dream

---

* I use *how* instead of *what* here because I want to invoke meaning as a living quality. Just as we observe how someone slumps if they're feeling defeated, how a squirrel flicks its tail when it's irritated, so too is meaning fluctuating in motion. When we say, "*What* does it mean?" it freezes the symbol in amber. *How* conveys manner and movement, which is personalizing rather than objectifying.

about going into labour and not having the resources to care for a child relates to the new film project you're about to launch into the world. Knowing this gives you agency you didn't previously have. You can make different choices in waking-life, such as giving yourself grace in a demanding and sacred time, or asking for the "midwifing" help of an assistant or friend.

As you claim agency in waking-life, so too will your dreams begin to change. If you find yourself in a recurring dream of panic during labour, a degree of lucidity may carry into the dream from your waking dreamwork. You'll find you're able to summon new resources, maybe feeling supported and nurtured by an inner mother figure, or even jumping ahead in the narrative to see your healthy toddler running around independently.

With these pieces of wisdom in your dream travel bundle, I hope you will feel more oriented in the wild world of dreaming. When you feel bewildered, remember that not-knowing is a requirement for transformation. Let yourself play with seeing through many eyes, even inhabiting strange perspectives. You'll be surprised by what can be found in the most unusual places. Remember that you are in a divine conversation. While it may be in a language you haven't yet learned, one day it will become second nature to you. When you experience lucid and mystical dreams, consider them gifts for the work you've done, and take a moment to bask in and celebrate yourself. The best way to give thanks to Sophia is by contributing the beauty of your healed heart to the world.

CHAPTER 4

Types of Dreams

RATHER THAN THINKING of dreams as an indistinguishable mass, it can be helpful to know that they come in a variety of different genres. While it's just as impossible to name every kind of dream as it is to categorise our life experiences, knowing the most universal types of dreams can help you deepen your discernment and mastery of dreamwork. There are dreams that defy interpretation, dreams that aren't personal, dreams that predict the future, and many more. While we will be focusing on the symbolic value of dreams in this book, let's first take a look at some species of dreams that require a different approach.

Compensatory: If you're too one-sided in your conscious attitude toward a situation in your life, your dreams will give expression to the opposite perspective to help you move to a more vital middle ground. In other words, these dreams compensate for what's unconscious, neglected, or unacknowledged. Like walking a tightrope, if you lean too far to the left you will never keep your balance—so the dream pulls you to the right to keep you from falling. For example, when you've been too accommodating in waking-life, you might be full of rage in your dream. This isn't to say that rage is the right response in the waking-life situation—the dream had to exaggerate unacknowledged anger to help you to come to terms with the full spectrum of your feeling. Another example is if you have been spending all your time working on your business, your dreams may counterbalance by introducing a foolish character who takes nothing seriously. Compensatory dreams are often recognizable by how deeply they contrast with your waking-life situation or attitude.

Prospective: Different from a prophetic or precognitive dream, these dreams are like trying on probable futures in which you get a glimpse into who you are becoming. You'll notice spates of these dreams during big transitions like moving or changing careers. Far more powerful than the conscious mind, the unconscious is able to draw upon all kinds of data to sketch out a rough plan for the future. It can even offer solutions to your hurdles along the way by showcasing what's possible. Using a vast storehouse of sensory input, historical patterns, memories, and other forms of experience, your dreams may offer a version of the future showcasing how you could grow. For instance, you might dream of a future home or career, and eventually discover that, while the details aren't exactly like the outcome, the dream was uncannily predictive.

Rehearsal: Often reported by athletes and musicians, these dreams are for practising something that you're attempting to improve upon in waking-life. When I was twelve years old, I loved swimming and diving but was terrified of the "inward" dive, because I always thought I'd hit my head on the diving board on the way down. For weeks, I would stand on the diving board with my back to the water, too afraid to take the dive. One night I dreamed that I did a perfect inward dive. I experienced exactly what needed to happen in my body—a focus on my core strength and using the board to gain height, followed by a simple 180-degree turn to the water. The next morning I went to diving practice and did a perfect (for a twelve-year-old) inward! I was never not able to do it again. A rehearsal dream might also take the form of navigating conflict, holding your ground, or public speaking. The dream becomes a safe and supportive way to practise something you'd like to consciously improve.

Precognitive and Warning: Sometimes called a prophetic dream, this is when we dream of something before it happens. The details may not match exactly, but there is usually a significant foretelling that comes to pass. For instance, I was once woken up in the middle of the night by a dream of intruders. I sat up in bed with my heart pounding and told my partner about my dream. About ten minutes later, we heard men climbing our fire escape! Because we were wide awake, we were lucid enough to lock the access to our loft from the roof and call the police. After arresting the two men, they told us one of them was actually carrying a gun!

Some might say these dreams are coincidental but I believe time is a lot less linear than we think. I believe we can actually have "memories of the future" and this phenomenon isn't limited to nocturnal dreams. I have personally experienced many waking-life moments of clairvoyance witnessed by others, and I can say that this capacity for knowing things before they happen is enhanced by focused dreamwork.

Quite simply, the more dreams you remember, the more likely you are to receive valuable information from the subtle realm. The tricky part is being able to discern between a precognitive dream and a symbolic one. While precognitive dreams do seem to have a charged or lucid quality to them, I haven't yet found a way to reliably tell these dreams apart except by witnessing their actualization in waking-life.

As we touched on, the trouble with being quick to warn others about a dream you had about them is, more often than not, it says more about your projection onto them than it does about their fate. In spiritual communities, I've frequently met people who take their dreams as prophetic, sharing unwanted advice with others without their consent. I believe this is a tell-tale sign of someone unwilling or unable to do their own shadow work. Projecting your shadow under the guise of "prophecy" onto a person who trusts you, or is vulnerable, can result in real harm. It can cause them to feel worried and upset and, in some cases, even traumatized. I knew a woman who was at a psychic fair when a stranger calling himself a spiritual healer came up to her and informed her that she had a dark entity attached to her and her family's psychic field. He was just a charlatan, soliciting his services, but years later the woman carried around a fear that she was being stalked by evil spirits. While this wasn't a so-called dream prophecy, the effect can be the same.

There are many famous examples of precognitive dreams, like how Abraham Lincoln dreamed of a president being killed before he was assassinated, and Carl Jung dreamed of rivers of blood engulfing Europe, that he believed was foretelling World War II.[1] But to be safe, it's advisable to always begin with a subjective approach to find the dream's parallels with your own life. If, after doing depth work, you still can't find a connection to the dream, you may consider sharing it with the person you dreamed of—but always ask for consent and acknowledge that what you are sharing may simply be your projection.

Paranormal: Paranormal dreams are those that fall outside the boundaries of what we consider the "normal" range of dream experiences. This includes things like telepathic dreams, visitations from the afterlife, and the appearance of entities. It's a huge topic, but it's worth making a space here to speak about a few of the most common dreams in this category.

A telepathic dream is the ability to receive non-local information while in a dream state. This can happen spontaneously. For instance, you dream your aunt decides on a whim to cut her long hair into a pixie. When you call her the next morning, you discover she did just that. Or, if you were conducting an experiment in dream telepathy, one person could secretly choose an image and focus on it while another person tries to dream of what it is.

Telepathy in the dream state has long been a subject of interest to scientists, but attempts to replicate it haven't been successful. That being said, I don't think waking telepathy is that unusual, especially as you develop your dreaming ability. I remember waking up one morning in my twenties to "hear" in my thoughts that my musical heroine Ella Fitzgerald had died. I immediately turned on the radio to discover that she had, in fact, died the night before. Another time, I was at an event when a stranger sat down at our communal table, and I "heard" her name in my head. I said, "You are Katia?" and she looked shocked. She said it was her name, but she never told anyone that—she usually introduced herself as Katy. In both these cases I was awake, so we cannot officially call it dream telepathy. But if we follow the idea that dreaming isn't restricted to our nocturnal state, and more like a channel we tune into while also awake, then perhaps the distinction falls away. Waking or lucid dreaming may be more conducive to this kind of non-local receptivity.

Most of my experiences of telepathy have occurred spontaneously, but it's easier to practise with people we are close to. When we share intersecting psychic fields with a loved one, we grow accustomed to reading each other's energy and carrying each other's concerns as our own. My partner and I have gotten so good at "shared brain" moments that we try to beat each other to the punch in saying ideas out loud. We get into laughing arguments over credit for who originated the thought form first. While telepathic dreams fall under the category of "paranormal," I see this ability as quite common.

Whether experiencing telepathy, having a precognitive dream, or receiving visitors from the beyond in our dreams, it's hard not to wonder about the nature of spacetime. It may be far more flexible than we realize. There are some fascinating discoveries being made in the sciences and philosophy to answer for these quantum entanglements.[2] Similar to "memories of the future," I have also had visits from my ancestors and relics from my heritage appear in my dreams. I knew these dreams were different from symbolic dreams because of their unique tone and texture. They had a lucid quality, rich with the gravitas of guidance being passed on to me from my long-dead elders. They also contained symbols that I had no personal experience with but which later turned out to be artefacts of my ancestry.

Many people report meeting their ancestors in their dreams and there are intriguing stories from people on their dying threshold who describe being reunited with their deceased loved ones in an adjacent dimension. Ancestor dreams are precious and life-altering for the dreamer because they are often course corrections or carry medicine to heal ancestral wounds. I have also dreamed of my ancestors in a symbolic sense, so I try to hold the paradox of these two ways of seeing when working with a visitation dream.

Many people report dreaming of ghosts or demonic entities who appear to manipulate their dreams, as if from outside one's own psyche. I'm reminded of something I heard the author Paul Levy say along the lines of, "dark entities exist for those that believe they exist."* The way I see these entities is like maladaptive clusters of thought/energy in psyche, or what Jung called "complexes." They are autonomous, living beings, in the sense that they have an agenda separate from our own. We can't control when they appear or how they'll subside. As we explored, we are all susceptible to being seduced by archetypes when we are afraid of our own shadow, or too rigid in our perceptions, but these are all helpers, in the sense that they contribute to our individuation.

Shadow work is about bringing these patterns to light, integrating traumatic experiences, and reclaiming our agency over intrusive thoughts and emotions. The psychoanalyst Hans

---

* Paul Levy and I went back and forth on this topic in December 2023, and indeed share similar views on the subject, but neither of us was able to find the original source of this quote.

Loewald wrote poignantly on the subject, saying, "Those who know ghosts tell us that they long to be released from their ghost life and led to rest as ancestors. As ancestors, they live forth in the present generation, while as ghosts they are compelled to haunt the present generation with their shadow life."[3] So long as we have the necessary support to do so, we can turn the ghosts of our past into ancestors. On the other hand, if someone isn't doing their shadow work—a topic covered in Chapter 10: Poison Is the Medicine—they may believe they need protection from a dark force that gains entry into their dreams. They will likely dream of and experience events in waking-life that seem to corroborate the existence of that intrusive entity.

There are objectively destructive forces both in the personal and collective psyche that have influence over us *because* we have a matching vulnerability to those shadows. The truth is that each of us carries the potential for what we call evil, but a "dark force" is often a thwarted vitality that has fallen into a negative aspect because it has been ignored or denied. Most extraordinarily, we find some of our greatest creative endowments hidden in the darkest places.

Anxiety: Somewhat less intense than a nightmare, anxiety dreams tend to reflect stress or ambivalence in your life. You may dream of getting into trouble, running late, being ill-prepared, unable to find something or get where you're going. In general, anxiety dreams are characterized by the feeling of a loss of control. You find yourself unable to accomplish something in the dream because of obstacles in your way. The more you try to overcome them, the less successful you are—and the more anxious you get. Often these dreams come out of uncertainty and overwhelm in waking-life, and it's important to pinpoint what's causing your distress to see if the choices you are making are supportive of your well-being. Anxiety dreams may be trying to alert your conscious self about an unhealthy situation you're in. They are ultimately a signal to find a place of peace and firm resolve in your life.

While some anxiety dreams are isolated and transient, arising during stressful moments in our lives, a pattern of anxiety dreams may be more significant. For instance, if you have repetitive dreams of overflowing toilets, it might be symbolic of feeling emotionally "backed up." These are signs of carrying around old, unprocessed conflicts that you've been unable to resolve. The dreams show how neglecting those issues can overflow into the present, causing tension and a lack of clarity. In waking-life that might look like a generalized anxiety, overwhelm, or persistent conflict in relationships. If this is the case, it's a great time to seek support in tending to and processing old issues so that they don't keep coming back up to haunt you.

These dreams can be typical for those who suffer from chronic anxiety. Whether due to personal, social, or environmental trauma, anxiety disorders are becoming universal. According to the World Health Organization, one in thirteen people globally suffers from anxiety.[4] It is growing increasingly common to experience some form of anxiety, especially as we navigate the age of the Anthropocene. So it's important to distinguish between the type of anxiety that is a healthy response to an objective threat and the anxiety that arises from what Jung called neurosis.

Neurosis, as Jung redefined it, is a psychological crisis when we are at odds with ourselves.[5] Who we think we are may be different from who we are meant to become—and the result of that conflict is neurosis. For instance, perhaps you were raised to be a doctor in a family of doctors, but in your heart of hearts you always wanted to dance. Though we generally think of the word in a pejorative sense, Jung believed neurosis served an important function as psyche's attempt to find harmony. "Neurosis is really an attempt at self-cure," he said, "It is an attempt of the self-regulating psychic system to restore the balance, in no way different from the function of dreams—only rather more forceful and drastic."[6] So even though anxiety dreams may feel as if they are just exacerbating our stress, they are attempting to bring our attention to an area of our lives that needs recalibrating.

Though neurosis often has its roots in the past, the work of anxiety is to discover where you are at odds with yourself in the present. Through the context, settings, and dynamics of a dream, your dreams will show you what area of your life is in conflict. The next work is not to get rid of the neurosis, but to find a way to live with it. To say it another way, the things that make us neurotic can oftentimes be our *raison d'etre*. How many stories have you heard of people whose lives became extremely useful to others as a direct result of their disadvantage?

To discover what your anxiety has to teach you, try reimagining your dream. Ask yourself what the most satisfying outcome would be. For instance, if you dream of missing your train, instead of ending in a sweat of anxiety for letting everyone down, consider how being late and lagging behind might lead to a mystical adventure. Try rewriting the dream in your journal and then consider how this new solution could be expressed in waking-life. Would it look like changing habitual behaviour? Accepting your unique difference? Taking some new direction? If you're contending with a deeper wound, finding a therapist or mentor can be the first step in introducing internal and external resources to shore up your nervous system. But perhaps the most remediating approach is finding a creative way to use the energy bound up in your anxiety to offer something of value to the world. In so doing, you are voluntarily partnering with the source of your suffering, which is what makes it meaningful.

Jung once said, "Neurosis is suffering which has not yet found its meaning."[7] When you realize that what you're going through is important and leading somewhere, this is when meaning is made. You discover the connection between your suffering and the pattern of your overall story. Inhabiting that unique story is also tied to the fate of the world: your well-being matters to us all.

Creative: In every creative field, there are tales of breakthrough discoveries that have come directly out of dreams. In many cases, the individual is sufficiently obsessed with a subject already but is only able to reach a solution with the help of the imaginal. Take the famous anecdote about August Kekulé, the German chemist, who was trying to understand how the atoms in benzene were arranged. After wrestling with it for some time, he fell asleep and dreamed of atoms dancing around before his eyes. When they finally settled into place they were in the shape of a snake eating its own tail. When he woke up he realized benzene arranged itself in rings, a discovery that revolutionized chemistry.

Dreams are an inexhaustible wellspring of inspiration for any creative individual. Many of modern culture's greatest achievements have come directly out of dreams: Einstein's theory of relativity, Niels Bohr's model of the atom, The Rolling Stones' "Satisfaction," and Elias Howe's invention of the sewing machine all came from dreams. Mary Shelley dreamed *Frankenstein* before she wrote it, and *The Strange Case of Dr. Jekyll and Mr. Hyde* came right out of one of Robert Louis Stevenson's dreams. Paul McCartney found the melody for "Yesterday," the Russian chemist Dmitri Mendeleev discovered the periodic table for the chemical elements, and somewhat ironically, Rene Descartes found the basis of the scientific method—all in their dreams!

Perhaps it is because we are dipping into a much vaster pool of knowledge, or maybe it is because we have to shut down the rational side of the brain to set our creativity free. But there's no denying that paying attention to our dreams enhances the imagination. Remember, everything that ever been invented first appeared in the imaginal realm.

Assimilative: When you find yourself on a learning curve in life, overwhelmed with sensory input, your dreams may need to sort through an overabundance of information to find what's useful and valuable. These dreams tend to replay the previous day's events in a loosely similar way. For instance, I once did some work for a friend by pulling a whole field of invasive knapweed over the course of a week. As simple as it sounds, it was a learning experience for me, figuring out how to wait for the flower stem to bolt, how it pulled easier when the soil was moist, and so on. During that period, I often dreamed of knapweed. There are times when psyche needs to consolidate what is worth keeping and what needs to be discarded. In waking hours, the assimilative process can be helped by physical activity, meditative rest, talking with a trusted other, or writing in a journal. But dreaming provides the ideal conditions for the consolidation of memories and emotions, due to the absence of new sensory input during sleep.

In one study, participants were asked to play the video game *Tetris* the day before, and 67% reported unambiguous *Tetris* images in their dreams that night. The takeaway was that "engaging learning experiences may have a particularly robust influence on dream content."[8] Similar to what we discovered with the dreams of creative people, when we are sufficiently engaged in novel learning, dreams take up the task of consolidating (and furthering) those developments into our memories. Furthermore, it's been discovered that when we dream of the content we are learning, it enhances our memory in waking-life.[9] A good example of this is when we are learning a new language and begin to dream in that tongue.

Neuroscience has also discovered that the amygdala (which processes emotions) and the hippocampus (which helps move short-term memories into long-term storage) are especially active during vivid dreams, suggesting that dreaming serves an important role in both consolidating memories and processing emotion.[10]

Without any intervention, dreams help us integrate our waking-life experiences, learn from our failures, and prepare for the future. But before you discard assimilative dreams as simply replaying your waking-life events, consider if they might also have symbolic value. Coming back to my dreaded week of pulling knapweed, there was one dream in which a bright pink bloom of knapweed was sealed in resin, mounted beautifully onto a piece of reclaimed wood. At the time, the dream provided a powerful teaching that related to my life on the importance of elevating and preserving that which others reject.

Archetypal/Collective: A collective dream often contains symbols that the individual doesn't recognize or has no personal association to, but which can be found throughout history in various cultures and mythologies. These archetypal images arise from the collective unconscious and often address larger cultural themes. A dreamer I once worked with received a powerful dream of a pyramid with an eye in its centre. She had no personal associations to the image, and was amazed to learn that it appeared throughout history in Christianity as the symbol of Divine Providence, on U.S. currency, in Freemasonry, on the Lithuanian coat of arms, and many other locations.

The "collective unconscious" is the term Jung coined to describe the inherited part of the psyche. In his own words, "The collective unconscious contains the whole spiritual heritage of mankind's evolution born anew in the brain structure of every individual."[11] I might take this one step further and say that it isn't just human evolution that we have inherited, but the entirety of the ecosystem with which we have co-evolved. At any moment we have access to this great library of experience and diverse ways of knowing I call the ecopsyche.

Jung believed that myths, legends, fairy tales, and even religions are a kind of collective dream where the substance of the species, race, or even all of humanity is being projected. For instance, the ubiquitous stories of princesses trapped in towers speak to the collective problem of the imprisoned feminine principle. A collective dream holds broader meaning in the same way that a myth or fairy tale will have significance for a great number of people. You'll notice when you share one of these dreams in a group, it comes across as a teaching for all.

But, as is the way with dreams, there is no clear demarcation between a personal or collective dream. They often speak to both the individual and to the culture and epoch in which one is living. Learning how to live with this paradox is one of the great lessons of dreamwork. As Jung says of a layered metaphor, "If such a content should speak of the sun and identify with it the lion, the king, the hoard of gold guarded by the dragon, or the power that makes for the life and health of man, it is neither the one thing nor the other, but the unknown third thing that finds more or less adequate expression in all these similes, yet—to the perpetual vexation of the intellect—remains unknown and not to be fitted into a formula."[12]

If you receive what you think may be a collective dream, consider consulting someone with a strong knowledge of mythology. Or try researching the images in a fairy-tale database, an ecyclopedia, or in the glorious *The Book of Symbols: Reflections on Archetypal Images*.[13] As the clues assemble themselves, use the Keys to Courting the Dream found later in this book to allow the constellation of Wisdom to take place. It can sometimes take days, months, or even years to understand these big dreams, so do your best to stay curious and open while you're still gathering layers.

Initiation: Even if you were not raised in a culture that observes shamanic practices and beliefs, you may still have dreams that contain archetypal symbols of initiation, ritual wounding or healing, and the appearance of guardians or spirit helpers. These dreams may progress in a series across a span of time. They may start with being pulled underground, swallowed, or having to make a descent of some kind. In waking-life, you might experience a simultaneous depression or extended confusion regarding your direction in life. There may be the sense of a long journey ahead of you or a near-impossible mission to accomplish. Initiation dreams often involve some kind of ordeal, like an animal or insect bite, dismemberment, abduction, or even death. This is because you are being reconfigured at the most foundational levels of your being. It's normal to feel reluctance and fear, but if you understand the larger patterns of initiation, you can take some comfort in knowing that eventually the ordeal will be followed by rebirth. While it's easier said than done—and these periods can last much longer than we'd like them to—it's best to go willingly; accepting and honouring that which is being taken from you with full-hearted grief. Keep your eyes peeled for dreams of helpers and guides who carry a new symbolic attitude. Follow those faithfully and eventually you will emerge with a story to tell, a new set of skills, and a greater personal capacity.

Healing: A friend once told me that when she was seriously ill she had a powerful dream of her mother feeding her oranges. She described the dream as being full of love and warmth and when she woke up her fever had broken and she had recovered. Dreams like this contain healing energetics unto themselves that defy interpretation but provide constitutional support.

Though not all dreams offer healing in such a direct way, many do bring warnings of disturbances in the soulbody. There's a wonderful book by Marc Ian Barasch titled *Healing Dreams* in which the author discusses being diagnosed with cancer. After receiving several dreams about his illness, including the one that pushed him to get diagnosed, he undertook fifteen years of research with people who had similar dreams.[14] It's not always as straightforward as you might hope to find solutions for your illness in dreams, but they undoubtedly nudge you to live more centred in your truth. They may not give us a miracle cure to alleviate medical problems, but often address the hidden causes that give rise to illness. Tending to these roots can lead to various other kinds of wellness. I usually take dreams that indicate issues with the body seriously and will always suggest the dreamer get a checkup, test, or scan to rule out any concern for their physical health.

Healing relationships can also take place in dreams, even when the parties aren't in contact with each other. You may dream of finally forgiving someone, or getting the validation you'd been longing for, or being able to say out loud the thing you most need to express. Sometimes when you are unable to come to terms with someone in waking-life, dreaming provides a safe forum in which to find the healing you need. It is possible that this healing is also felt by both people in your shared resonant field.

Lucid/Out-of-Body Experience (OBE): Lucid dreaming is the ability to become awake within a dream and know that you are dreaming. You may remember my dream about the subterranean temple called the Hypogeum that was built to house individual dreamers on vision quests. The Tibetan Buddhists call this practice Dream Yoga, and it is considered spiritual preparation for dying consciously. They say that if you get really good at it, you can opt out of the cycle of samsara (karmic rebirth) at the time of your death.

For medicine people in various Indigenous cultures, what we call lucid dreaming is not limited to sleeping hours. Visionary or out-of-body experiences can also be accessed through the use of sacred plants, drumming, and meditation. They may enter the dream state consciously in order to retrieve lost or stolen pieces of an ill person's soul.

Though some form of lucid dreaming has been practised for thousands of years, Western science maintained it wasn't possible until the 1980s when psychophysiologist Dr. Stephen LaBerge proved to the scientific community that one could be awake and dreaming simultaneously. When you fall asleep, the brain generates inhibitors that render you physically paralyzed so you can't act out your dreams while sleeping. With the exception of some twitching in the fingers, the eyes are the only body part that still moves while you're in REM sleep. Knowing this, LaBerge devised a simple but groundbreaking experiment. Wired with electrodes in a sleep lab, the dreamer could perform a set of prearranged eye movements to signal back to the lab technician at the onset of lucidity. Not only were they able to communicate with someone in a state of lucid dreaming for the first time, but they went on to measure things like the passage of time in a dream versus waking.[15]

Since dreaming is not constrained by physical limitations or social taboo, much becomes possible in the lucid state. While the Maltese may have practised it for incubating healing dreams, and the Tibetans for spiritual awakening, lucid dreaming can also be used for skills rehearsal, creative idea incubation, spiritual learning, and the overcoming of social obstacles.

Any kind of meditation or yoga practice that heightens your overall awareness will enhance your ability to lucid dream. As you begin to wear away at the idea that dreaming is less real than waking, your reverence for the practice will deepen. The next time something unusual happens, ask yourself, "Am I awake or dreaming?" You might be surprised to find the answer is both.

Earth Dreaming: As we'll discuss in finer detail in the later chapters of this book, psyche is inseparable from the larger ecosystem in which our bodies are embedded. It's common to have dreams that are concerned with the climate, as well as the more-than-human species in our environment and the needs of our surrounding ecology. Rather than saying that we have dreams about the earth, it's more accurate to say that the earth is dreaming through us, since we are just smaller organisms living on her larger body. Our psychic concerns and fluctuations are intricately linked with hers. This might look like having more vivid dreams around the new moon, during your menstrual cycles, or at especially potent seasonal thresholds or weather events. You may have dreams set in the habitat of your formative, native geography and of the kin that share it with you. Depending on the state of things, these dreams may express a state of distress or imbalance requiring attention, or they may offer the unique wisdom of that ecology. The more engaged we are with the land where we live, the more linked with its knowledge and needs our dreams become.

Numinous: The word "numinous" comes from the Latin *numen* and means "arousing spiritual or religious emotion; mysterious or awe-inspiring."[16] Echoing the concept of resonance, we can have a numinous experience in an encounter with another person, in a state of contemplation, during psychedelic experiences, in nature, or in synchronicity. The numinous is the experience of coming into contact with Divinity itself, an encounter that often has a combined quality of fear and awe. Not the kind of fear that might come in the presence of evil, but in meeting something Holy and more powerful than us. There is a Hebrew phrase in Psalm 111:10, which translates to, "The fear of God is the beginning of wisdom."*

When you wake from a numinous dream, you are altered. It is as if the encounter has changed you or requires you to transform your life. No matter how hard you try to articulate what you experienced to others, the words fall flat: the depth and dimension of the numinous defies language. Whether you saw the entire cosmos in an orchestra of coordination, discerned God in the body of a Black woman, or heard a disembodied voice whispering a healing truth in your ear, these dreams often give us a radical shift in perspective or worldview, and may stay with us for years (or even a lifetime) until we develop the capacity to understand them.

I consider these dreams gifts of grace. While they aren't terribly frequent, I dare not complain because they often appear in the depths of turmoil or tragedy and guide me with a strong hand onto the right path. The Merriam-Webster dictionary defines *numen* as a "figurative nod of assent, or command," so we can extrapolate that the Holy is in some way affirming or commanding our destiny.[17] Dreams of this nature are thought to emanate from the realm of the transpersonal, which is to say, beyond the personal. I tend not to interpret these dreams so much as honour them with gifts of gratitude on my altar and in my prayers, let myself live into their wisdom, acquiesce to the nod.

---

* Fear (יְרְאַת) in this sense means reverence, and God is eternal (יְהֹוָה), so another way to interpret this is that reverence for the eternal is the beginning of wisdom (חָכְמָה). Psalm 111:10 King James Version.

While these are just some of the most common, there are as many kinds of dreams as there are life experiences. There are those dreams that wake you from sleep, or into another dream—like awakening through layers of consciousness. There are those dreams called sleep paralysis, that wake you up only halfway while your body remains immovable, and may come with frightening visions and encounters.[18] There are also passive dreams—when you are not an active participant but observing from a distance, like watching a film—which may speak to how close or far you are from engaging with the matter. Dream categories are useful in giving us language for these ineffable experiences, but the boundaries tend to dissolve when you consider that even the most literal-seeming dreams carry symbolic value. In strengthening your capacity for metaphor, you are learning to see the intersecting patterns of meaning in the world, blurring any definite borders between waking and dreaming.

CHAPTER 5

Metaphor: Language of Kinship

METAPHOR IS OUR FIRST LANGUAGE. It is the vocabulary of the body, made up of images that serve to restore connectedness to the world.

The Oxford Learners Dictionary defines *metaphor* as "a word or phrase used to describe somebody/something else, in a way that is different from its normal use, in order to show that the two things have the same qualities. For example, 'She has a heart of stone.'"[1] But it's important to remember that before becoming words, metaphors are images. Even the definition of metaphor as a "figure of speech" is a metaphor from the Latin *figura,* meaning shape, body, form, or symbol. Our dreams are made up of metaphors: symbols that generate wisdom by revealing kinship between seemingly unrelated situations. If Wisdom is the *anima mundi* connecting all beings in nature, metaphor is the language that makes our relational links visible.

We tend to think of metaphor as a literary device that poets use to embellish text. But metaphor not only precedes the written language—it precedes speech. Aristotle framed metaphor as the "underlying condition of all learning."[2] You could say it is our most intimate language because it's the very basis of how we experience and conceptualize the world within our bodies. When we say, "I'm drowning in debt," we are invoking the embodied experience *before* the words: of not being able to catch our breath, of feeling sucked into an undertow, of a dire need for solid ground. Metaphor brings those two truths together so they can exchange ideas. If a dream provides this metaphor, the dreamer can begin to think in terms of what a drowning person needs, and how urgently. This first language of symbols, which draws things into correlation, is how wisdom communicates.

When speaking, we use an average of six metaphors a minute—that's once every twenty-five words. We don't recognize them most of the time because the metaphors we use have become so culturally ingrained that they are no longer evocative. When symbols lose their potency and become cliché, we call these "dead metaphors." Through overuse, the connection to the original image is forgotten. But even when used unconsciously, metaphors have the power to shape the way we think about, communicate, and interpret the world.

Kristen Elmore, a social psychologist at Cornell University, conducted a fascinating study that looked at how different metaphors for genius reflect and reinforce gender stereotypes.[3] The study was called "Light bulbs or seeds?" and tracked how people relate to these two metaphors for scientific discovery—ideas that appeared suddenly and effortlessly (like a light bulb switching on), and those that were nurtured over time (like seedlings). Participants were exposed to an array of male and female creators whose innovations were described in both of these ways. "We found that an idea was seen as more exceptional when described as appearing like a light bulb rather than nurtured like a seed," said Elmore, but only when associated with men.[4] The reverse was true for women's ideas, which were viewed as more valuable when described as having been "cultivated" over time, like a seed. The results echo the stereotypical view of men as geniuses and women as nurturers.

The implicit biases in the metaphors we use have far-ranging implications in the world. In the above example, they reinforce the perception that women have to work long and hard on an idea, while men are predisposed to brilliance. This adds to the barriers women face when entering the sciences or receiving recognition for their achievements.

In another study at Stanford, participants were given contrasting metaphors to describe an eruption of crime in a hypothetical city. In one metaphor, the crime was described as a "virus" and in the other a "beast." When asked how best to deal with the problem, participants who were given the beast metaphor advocated for strong intervention by authorities, whereas those who received the virus metaphor were more interested in looking for the underlying cause.[5]

When we become conscious of the metaphors we are using, it changes the way we conceptualize and experience the world. We may choose, for instance, to opt out of the many war-and-battle metaphors we use every day like, "He *attacked* me in the comments," or, "She *shot* down my argument," or, "His claim was *indefensible*."* When we cultivate fresh metaphors by tending to our dreams, we tap into the generative power of nature to make and remake the world.

Etymologically speaking, the word "metaphor" comes from the Greek *meta*, meaning "with, across, or over" and *pherein* meaning "to bear, or carry." Metaphor serves as a kind of bridge across which our perspective is carried into a new understanding. We can imagine two banks separated by a wild, unpredictable river. In waking reality, we stand on the bank of certainty: the domain of matter, the explicit, physical, quantifiable universe. The wild river is everything we can't explain or don't accept—chaos, ambiguity and the complexity of nature, including sacred and imaginal

---

* Examples inspired by the classic *Metaphors We Live By*, George Lakoff and Mark Johnson, University of Chicago Press, (1980)

phenomena. The opposite bank represents the ground of wisdom, where we arrive when we are able to hold the equivalency of those worlds together.

The essence of a metaphor is to understand one situation in the shape and gestures of another. For instance, your marriage might be in trouble and you use the metaphor, "our relationship is on the rocks." This may strike you as a benign phrase, but in a dream, you are in that embodied metaphor: You and your partner are shipwrecked, clambering for safety over steep and jagged rocks. In waking-life, you are not literally standing on rocks, but you are having to navigate difficult, sharp edges in relating to each other, and you aren't certain if your relationship will be seaworthy again. More than just analogy, metaphor shows us the connection between situations with a similar feeling tone. And in so doing, it carries our perspective across an implied divide. In revealing a meaningful connection between contexts, metaphor liberates us from the isolation of prosaic thinking, catalyzing psychic movement.

In our dream of the "relationship on the rocks," the metaphor sets one thing beside another and says, "See, they have different forms, but they make the same gesture. They *mean* in the same way." You are not literally shipwrecked, but the metaphor offers you a powerful new perspective, a different way of inhabiting your situation. So instead of feeling muddled and emotionally fraught, you can now conceive the full precariousness of your relationship. Depending on what pulls at your imagination from the dream, you might decide to wait until *the tide ebbs* in its emotional intensity before trying to *navigate* your way out of conflict. Or you might look for tools you can draw upon to *repair your craft* of togetherness. Or perhaps you will aim to be kinder, doing your part to soften the *sharp landscape* of your communication. In making the connection between the two experiences, symbolic solutions become more readily apparent.

As Jan Zwicky writes, "the metaphor tells two truths at once."[6]

In the dreamwork process, neither prosaic nor mythic realties are discarded—both are enhanced by their encounter. The echoing of their similarities is the sound of wisdom at work. But it's important that they also retain their differences. Unlike dream dictionaries that give a symbol a this-means-that definition, a living metaphor allows both realities to exist. As soon as you say the boat = relationship, you lose the *suchness* of the boat and its ecology of analogies. It is the dynamism of their tension that allows an ongoing exchange between the worlds. For example, the precariousness of the vessel out at sea, its vulnerability to invisible currents running beneath the surface, the sense of being on a journey together: all of these details continue to enhance your understanding of the dream so long as you keep that combinatory play alive.

Wisdom catalyzes movement by overriding old and familiar patterns of thought with fresh ways of seeing. This is why art and poetry are so important to culture. It is the job of the artist to catalyze consciousness on behalf of the collective. They must be courageous enough to enter the imaginal in order to find living metaphors to bring back to this world and in doing so, redeem culture. It is an act of overcoming. As the poet Louise Glück says, art removes "the misery of inertia."[7] A metaphor unrecognized will do nothing to shape us, and so in turn we can do nothing differently to shape our world. What's needed is a true encounter in the imagination, a resonance with the metaphor to shift one's gestalt.

Resonance is a musical term that describes the sympathetic harmony between two instruments. Though they may not be in contact with each other, one may still respond to the vibration of the other. A good example of this is when someone speaks or sings in a room with a resting guitar. If they hit the right frequency, the guitar strings will vibrate in harmony with that voice. This is what happens when we hit upon the right note in dreamwork. We may try on several different ideas and associations, but when just the right chord is struck, we can feel it hum in our body; we become that resonating instrument.

Resonance occurs when the unique vibration of our truth is being sung and we recognize it with an effervescence of emotion and sensation. This form of remembering is called *anamnesis* in Platonic philosophy. It's the recollection of innate wisdom from a time previous to birth, or perhaps a fold in hyperspace that gives us a brief memory of the future. This is why great teachers aren't necessarily telling you something new so much as affirming what you already know but haven't yet been able to articulate for yourself. *Anamnesis* is the opposite of empiricism, which says that we can only acquire knowledge from direct experience and sensory perception. When Joseph Campbell said "follow your bliss," I am quite sure he was describing resonance—not as an isolated moment, but as a string of moments across a lifetime, like lights along a path, that we can follow.

Without a relationship to the animate world of symbols, our energy can feel stagnant and disconnected. When we're unable to relate our personal hardships to anything greater than ourselves alone, we may begin to believe that our life has no meaning. But metaphors reconnect us to the symbolic dimension of life, to the animism behind the surface of things. They ground and locate us in our own mythic story. This helps us recognize the value of the stage we are in by connecting us to the larger cycles and patterns of existence. As we forge those connections, our dreams and symbols begin to move again, evolving in a purposeful direction that generates energy in our body. To understand how this movement works, it's important to remember that metaphors are not single images, but exist in an ecology of other images that are following a creative pattern.

Just as it is in nature, every dream has a longing to thrive. Our job is to collaborate with our symbols to discover how to support and fulfil that longing. To further explain, let's look at a dream that shows how a chain of metaphors works together to shift our gestalt.

I'll Always Come Back: Fatima's Dream

I dream my husband has abandoned me and left me with all our financial responsibilities. I feel lonely and devastated. I wander around looking for connection in the town, but everyone is too distracted and busy to notice me. After a few months, my husband returns and to my great relief declares, "I will always come back!" And with that, he begins to pay off the debt that accumulated in his absence.

In dreamwork, I always like to begin by laying the objective situation beside the dream to find any immediate similarities and differences. Knowing Fatima was married, I asked if she was at all concerned about their relationship and/or money matters. She said, "Not at all. We are in a stable, loving marriage. Our devotion to one another is strong, so I can't imagine him abandoning me like in the dream. I do feel like the more financially responsible partner in the marriage though, and this causes a lot of tension between us."

There are some similarities between the waking and dreaming worlds, but given her confidence in the stability of the outer relationship we can begin thinking in symbolic terms. If we consider the husband as a metaphor, we need to understand the role he occupies for her in psyche. So I asked, "Tell me about your husband. What kind of person is he?" Fatima replied, "He is a generous, wise, and creative person. I would say he's the one person in the world that really gets me, who advocates for my soul." If we follow the idea that "husband" is symbolic of support and advocacy for Fatima's soul, suddenly the dream opens up with possibility. Even with this little detail, we can see that the metaphor exists in an ecology. The soul-husband has left; there is an atmosphere of burdened responsibility, a search for connection in the social world, underwritten by a deep sense of abandonment. But there is also a return, a promise, and a replenishment of debt.

In the dream, the husband leaving and the dreamer feeling financially burdened are related, so it felt important to discover why. I asked Fatima to tell me more about her finances in the marriage. She described feeling overwhelmed by the family's responsibilities, because her husband took little interest in money matters and retirement planning. "I don't mind taking care of that stuff," Fatima explained. "I actually enjoy it, but I barely have any time for my work in the studio."

I found myself curious about her neglected work in the studio, so I returned to the idea of her husband as soul-advocate. I asked, "You said your husband really gets you and advocates for your soul; in what way does he express his support?" Fatima said, "I've never quite believed in myself as an artist, but from the day we met he has always been my biggest fan. He constantly tells me how much he admires and respects my work. We joke that I outsource my confidence to him, because despite the success I've had with my painting, I always feel inadequate to the work. He's the one who cheerleads me in times of doubt."

This touching revelation helped me imagine what it must be like for Fatima to be without that support. So I asked, "Have you been going through a period of doubt lately?" Fatima instantly related to a months-long creative drought. "I haven't felt like I have anything of value to offer with my paintings lately. I'm so convinced this is true that I rarely even give myself time in the studio. I feel like I'm neglecting what I love most," she said. With this new association, tears sprang to her eyes. We both felt the resonance of how this act of self-abandonment mirrored the dream's metaphor of being deserted by her true love.

In the next scene of the dream, she goes out wandering, looking for connection "in the town," which is another metaphor for the social world. "Tell me more about the loneliness you expressed in the dream. Is this longing for connection part of what you go through in a creative drought?"

"Totally," she replied, "All of my friends have normal jobs and they don't really get my struggles. It feels like everyone I know is too distracted or busy to see me in the way I long to be seen." She thought for a moment and continued, "But the truth is I am the one who distracts myself with stuff like bookkeeping, or scrolling on social media. It feels easier to spend my time doing unchallenging tasks, but avoiding my creative work just makes me lonely. When I'm in a creative flow, I feel connected to myself and never get lonely." This was another big moment of resonance for us both, because we could now see how the abandonment of her creativity was connected to the other metaphors. Though there were legitimate money concerns in the marriage, we also played with the idea of the dream-debt as symbolic of her lack of investment in her own work. This opened up a conversation for us about how creativity requires a confrontation with our own vulnerability and fears of inadequacy.

Knowing that the dream ends with return and redemption, Fatima could take comfort in knowing that the abandonment was temporary. The intensity of the fight against our inner critics, the struggle with feelings of inferiority or even exhaustion, can occasionally become too much to bear for any artist. So we break away like an immature lover who isn't prepared to move through conflict. But for the one who is committed, the dream seems to say: there is always a return. The lover returns, and does his best to pay into what he's neglected. Fatima's creativity may not look like a methodical kind of attentiveness, but she always renews her commitment and balances the scales.

Before the dreamwork, all Fatima could feel was the weight of her depression, but making the connection to this inner desertion empowered her to make different choices. She was able to forgive herself for the period of disconnection from her creativity, knowing the deficit would eventually be paid. This act of grace helped create connection for her again. The power of this dream was enough to give Fatima the courage to return to that thorny threshold where she'd left her work. Knowing it was herself abandoning her creativity inspired her to show up in a more steadfast way to her own soul, instead of "outsourcing confidence" to her husband. She played with inhabiting the role of a supportive inner husband. It helped her move through some of the fears and obstacles in her path to contribute more steadily to her projects.

Once I've worked with a dream, I like to name what I love most about it and suggest a ritual to enhance and give thanks for its medicine. In Fatima's dream, what I loved most was the declaration of the husband, "I will always come back!" It is a powerful mantra to remember in times of creative difficulty and resistance. That despite any doubt that arises, a deeper commitment exists. While she may need to abandon the work occasionally, it is never permanent. Her soul will never leave her. In closing with our dreamwork, I suggested a small ritual for Fatima: put these words in a prominent place where she works. She painted "I Will Always Come Back" in brilliant blues and greens above her easel in her studio. Years later, she described still feeling supported by the dream's wisdom every time she read those words.

A metaphor in a dream is rarely a single image, but embedded in a whole world of interconnected metaphors that are collectively moving toward a goal. In dreamwork, we consider each image separately, but we must not remove it from its context. It must be contemplated in its larger context for cohesion to become possible. If we had stopped at an interpretation of Fatima's dream being about her objective money stress, we would have missed all the other jewels the dream offered regarding her own sense of value and self-support. This is important to note, because whenever you have a hypothesis about a dream, it must be tested against the other metaphors in the dreamscape to see if they all fit, and if they form a larger overall pattern. The soul-abandonment followed by loneliness, as well as the eventual reunion and repaid debt were all essential to this ecology of metaphors. When you have successfully understood a chain of metaphors, you will be able to walk across that bridge into a new way of seeing, as Fatima was able to do. Of course not all dreams have such a redemptive ending. In these cases, the "new way of seeing" may be subtle, enabling you to refine your perspective over a course of dreams.

Metaphor is our mother-tongue. It's a natural language that transcends race, culture, and possibly even species. It is believed that many animals dream, including reptiles, spiders, octopi, birds, and all mammals, so we might guess that their dreams are also made up of the symbols that represent their worldview. Songbirds, for instance, were found to be improvising new songs in their sleep.[8] Octopi change their skin patterns during REM periods, suggesting they are dreaming of moving through environments and having encounters.[9] From the perspective that we are all descendants of the same earth, metaphor is nature's way of communicating through us. By learning to think analogically, we are learning the interconnected and participatory language of the earth.

If we could visualize psyche, it would look like a vast and intricate network of nodes and branches. Like mycelium, it is invisible to us, yet it is the largest single organism in the world. It is actively transporting nutrients from both above and below environments across its branching fungal threads, decomposing plant material and transmitting nutrients where they are needed. Creating efficiencies and resilience for all, providing health, nourishment, immunity, and growth to everyone in the forest. Like mycelium, psyche does not discern who deserves its beneficence, since we are all connected. Across the mycelial-like threads we call dreams, we receive practical knowledge, transmissions of wisdom, creative solutions, opportunities to grow, and yes, even a place to compost our dying material.

Zwicky writes, "Those who think metaphorically are enabled to think truly, because the shape of their thinking echoes the shape of the world."[10] By following the metaphors in our dreams, we are yielding to the inclination of nature itself. What is healing for us personally is in keeping with a greater good for all. Perhaps Fatima's work to forgo busyness and distraction to support her own creativity is the same capacity all humans need during social and environmental collapse. Maybe it is time for us all to consider the ways in which we are abandoning our own souls, and by extension, the soul of the earth. Maybe Fatima is one of many who are being similarly called to dismantle the obstacles to grief so we can meet the urgency of our times with creative originality.

COMMON DREAM METAPHORS

To develop a sense of how to begin thinking symbolically, let's explore some common dream metaphors. The purpose of this section is to help you recognize how everything you need to know about a symbol is contained within your knowledge and experience of the world. I will offer multiple perspectives on each symbol to demonstrate the variety of ways one image may speak to different people and contexts, or in a multi-layered way to one individual.

Water: Many people say that water is symbolic of emotions. While it's a perfect symbol to express the fluidity of some states of emotion, it is so much more than that. Water is the birthplace of all life. It covers 70% of the earth, and makes up 60% of our own bodies. This elemental substance is the vital life force of all earthbound creatures. As a symbol, we know that water is fundamental, even synonymous with "life force," but it also has a vast repertoire of expressions. When you dream of water, you need to look at what your water is doing to understand *how it means* for you. It could feel baptismal as you wash away your cares under a summer shower, or it may express itself as grief leaking out of faucets for a love lost or longed for. It may be in short supply, like a thirst in too arid a place, or it could overwhelm you in a tidal wave of desire. It might be small and contained in a pond of vitality filled with brightly coloured koi, or boundless as an ocean where something precious is lost. Like the fathomless depths of the unconscious, water has a way of rising up in waves to indicate powerful forces beyond our capacity to understand them. But water can also be turbulent, stagnant, trapped in an eddy, or dried up in a desert. So consider the particular expression of water in your dream to understand how your own life force is flowing. A dream of water and its inhabitants may also be about your concern for the wild water where you live. Has it been privatized, dammed, polluted? Keep in mind that even if your dream is dealing with an objective situation, it may still have symbolic layers, so notice how this elemental life force expresses itself in your dream.

Weather and Seasons: Dreams featuring climate and seasons tend to describe the elemental atmosphere and mood of your situation. You can rely on what you know and feel about weather and seasons to understand the overall feeling of your dreamscape. For instance, if your dream is set in winter, you may instantly think of hibernation, rest, and incubation—but it is also dormant, cold, and snowy. You might ask yourself, in what way does my energy feel cold or frozen? Depending on the context of the dream, you may be in a necessary dormancy to gather new energy, or shutting down your flow of feeling. A dream set in spring will have a far different mood than winter. It is the season of beginnings as new life pushes up and out after a long incubation, but it can also be exposing to those vulnerabrave plants who've been underground for so long. Summer is extroverted, full of activity with everything in its peak expression of beauty, but it can also be unforgivingly active and demanding. Autumn is both a time of ending and of harvest, when the earth's life force begins to pull inward and a shedding becomes necessary to conserve energy. Powerful weather like tornadoes, earthquakes, and tsunamis can indicate large-scale change and upheaval. These apocalyptic dreams may speak to legitimate fears around climate change, but it's always worth considering their symbolic dimension as well. Apocalypse dreams are often symbolic of something in or around us seeking this complete renewal. As Edward Edinger writes, these dreams are, "the momentous event of the coming of the Self into conscious realization. The shattering of the world as it has been, followed by its reconstitution."[11] Psyche tends to pick up on big changes before we become fully conscious of them, so if you're having weather disaster dreams, you might need to consider in what way your life may be shifting at the most fundamental level.

House and Rooms: Dreams of a house, whether familiar or not, are extremely common and often symbolic of how you may or may not feel at home in yourself. If a particular room in the house is featured, it may allude to that symbolic area of your life. For instance, the basement is the underground part of the house so it can be a metaphor for the unconscious, where things are hidden, stored away, or yet to be unearthed. Horror films often set their scariest scenes in the basement to play on our fear of the dark and unknown. It's almost always unlit, or unfinished, to build the tension as the protagonist makes their descent. But in dreams, the basement and other underground places are the sites of remarkable symbolic discovery. While we may at first be afraid of what we could discover in our descent into the underworld, our shadows tend to obscure hidden gold.

The kitchen, on the other hand, is the heart of most homes. It's the alchemical centre where food is transformed from raw into digestible states. There's a reason why people tend to gather in the kitchen—we associate it with comfort, connection, and nourishment. A dream taking place in the kitchen will often touch on these themes of alchemy, hearth, and nurturing. The bedroom is one of the most intimate rooms in the house. It is where lovers meet, where we finally rest, and it is the domain of dreaming. Many dreams take place in the bathroom, which is usually the most private room in a house. It is the part of your life where you cleanse yourself of outside influences, release tension, process your experiences in solitude, and prepare yourself to meet the world. Depending on the state of your dream-bathroom, you'll get a very good sense of where you are symbolically with regards to self-care. One of the more wonderful dreams that people report are those ones where you discover rooms in your house you've never seen. These may arise during thresholds of enormous growth and self-discovery. These periods are often characterized by learning so much more about who you are, what you are capable of, or what you've left unexplored. Pay special attention to your house dreams to get a sense of what area of your life or parts of your self are undergoing change.

Vehicles: The transportation in our dreams often indicates how we are moving through life. Whether we are speeding, taking flight, travelling in a collective, or moving along predictable tracks, our dream-vehicles are symbolic of how we get from here to there. Not in the literal sense of distance, but travelling as a metaphor for our direction in life, and how we are moving through particular experiences. Cars can be symbolic of our bodies as well. If your car is broken down, you may be feeling "burnt out" or "low on fuel." If someone else is at the wheel, you might need to ask yourself if you are being unduly influenced by an unconscious attitude. Likewise, if someone's in the backseat telling you how to drive, you may have a complex giving you more help than you need. A bus or train might suggest a commonly accepted route, or habitual pathway— one often shared by others in the collective. A bike might suggest a self-powered journey. Planes take us up into completely different atmospheres, above the fray, into new heights, so a flight might be symbolic of escaping the familiar, travelling into the unknown, or even reaching for new *planes* of consciousness.

Colours: The symbolism of colours varies greatly from culture to culture and throughout time, even amongst the same people. But there are some archetypal associations that we share about colours that repeat around the world. As an example, red is the colour of blood and tends to be associated with vitality, passion, and eros. But it can also be symbolic of danger and aggression (as in the idiom *red with rage*). Green is often associated with life, the healing power of nature, and newness (as in *green behind the ears*). Black is the colour of darkness, the absence of light, in which we lose our ability to see colours. This may be why we associate black with death, mourning, and the unknown. But like that symbolic basement, the rich soil in early spring, or a peaceful night, black is rich with potential. Rather than drawing upon any one dictionary of colour symbolism, it's far more important to follow your own feeling and associations to any colour in your dream. Whether your impressions and connections to a colour are personal or culturally inherited, you can trust that what comes to mind when you visualize the colour will lead you to the right symbolic interpretation.

Body: Perhaps the most common symbol of all, the body can signify many things depending on how it appears and what it is doing. The body is, of course, the way we incarnate in the world, but it is also the vessel of our health, and a huge part of our self-image. If your dream focuses on a particular body part, look to its function to get a sense of why it is important. Hands, for instance, are what we use to make and create, but they are also how we touch each other and grasp the world. There are a million gestures that we enact with our hands—from high-fives to fists, strokes to slaps—sometimes to protect ourselves, other times to draw others close. If your hands feel important in a dream, look at what they are doing (or failing to do) to get a sense of their symbolic importance in relation to the context of the dream. For instance, a dream of wounded hands that are unable to play an instrument might suggest a creative injury. Similarly, feet are how we stand up (*on our own two feet*) and walk in the world. So a dream of not being able to stand or move might have to do with feeling a lack of confidence, not being able to *take a stand*, or maybe feeling stuck in your situation. If your body is distressed or diseased in a dream, it's always a good idea to visit your doctor for a checkup in case it's a warning dream. But do consider the symbolic dimension as well. Dreams often have multiple layers of meaning.

Money: Money in dreams often has to do with the value we place on a thing, and the sense of worth we give ourselves or others. If you lose money, it might indicate that you're experiencing a loss of self-worth in waking-life, or feeling undervalued in some way. Likewise, if you owe a debt, you may be feeling under-resourced or symbolically indebted in some way. Money disparity is the basis of many inequities in cultures and relationships, so a dream of imbalanced wealth may be pointing to a lack of fairness or justice. If you dream of coming into a windfall, it may suggest a sudden experience of abundance or self-worth. Of course your waking-life money concerns can express themselves in your dreams too. As we discovered with Fatima's dream, there was both an objective financial disparity in her relationship and a lack of investment in her creative work.

Sex: Sex dreams are usually about connection, intimacy, and union with the parts of ourselves and others represented by dream characters. Rather than taking these dreams literally, look at the symbolic characteristics of your partner and ask yourself where you might be coming into more intimate relationship with those qualities in your life. If the union is pleasurable and loving, consider that you are coming into contact with something nourishing. Even if that union is taboo in waking-life (like having sex with a family member, co-worker, etc.), remember that our dream characters are also symbolic.

If the sex is violent or unwanted, you'll need to discover what active complex may be giving rise to this violating inner figure. Shadow dreams are covered in depth in Chapter 10: Poison is the Medicine, but if these sorts of dreams are common for you, it's best to seek mental health support in caring for these places of vulnerability. People who have experienced sexual trauma are known to have recurring dreams of some version of their assault. Though it may seem cruel of psyche to keep producing these scary dreams, I believe nightmares are adaptive in nature. They are attempting to re-integrate the splintered self that gets fragmented in trauma. With the right kind of help to look directly at these dreams in a safe container, where you can express everything that needs to be felt and spoken, it is possible to shift the pattern of these dreams over time. If you aren't having trauma-related dreams, you can begin to explore the ways in which a violent inner voice or attitude might be stealing energy from you. By looking at some of the surrounding elements in your dream, you can narrow in on what precipitated the event, and in which area of your life you may be feeling overpowered.

Another really common sex dream is having a partner cheat on you. If there is no basis for that fear in your waking-life relationship, you might want to look at where you are losing an inner connection or sense of support. Like Fatima's dream partner was symbolic of her soul-support, you may discover that your inner partner has been unfaithful. Cheating could be about abandoning love, devotion, and care for who you are at a fundamental level, so observe the qualities of the other dream characters to get a sense of what's coming between you. Sometimes sex dreams compensate for a lack of intimacy in our waking lives, expressing the natural desires and drives of the body. Dreams can be generous in this way, so enjoy!

Clothes: The clothing we wear (or don't wear) in a dream relates to how we present ourselves to the world. We wear clothes for practical reasons, like staying warm and protecting our skin, but the type of clothing we wear is also chosen to project a certain image to the world. If your clothing is inappropriate for the dream situation, you might be feeling socially out of sync, or you may be in the process of changing your identity. As an example, let's say you are wearing a dress you used to like, but it no longer suits how you want to present yourself. You might ask yourself, in what way am I still *wearing* an old identity? One of the most common dreams people have is being naked in public. In the same way that we use clothes to project an identity to the world, wearing no clothes is about feeling vulnerable, *baring yourself* for others to see. You'll notice that while we often feel embarrassed in these dreams, others don't seem to notice. I think this is true of vulnerability overall. It tends to feel riskier to be authentic than it does to witness it.

Tests and Exams: Dreams of having to take a test or an exam may have to do with the pressure you feel to measure up to social standards, so be successful, or graduate to a new level in life. Often these dreams are tinged with feeling unprepared, not knowing the subject, or arriving late. Standardized testing was the norm for so many of us in school, so it was our first and enduring experience of being coldly evaluated. If we didn't do well on those tests, we were prohibited from moving to the next level with our peers. While we may no longer have literal examinations to pass, many of us still feel pressure to compete and keep advancing our social status. So when you have a dream like this, it's a good idea to ask yourself if you are feeling watched and judged by others ... or by an inner critic. Where in life do you feel competitive or like you have to prove something? If you feel unprepared or out of sync, ask yourself if those are your legitimate goals or just internalized pressure from the culture.

Death: It can be shocking to have a dream of a loved one dying, but even these dreams can be taken symbolically. Psyche recognizes pivotal moments in a relationship when something dies between two people. This doesn't necessarily mean the relationship is over—though sometimes it can suggest just that—but more often than not it is a symbolic ending. When a young person grows into an adult and needs to make separations from their parents, they may dream of a parent dying. Similarly, a parent may dream of a child dying as they step more clearly into their independence. But it's important to remember that even these most intimate relationships are often symbolic of the *inner* child or parent, and how those core dynamics are changing within the self. In this sense, death can be an extremely positive symbol, though some grieving may still be necessary to help the change progress. All long-term relationships go through phases of maturity, ultimately leaving behind the old versions of ourselves so that we can grow into who we are becoming. To psyche, this is a kind of death because it is irreversible and will almost certainly give rise to new life. You may even dream of your own death as you step out of an old way of being, or when a new attitude or outlook supersedes an old one. You may also dream of a loved one's death if you are concerned for their objective well-being. As always, tend to your symbols on both explicit and intrinsic levels.

These brief examples show that everything you need to know about dream symbols is contained within your existing knowledge and common sense. You already know what vehicles and clothes are for, it's just a matter of shifting your perspective from the literal to the symbolic to see the metaphor at play. It can be helpful to give yourself a very basic definition of the element you are working with in order to see in plain terms what you take for granted about the things that make up your world. For instance, you might need to define an exam as "a standardized evaluation of skills that allows one to progress" before you can see how it is a metaphor for getting stuck in the fear that you don't measure up. Once you have a basic definition, you can amplify that image through your particular associations to the symbol and the context it is embedded in.

It's wonderful to have an arsenal of tools to rely on when navigating the mysteries of the Imaginal but there is no skill greater than the ability to remain curious. If we can withstand the discomforts of not-knowing what a symbol might mean, we gain the chance to be led by and surprised by a dream's revelations. It's less important to get to the bottom of a dream than it is to remain curious about it. I use the word "courtship" to describe my approach to working with dreams because it puts us in right humility with the mystery. It acknowledges that there is something we love and wish to get closer to, and yet we are in the humble position of approaching it without guarantee. I believe this should always be the starting point with dreams: to acknowledge that we know nothing, but that maybe, through the hospitality and earnestness of our presence, the mystery might decide to approach us.

We all possess a natural ability to understand metaphors, but like learning any new language, it takes time to gain competence. Be patient with yourself, and trust that an open heart and mind is everything you need to dialogue with your dreams. Eventually, and with enough practice, thinking symbolically will become automatic and run like an undercurrent to your other ways of thinking. You may even begin to see how often metaphors appear in your waking life.

CHAPTER 6

Patterns in the Unknown

WHILE DREAMS ARE WILDLY unpredictable and chaotic, they are also made up of patterns. They have universal elements, typical shapes, repetitive gestures, and an inherent narrative structure that we can follow. While dreams may appear random to the casual glance, they have a pattern language that can be learned. By studying the archetypes found in dreams, in myths, and in stories from around the world, what emerges is a map by which we can orient ourselves in times of doubt and ambiguity. As the organizing intelligence that animates all life, Wisdom is the pattern-maker who stitches together our dreams in an intentional order—each event giving rise to the next, pulling us into purpose.

Patterns can't be found in a standalone dream. But when we map them out over the course of months or years, recurrent symbols and motifs begin to emerge. And when we zoom out beyond our personal dreams, we find the same archetypal patterns repeating in distant cultures, in the myths and the dreams of people around the world throughout history.

We find this patterning phenomenon in the rest of nature: in the symmetries of an orchid, the radial patterns of snowflakes and starfish, the branching of trees that, like fractals, grow in self-similar iterations, the mighty spiral found in the nautilus shell, the twirling growth of plants, the seed-heads of a sunflower, spiral galaxies, and in meanders, which is the lovely name for the curves and bends created by rivers and streams. We find universal patterns at different levels and scales throughout the living biosphere. So why shouldn't they also be found in the ecosystem of the imagination?

There's a wonderful book from 1977 called *A Pattern Language* that is still one of the most popular books in architecture today.[1] The authors sought out and named 253 enduring patterns in the design of homes, streets, and communities. These patterns developed organically from the common habits and needs of those living in houses around the world. But by naming those patterns, the authors assembled a new language, a way of *communicating* architecture.

When we find an existing pattern in any discipline, whether it's in mathematics or architecture, it helps us anticipate what typically comes next in a sequence of events—what problems might arise, what actions lead to what outcomes, and how others have solved similar dilemmas. Solutions in *A Pattern Language* are never fixed or generic, but presented as an array, existing in a field of dynamic relationships. Similarly in dreamwork, having some knowledge of archetypes—such as how the narrative progresses through scenes of a dream, or what each of the stages in one's heroic journey might hold—can help us recognize the parallels in our own dreams. Once we have discovered a recurring pattern in our dreams, it spontaneously gives rise to emergent solutions.

Unlike fixed interpretations, pattern recognition allows us to see the elemental structure of a symbol, though its outer shape is always changing and new. Once we identify a pattern in our dreams, we can more easily find variations of it in other places. We may notice it in our internal dialogue, or spot its dynamics in our external relationships, see how it travels across the generations of our family or plays out in the larger culture. Knowing what anchors patterns in place gives us insight into what changes can emerge from them.

To dispel the notion that dreams are nonsensical or chaotic, I'd like to offer you a few different lenses through which to recognize the pattern language of dreams. Over the next two chapters, we will explore the architecture of dreams, looking at some of the structures in psyche so we can spot the recurring forms and elements in our own dreams. While dream dictionaries render symbols lifeless by assigning them static definitions—like "a dream of a banana means pleasure and happiness," the art of dreamwork is in discovering that though your dreams contain universal symbolic patterns, each symbol is also distinct. While dreamwork is an artform that requires us to be open and curious—and is the focus of Chapter 9: Courting the Dream—knowing something about the architecture of dreams can steady us in our wonder. It is by holding the tension of these two things together that we arrive at wisdom.

ARCHETYPES: ANCIENT BLUEPRINTS

To describe the ancient patterns found in the psyche, Jung coined the term "archetypes." Having studied world mythology and religions, Jung found repeating motifs in creation stories, fairy tales, and myths from around the world. He was astonished to discover remarkably similar imagery in the dreams of those he worked with, even when they'd never come into contact with those myths. He also discovered the meaning of those dreams would correspond with that of the myths; they would *mean* in the same way.

He called these patterns archetypes, from the Greek *arkhetypon*, meaning "original pattern from which copies are made." Combining the words "archaic" and "typical," Jung saw archetypes as heritable patterns in the human psyche that influence how we see and experience the world. He believed that rather than coming into life as a *tabula rasa*, or blank slate, all humans carried these blueprints that—for better or worse—behaved like primordial reflexes. These reflexes determine how we experience and move through the world. Jungian analyst Ann Belford Ulanov explained it succinctly when she wrote, "As the instincts are to the body, so the archetypes are to the psyche."[2]

Though we tend to equate archetypes with characters like "witch," "hero," or "wise old man," it's more accurate to say that these images are the manifest expression of archetypes. We are unable to observe archetypes directly, so we need to use symbols to describe and understand them ... but no two witches are the same. You could say that myths, made of archetypal imagery, are humanity's way of engaging with those unknowable patterns in the substrate of our collective psyche.

While archetypes manifest in different imagery for every culture, and for each individual, they tend to hold the same basic structures. For instance we find variations on the ouroboros symbol in ancient Egypt, neolithic China, Norse mythology, Vedic texts, and Alchemy, just to name a few. Sometimes visualized as a snake eating its own tail, other times a dragon, or even abstracted into a joined circle, the ouroboros always has its end embedded in the beginning, symbolic of the great cycle of life, death, and rebirth. The form an archetype takes is reflective of the culture and epoch in which one lives, but the archetypal structure below it is eternal.

The fourth-century Roman commentator Sallustius wrote, "Myths are things that never happened, but always are."[3] The first half of this phrase reminds us that myths aren't meant to be taken as historical fact: their purpose is not to explain or provide evidence for anything. Rather they are meant to excite our mythic imagination and engage the part of us that is connected to universal truths.

Archetypal psychologist James Hillman once said that if we make the mistake of taking myths as fact, it puts us in danger of becoming a fundamentalist.[4] When we get caught up in the strict, literal interpretation of scriptures and myth, we overlook the universal structures below the images. As the second half of that phrase explains, myths "always are," meaning the archetypes within them are *eternal*. Eternal in this sense doesn't refer to an abstract theological realm, as Hillman points out, but to that which is ever-present.[5] In other words, a story can be told in a hundred different ways in a hundred different languages but still share mutual, relevant truths. So when we are thinking mythically, we are experiencing the immanence of that which always was and will forever be.

This is the fundamental problem people face when understanding their dreams. We are so used to thinking literally that we take dreams as predictions of our future, or comments on our day-to-day lives and relationships. But while dreams occasionally speak in this direct way, more often than not they are speaking symbolically. They come wearing the wardrobe of scenarios and locations that are familiar to us in order to communicate corresponding patterns and movements in psyche.

You may have noticed how the same archetype can show up in different guises across a series of your own dreams. As it attempts to show itself from multiple viewpoints, you may dream of trying to give a public speech when people start leaving the room. The following week you dream of approaching someone you admire, only to have them ignore you. In another dream, a peer is being recognized for their accomplishments while you are excluded on the sidelines. Each of these metaphors are different, but the elementary archetype is that of an outsider, a figure who typically lives life outside the mainstream while secretly longing for connection.

Unlike a static image, archetypes are forces that grab hold of us and push us into action, usually causing us to behave in ways we don't consciously choose. This might look like having exaggerated reactions to certain triggers or making choices that play out in destructive ways. Following the example above, a person possessed by the outsider archetype may perceive a slight where there is none, and assume others are rejecting them. They might even abandon a relationship before they get hurt—even though what they most long for is connection. But when you engage with archetypes consciously, learning what they want and *how* they mean in your life, you begin to see them as powerful guides in your psychic development.

The aim is not to control or avoid these ancient patterns. But learning how they typically unfold gives you a chance to discover their corresponding meaning for your life. This is why stories are such powerful conduits for healing. When you listen to myths and wisdom stories, you recognize the activated archetypes within them and realize that your situation is not isolated or meaningless. You see how protagonists move through their own hardships. It can reassure you that the times you may feel stuck or frozen won't last forever. Many travellers before you have survived this same passage and are wiser and more resilient for having experienced it. Myths give us an imaginal map, showing us there is life and meaning beyond the crisis of the journey if we keep moving in conscious cooperation with the archetypes.

THE UGLY DUCKLING

To give you an example of how an archetype moves through stages of development, let's look at the classic outsider story of *The Ugly Duckling* by Hans Christian Andersen.[6] The story begins with a mother duck sitting proudly on her brood of eggs. There is one egg in particular that is larger than the others, and she is dubious of it—especially when it takes longer than the others to hatch. Finally, this last duckling emerges out of his huge, grey egg looking very different from his siblings. As he grows up, the ugly duckling is ruthlessly teased and bullied by his siblings for being different, and his own mother even wishes he'd never been born.

The poor duckling is bitten and pushed and kicked, driven out by everyone in the farmyard. One day, when it's worse than worse, he runs away. He flies over the hedge and, closing his eyes, flies still farther into the wild moor beyond. Along his journey he meets all kinds of creatures—a cat, an old woman, a hunting dog, wild geese, hunters, and a prize hen—but he has negative experiences everywhere he goes. Each one tries to make him like themselves instead of valuing him for who *he* is, and both are frustrated with the results. After the tom cat calls him crazy for wanting to play in the water, he yells out, "You don't understand me!" And as he dives under and over the water, he finds real joy for the first time. He frolics in this way for a long time in solitude though his loneliness is always present.

One autumn evening, a flock of wild swans emerges from the bushes with their graceful curved necks and dazzling white plumage. When they they spread their glorious wings, singing as they begin to take flight, he marvels that he has never seen such beautiful birds. He watches as they rise up and up into the sky. The duckling is filled with such a happy sensation that he lets out a cry "so strange that he frightens himself."

The water in the pond begins to get colder as the days grow shorter. Eventually it cracks with ice when he swims, making it harder to keep even the smallest space around him free. Before he knows it, he is trapped in the frozen ice in despair. The next morning, a passing peasant sees and rescues him from near death, letting him warm up in his home for a time. But soon he realizes he doesn't belong there either. He is left in the cold to survive the great hardships of winter alone.

When the spring finally begins to warm, he comes upon the same glorious birds he'd seen before. This time, although he is wary and quite sure they will reject him, he swims toward them nonetheless. He believes he is so ugly and unworthy of even approaching them, the first thing he says to the royal birds is "Kill me." It's only then, with his head bent in shame, that he glimpses himself in the clear stream. His reflection is no longer an ugly duckling but a beautiful white swan. To his surprise the others fly toward him with outstretched wings! All his life, he'd been persecuted and despised for his ugliness, and now the children playing nearby are saying he is the most beautiful of all the swans. He has never been so happy in all his life.

This wonderful story of individuation resonates for many outsiders because it illustrates those movements in the archetype from ugly duckling to beautiful swan.* Before tugging on a few of the story's threads, it's worth noting that there is no wrong way to interpret a fairy tale. One symbol or turning point in the tale may resonate more strongly for you than another, depending on where you are at in your own psychic development. This is why these tales are so enduring—because two people can pull on different threads, and both find the meaning they need.

In the first stage of the story, the ugly duckling is taught that he is ugly, big, clumsy, and wretched. Different from everyone around him, he is bullied, mocked, and made to feel like he doesn't belong. This is symbolic of that traumatic period in one's life when the archetype of the outsider first coalesces. Some people are just born wonderfully different, and have a unique perspective to offer the world as a result of their difference. But they aren't always able to recognize themselves as beautiful or unique because the world around them is accustomed to conformity. When we don't have our beauty reflected, we may internalize the ugliness and unworthiness we are shown.

When the duckling finally jumps the hedge "and flies still farther," we have our first movement in the archetypal pattern. It is that moment, either by force or will, when someone makes a painful separation from the group, driven to discover what, if anything, lies beyond the rejection they experience. In my book

* Individuation is the word Jung used to describe the process of self realization, in which a person becomes conscious of their shadow and divests themselves from the expectations of others in order to live in accordance with their own soul.

Belonging, I called this stage "Initiation by Exile."[7] It is often a catalyzing period in the story of the outcast when they are initiated in a period of solitude to find, after all seems lost, what remains.

In this wandering time, our duckling discovers his love of water. He dives deep and resurfaces again and again, feeling for the first time at home in his own skin. I like to think of that water as the domain of the imaginal. Like the duckling, so many outcasts turn to their dreams and the inner life in times of exile. On one hand it is a relief, but it's also where our true mettle is tested as we face our inner and outer foes and tyrants. During this movement, the duckling is harassed by hunters, threatened by a scary dog, and narrowly survives a storm by taking refuge in an old cottage. He is briefly adopted by an old woman who lives with a haughty tom cat and her prize hen. But when our duckling can't lay eggs like the hen, or purr like the cat, he is once again shamed and cast out for being useless.

He returns to his beloved water, the one thing that brings him joy, and that's when he has a mystical experience upon seeing the dazzling swans. He gets a fleeting glimpse of his imaginal self—his ultimate becoming. At some time or another we are all blessed with such a moment. We experience something or meet someone who resonates completely with our soul. If we are clever, we don't confuse this feeling for envy. We reach for the deeper current running underneath the moment of resonance, to find vocation, a calling homeward. Though he is still too young to fly and is unable to follow the swans as they rise into the autumn sky, the duckling is so overcome that he lets out a glorious sound that both surprises and scares him. You can feel the archetype moving again here— how it no longer completely identifies with rejection, but is able to vocalize something that's glorious in him, even though it's still frightening and out of reach.

It is no mistake that what follows is the duckling's near-death experience. It's often when we venture one step into a new way of being that the old attitude feels threatened and rears up twice as fiercely. As winter descends, he has to swim harder and harder to keep the water from freezing and, "every night the space on which he swam became smaller and smaller." This is the crisis point in our story: our little duckling becomes frozen in place, paralyzed with inadequacy against the conditions of his life. Symbolically speaking, this is when we lose track of our own story, when the divine thing we glimpsed grows faint and feels inconsequential, so we lose hope that life will ever be different.

It's fascinating to note how the archetype doesn't move in a linear direction. There is often a necessary period of contraction after that initial excitement and expansion. The winter is symbolic of a season so heavy with hardship that the author makes his only appearance in the story to say, "It would be very sad, were I to relate all the misery and privations which the poor little duckling endured during the hard winter."[8] But this complete defeat is also necessary for the story. After every attempt to fix the problem fails, the ego must surrender to a higher power. As Jung famously put it, "the experience of the Self is always a defeat for the ego," meaning when an old identity shatters, wisdom can finally prevail.[9] There's a beautiful haiku written by the seventeenth-century Japanese poet Mizuta Masahide that sums this up well:[10]

Barn's burnt down—
now
I can see the moon.

A passer-by sees the duckling frozen in the ice and breaks him out with his shoe, bringing him into the warmth of his home for a while. This passer-by is symbolic of the sort of wisdom that comes out of nowhere. It may arrive in the form of an illuminating dream, a synchronicity, a chance encounter, or an unusual perspective that unexpectedly takes hold. Sophia often makes an entrance at our lowest point, when we are filled with anguish, to offer us confirmation that there is life beyond symbolic death.

The whole landscape of the duckling's life begins to thaw with warmth. A lark sings, the sun warms his feathers, and he finds his wings are strong enough to carry him into a nearby garden where, "the apple-trees are in full blossom, and the fragrant elders bend their long green branches down to the stream ... everything looks beautiful, in the freshness of early spring."[11]

Even so, he feels strangely unhappy as he spots those lovely swans he had seen before. He is so filled with learned unworthiness as he approaches the swans that he expects to be rejected. He even says, "Kill me." We can hear his utter humility. His love for those "royal birds" is so pure and complete that he knows there would be no sense in living life without them. Given that feeling of defeat, he still approaches that which he loves. This is another important movement in the pattern of the archetype, where instead of withdrawing into isolation, he pushes through his fear toward his true self. Indeed, it's only when he bows his head that he catches sight of his true self in a moment of honest reflection and is able to witness himself with the same admiration he gives so easily to the other swans. He is finally welcomed with open arms into a life of belonging.

The same archetypal patterns that appear in myths and fairy tales also appear in our dreams. For instance, you may dream of a closet full of dresses that are too small for your body. The dream conjures the ugly duckling in you who may have been pecked at and told he was too big and clumsy. But knowing that the archetype moves beyond this belief into the actualization of his inner swan can be held as a secret in your own knowing. You are not alone. You too are beautiful. And like him, you weren't meant for the small-dress life. Your camaraderie with the archetype can now be like a secret energy reserve to draw on in times of despair.

* * *

The archetype is not simply a pattern that you observe—it has an energy that can possess you for better or worse. For the ancient Greeks, it was understood that when you fell hopelessly in love, or were consumed with rage, or hungry for power, you were being physically and emotionally inhabited by gods. Whether you are conscious of it or not, you may find yourself possessed by one of these primordial patterns, embodying its qualities, or enacting its fate. But when you tend to your dreams, those archetypes are given form that you can observe and relate to, rather than getting swept up in incomprehensible drives and swells of emotion.

Perhaps most fascinating is how an archetype can appear in dreams without you having any personal experience with its images or story. I once worked with a woman who was experiencing a painful separation from her daughter who was in the clutches of an eating disorder. While she worried for her unreachable daughter, Marjorie felt as if her whole world had gone fallow. One night, she dreamed of a field of golden wheat. This image prompted me to invoke the myth of Demeter, the Olympian goddess of agriculture. Though she'd never learned about the abduction of Persephone by Hades, she was shocked to relate so powerfully to Demeter's loss. She learned how Demeter was so stricken with grief that she wasn't able to tend to her crops and the whole world fell into the famine of winter. She related this acutely to her own daughter's famine, and her own inability to provide for others while her daughter was unwell.

When Marjorie learned that the mythic daughter and mother were eventually reunited by striking a compromise with Hades, it opened her to consider how she might need to let her daughter venture into the underworld for her own initiatory process. Over time, she learned to see their separation and reunification as part of an ancient and necessary process. The myth gave her hope that in time her daughter would return. Though it was an incredibly difficult passage, they reunited on the other side of that hardship, creating a more autonomous and nourishing relationship for them both.

The value of working with myths and fairy tales is that they give shape to the underlying archetypes that are active in our lives. Knowing the pattern in the story helps us to anticipate what problems are on the horizon and what solutions may resolve them. While having knowledge of fairy tales, mythology, and literature can enhance your dreamwork, I don't believe amassing an intellectual library of archetypes is necessary. You contain everything you need to understand your own dreams. In fact, too much information can be a hindrance. If you immediately jump to previous knowledge of an archetype, you may lose what the dream is saying that is new.

Due to their lineage, certain words have the tendency to coagulate into a concept that abstracts us from an embodied encounter with its meaning. As an example, Jung's terminology *anima* and *animus* are still used frequently to describe the archetypal feminine in a man and masculine in a woman. But these words are loaded with a polarizing history that, for many, has lost relevance in today's gender-fluid landscape. It's not to say that we need to toss out old maps completely, because they are often valuable seed ideas. But in cartography, there is a process called *ground truthing* in which all maps need to be refined, redrawn, and checked against the changing reality. We need to keep pushing at language and the contours of our assumptions. What's more important than knowledge is the openness, curiosity, and love that draws us into relationship with our symbols. So long as we are respecting our images as if they are themselves alive, they might invite us below the surface, into their dynamic depths.

Sometimes our patterns appear as symbols that can be traced back to ancient art and literature, but they may also manifest as common dream themes shared by folks from different cultures. Some examples reported from around the world include dreaming of losing your teeth, or being chased, or falling from a height.

Patterns can also emerge as motifs across a series of one's own dreams, like recurring characters, places, dynamics, or symbols.

Recurring motifs don't usually stay with us for a lifetime, but they need more than one dream to express their complexity. A good example of a persistent pattern is when a relationship breaks up and we keep dreaming about the ex for months, or even years. This often happens because there is a wound we are unable to heal quickly, or a lesson in the experience that we haven't yet integrated. It may also happen that someone has made such an important impact that their image returns to us over a lifetime—to express the things they symbolize for us that continue to be relevant. Though it may seem as if persistent dream themes are just repetitive, they are actually taking us around the spiral, returning again and again to the matter from a slightly different angle, or from a greater distance, until we gain wisdom from the pattern.

Sometimes we get trapped in a pattern, or in a recurring dream, because we have forgotten our "dream bending" agency. We lose the lucidity of volition and begin to feel as if life is happening to us, forgetting that we too are happening to life. So we continue to make the same choices when faced with the same dilemmas. It's like sleepwalking through our own story. What's needed in these situations is a new perspective—but before we can conceive of a new solution, first we need to understand how and where we got stuck.

Several years ago, a brilliant woman came to me haunted by terrible dreams. Rebecca suffered with agoraphobia and depression and was afraid to sleep at night for the violent images that preyed on her would-be rest. Though she found them shameful and embarrassing, she bravely shared these dreams with me. Knowing that dreams are in perpetual service to our well-being, we cradled each one with compassion and curiosity, and they began to turn up powerful insights about the things blocking Rebecca from expressing her true nature in the world. As anyone who has undertaken healing knows, it was hard work, and there were many ungrieved wounds that needed tending. But eventually the nature of Rebecca's patterns changed. She no longer found herself threatened and intimidated by invalidating figures; instead she started swimming in her dreams. At first in pools, then in lakes, eventually she was diving under the sea and able to breathe underwater. Deep under the surface, she found shipwrecks and chests filled with interesting treasures not necessarily valuable to anyone else, but fascinating to her creative individuality. She would wake up from these dreams with a sense of wonder and excitement to sleep again for what she might find. This was a far cry from the woman who was haunted by nightmares.

After many of these treasure-diving dreams, Rebecca began to leave the house and even travel further afield for the sole purpose of going to charity shops. She began to recreate her dream experience, finding and collecting neglected objects that she refurbished to resell in what would become a thriving retail store. As a gift, she sent me a tiny bottle, capped with a cork, and filled with colourful beach glass. It still sits on my altar today.

There is an art to both reading and tending your dream patterns, which we'll explore in later chapters. But it's valuable to know before you start that you can change your patterns—or more accurately, that with the right attention and curiosity, your patterns will naturally evolve. Your attention is a kind of nourishment to the dreaming. Like any two beings in a relationship, your exchange of energy and resources inevitably changes you both. Like psychic metabolism, as you integrate a symbol's wisdom, it begins to shift its shape in you—sometimes in a subtle way with only small adjustments, other times dramatically, even disappearing altogether to make room for a new archetype. Simultaneously, you and the dream have been enriched.

People often ask me after a dream session, "But what should I *do?*" Taking some action that reinforces the wisdom generated from dreamwork is essential, but often this question comes out of our habituated anxiety that something must always be done with one's dilemmas. In fairy tales, the protagonist may begin with a mission, but the hardships they endure, and the initiations they undergo, are rarely about accomplishment. It is instead like an alchemical process in which the hero or heroine is changed by their experiences: they become the kind of person who knows which way to go.

Remember the line from the Hildegard von Bingen poem shared at the beginning of Chapter 2: Wisdom of Sophia, "With wisdom I order all rightly."[12] It's tempting to interpret this as saying there is a right and wrong way to go. But we have to remember that when it comes to following Sophia, we always have volition. The patterns of Wisdom offer solutions, but we always have a choice to accept or reject what's offered. There is no wrong way to go, because even when our decisions lead to hardship, they contribute to our next becoming. Purpose is not a path that fixes your direction, but an orientation of soul that blazes a trail.

THE DRAMATIC ARC

Nobody knows where the oldest myths and fairy tales originated, because they were orally passed on for thousands of years before they were ever written down. But when we study the architecture of myth, we begin to find a remarkably similar structure in our own dreams. As the great mythologist Joseph Campbell famously wrote, "Myths are public dreams, dreams are private myths."[13] They function as the communal version of our nightly dreams. So we might speculate that myths emerged from our collective biology—or more precisely, from the earth's own dreaming through us.

Understanding a dream is not so different from interpreting a film or piece of literature. I have often wondered if the structure of these art forms, storytelling itself, actually emulates dreaming: the narrative arc, the ensemble cast, the building of tension, abrupt jump cuts, even cliffhangers and satisfying resolutions. In both film and dreams, there are no mistakes in how, when, and where things are placed. Just like a stage play, every dream has a mission at hand and all of its elements are attempting to bring about a persuasive solution.

The earliest work on dramatic theory, *Poetics* by Aristotle (circa 335 BC), identified the core progression found in stories, plays, and poems that we now refer to as the "dramatic arc." In the nineteenth century, the German playwright Gustav Freytag refined Aristotle's theory into a model that is still used by playwrights, authors, and filmmakers today. Then in 1970, Carl Jung showed how this same dramatic arc could be found in a great many dreams.[14] Though he didn't go into much detail, he suggested that it could be a useful tool for working with dreams in four parts: Exposition, Development, Culmination, and Solution.

Looking at a dream through a rational lens, it can be hard to fathom any order in what feels like a maelstrom of random images and characters. But when you pan out from the details to appreciate the dream as a whole, you can see these pivotal turning points that together, and in sequence, form a narrative arc. Knowing this pattern can support your dreamwork process. It allows you to return to each of those anchor points when you're feeling disoriented. Even if you have nothing more than a fragment or single scene in your dream, you can still use this framework to spelunk its nuance.

Exposition: This is the opening scene in which the dream says something about the place, like "I am with a rebel army hiding in an underground bunker during wartime." It is also where we meet the protagonist, often represented by the dream ego (one's own dream-perspective; the "I" in the dream) as in the above example, or with other key characters like, "My spouse and I are packing to move." Usually in the exposition we get a hint of the problem or mission that will unfold across the rest of the dream.

Development: This is when tension begins to build as the plot develops. Let's say the next sentence in the bunker dream is, "I've been swept into something dangerous and could realistically lose my life." In this stage, the protagonist is filled with uncertainty regarding the conflict they are facing. To use the example of the couple who are packing, "We have to leave where we are staying, but I don't know where we are going." You can feel in both these examples how uncertainly is building the tension.

Culmination: This is the crisis or crux of the dream. It's when all that tension builds into a decisive action or brings about the development of the plot. In the bunker dream, for example, "Leadership decides to smuggle me onto a train for privileged classes." Or in the dream of the moving couple, the tension builds into a crisis when, "We are about to check into a hotel when someone steals my luggage. It contains all my precious valuables."

Falling Action: Jung didn't recognize Freytag's extra (fifth) stage. It's worth noting, however, because there is a downslope after the climax when things turn for the protagonist. This is when we see the success or failure of the actions taken in Culmination. It might look like a tragedy we must come to terms with or a reversal of fortune or internal attitude. In the bunker dream, there is a falling action when, "A porter tells me to get off the train, and I'm in a panic to gather my things knowing I am in hostile territory." Or in the case of the moving couple who just had their valuables stolen: "Without my luggage, I must borrow strange clothing from a friend."

Solution (or result): The final stage of the dream arc. Often the last line or two of a dream is when the plot has been cathartically resolved either by overcoming or failing magnificently. This leaves us with a new status quo in its wake. The bunker dream finishes with, "A woman intends to prosecute for her poor treatment on the train. We are in the same predicament with a common foe, and I tell her I'll be her witness." This solution seems helpful: wrongdoers are being held accountable and there is a gathering of support for the parts that feel maligned.

But many dreams leave us with a question rather than an

answer. The travelling couple dream ends with, "My spouse and I are now at odds, considering separation. I'm unsure if I'm staying or going." In this case, the solution is not yet cooked. We are likely earlier in the alchemical process, symbolized by the dreamer's ambivalence and lack of secure location. More important than making a decision, like staying or going, is to take what can be learned from the dream to refine your inquiry. So, the dreamer's loss of valuables may need to be reckoned with, or they may need to look at the uncharacteristic compromises they are making in their time of confusion. I always take it as a positive sign of adaptation when a dream suddenly awakens the dreamer from sleep. The individual is ready to "wake up" to the fear or stress they have been unconsciously harbouring. However frightening it may seem, those heart-pounding dreams that jar you from sleep mean that you are, on some level, ready to face the issue directly.

This model for understanding the stages of a story is extremely helpful because it serves as a map to orient yourself in the seemingly disorganized or complex landscape of a dream. If you know the significance of the exposition, you can focus on the first scene of the dream for clues as to what area or problem in your life the dream is speaking to. Knowing the crisis point of a dream is where the most intensity of emotion is clustered, you may be able to make a connection to similar feelings in waking-life. If you want to know where you stand with the issue at hand, the resolution of the dream will show you the state of your resolve or dislocation.

Looking at these dramatic pivot points, you should be able to name the problem of the dream, what action was used to navigate it, find the crisis or crux of the dream, and decide if the solution was successful or not. You can always play with different outcomes if it wasn't successful. Ask yourself: what outcome would you have preferred? What alternate strategies could you have used to get the resolution you wanted? In what way can this change-up be applied to your waking-life?

It's fascinating to consider how natural patterns emerge when comparing thousands of dreams, myths, and symbols. Whether in the arc of a gripping plot, the behaviour of an archetype, or similarity in sacred images from cultures around the world, these patterns are like imperishable truths that transcend our differences. A pattern language only works when it connects the smallest part to the very largest pieces in a system. In this way, a knowledge of the archetypes gives our tiny lives a bigger context in which to finally make some sense. But it also ennobles that small existence with an ancient wisdom that blazed the trails of the heroes and heroines before us.

CHAPTER 7

Universal Dream Elements

BY TRACKING what humans dream about and how often, researchers have been able to discover remarkable similarities between dreamers everywhere. While the dramatic arc shows us a dream's pivot points, knowing these universal elements that make up our dreams can help guide our dreamwork.

After collecting and analysing thousands of dreams from around the world, researchers Robert Van de Castle and Calvin Hall developed a coding system for the content of dreams.[1] They identified ten general categories into which all dream elements could be classified, creating a system that has widespread applications for scientists, anthropologists, and psychologists.[2]

For our purposes, I have adapted this system to explore seven of the most universal dream elements: Settings, Feelings, Actions, Dynamics, Characters, Animals, and Objects. While this won't cover every dream element, exploring these broad categories through a metaphoric lens will support you in developing your symbolic capacity, which can be put to practice with any image. As we move through each of these components, notice your ability to telescope between your literal and symbolic attentions.

SETTINGS

The setting, or the environment of your dream, is the context in which everything else takes place. As a symbol, it can reveal what area of your life the dream is addressing. In a well-told story, the opening scene sets the tone, introduces the characters, and gives us a teaser for the unfolding drama ahead.

Taken symbolically, the setting depicts the environment and mood of your psychic landscape. Remember our example from The Dramatic Arc: "I am with a rebel army hiding in an underground bunker during wartime." The first thing I notice is that the dream is set in wartime, which is symbolic of a large-scale conflict. Without knowing anything about the dreamer, we can guess that they are dealing with what feels like a life-threatening clash between opposing forces or ideologies. We are using war metaphors when we say, "I am *battling* cancer" or "I'm *besieged* with self-doubt." But what we really mean is that we are experiencing ourselves in opposition to something powerful, dangerous, and outside of our conscious control. The underground bunker is another fascinating symbol. It shows us that the dreamer's relationship to that conflict is yet subterrestrial or semi-buried. Perhaps the conflict is happening below the surface of consciousness. They aren't on the front lines, fighting the enemy, but in hiding—perhaps in an effort to protect themselves from perceived harm.

While there may be multiple settings in the course of one dream, take extra care to explore the opening scene as it will anchor the rest of your dreamwork. A wise friend once said to me, "If you want to know how something ends, look at how it begins." It's true that in many great films and books the outcome of the story is foreshadowed in its opening scenes.

As you write down your dream, make note of your immediate surroundings: Are you indoors or outdoors? If you are inside, is it a workplace, a house, a school? Just as settings have different functions in waking-life, they hold vastly different symbolic meanings. A cathedral, for instance, is a place of worship, so a dream in that setting will likely be symbolic of your relationship to religion or spirituality. Similarly, a workplace dream could be about a situation unfolding in your professional life, whereas a house dream will be about the more intimate aspects of your life. As we explored, you can take this further by exploring which room of the house you are in, each of which performs a different function in your life.*

When it comes to places that are most familiar to us, we have a harder time thinking about them symbolically because we are so close to them. It's very common to dream of being in your childhood home. But instead of dismissing that as "normal" because it's familiar, consider the significance of a dream set in that context at this particular time in your life. What was the prevailing atmosphere in that space? What memories do you associate with having lived there at that time in your life? What is the feeling or emotional tone of that house? Does revisiting it make you feel nourished, comfortable, safe, warm? Or does it bring up discomfort, longing, despair? How do those conditions relate to what's happening for you right now? A dream that takes place in your childhood home often speaks to core patterns from your family dynamics that are arising in present time. Like a Venn diagram, the two contexts overlap because they share a commonality.

For comparison, a hotel is a transitional accommodation. A dream in this setting might indicate a temporary situation or state of transition. A dream of packing up and moving house could be symbolic of making a foundational shift in your values or perspectives. As mentioned earlier, a dream of being in a car may have to do with how you are moving through life—especially as it relates to your body. Are you "out of gas?" Who is in "the driver's seat" of

---

* See House and Rooms in Chapter 4 Metaphor: Language of Kinship, under Common Dream Symbols.

this experience? Do you need to "put the brakes" on a specific situation or relationship? Are you "lost" or "afraid of crashing?" Each of these scenarios will bring about a precise set of descriptions and personal associations that will speak to how you're *navigating* the world. Notice how often we use metaphors in everyday language. They are so common in speech that we forget their origins and can't see the images we're using.

Another thing to notice about your dream setting is the time of day. Symbolically, we tend to think of the sun rising as a fresh start, the dawning of a new energy. But a dream of intrusive sunlight can leave you feeling overexposed. The daytime is when we are conscious, so dreams set in the day tend to be about our explicit concerns. A dream set at night may be more reflective in nature, like the moon, dealing with implicit matters. The night is when we sleep and dream and explore the limitlessness of psyche. But as anyone who's experienced insomnia knows, it's also when our anxieties are most ferocious. So depending on the other elements in the dream, darkness could be symbolic of that which is scary and unknown, or it may have a mystical quality to it. There may even be an overlap between these perceptions.

We use weather and seasonal metaphors to describe our moods —like feeling "stormy," or "grey," or discovering a new friend is like a "breath of fresh air," and has a "sunny disposition." The weather in your dream will say something about the elemental forces at play in your psyche. Notice if your setting is windy, snowy, or raining. Rain may be a symbolic climate of melancholy or grief, or it could feel sensual and baptismal depending on your *umwelt* in the dream. If there is snow, ask yourself where you are experiencing coldness, feeling frozen, or a lack of flow. The time of year and season can also play an important role in your dream. What might a dream set in spring say about this season of your life?

Maybe your setting is a different historical period. Are there clues that can help pinpoint the century or decade in which your dream is set? What do you associate with that time period? If it is set in your past, what was life like for you at that age? If you don't have personal associations with the dream era, say it is set in Victorian times, then what events or attitudes do you automatically associate with it? A woman I was working with recently dreamed of wearing a corset that she said reminded her of constrained femininity. Just taking a moment to explore *how* the dress meant for her was the key to unlocking the rest of the dream's wisdom.

Also consider the geography of your dream setting. Do you recognize something special about the landscape, or are you in a different country, city, possibly even universe? Places have as much character as people do, so take a moment to articulate what that is for you. If the dream is set in a mythical place, beyond anything you have encountered in daily life, you may not have immediate personal associations. But you can still describe what that mythical place looks like and what your instincts and reactions to it are. Does it evoke feelings in you like somewhere else you've been before? If the place is unfamiliar or unusual, see if you can name precisely in what way it is different. Incongruities in dreams often point to a meaningful contrast. For example, if your dream is in your childhood home but it appears to be decorated in a modern style that you love, maybe this acknowledges the work you've done to update an old *umwelt*.

Another thing to notice about your setting is whether it is private or public or some combination of both. Dreams that take place in private spaces (like a bedroom) are usually about your most personal developments, whereas dreams that take place in public settings (like in an airport, school, or mall) have to do with your relationship to the collective. Of course there are dreams in which your worlds intersect, just as they do in life, which speaks to the overlap of those contexts.

You may be surprised by what comes out of your associations

when you tap into your other-than-visual dream senses. Make note of what characteristics your setting has, what vibe it gives off, how it smells or sounds, how you feel in this place, and if it reminds you of anywhere you've been before. If you have an extremely detailed dream, it can feel overwhelming to render every image into descriptions. If this is the case, make broader strokes by tending to the most compelling aspects of each scene. You will know what to focus on by its quality of feeling. Some images and situations will have more intensity than others—and it's okay to let some of the smaller details go so you can tend to the key moments. On the other hand, if all you have is a brief or fuzzy setting, make do with what you have. You may not need more than three or four descriptors about the beginning of the dream to anchor you in your process. If you are feeling disoriented or confused about your dream location, consider that this too could be symbolic of an overall feeling of dislocation in some area of your life.

FEELINGS

Feelings are the greatest portal into understanding your dream. For clarity, in this context I am not speaking about the judgements and feelings you have *about* your dream after waking up, but *within* the dream itself. While the feelings you have upon waking are usually coloured by your conscious biases, dream-feelings are your undiluted responses to the situation at hand. Most symbols in a dream need to be courted for their underlying meaning, but feelings are the raw and unvarnished truth of your soulbody experience.

As an exercise, you can start by circling all the feelings in your dream. If you haven't written any down, you may need to plumb a little deeper to make your dream-feelings explicit. If you do no other form of dreamwork, you can often get to the heart of the matter by asking, "What is the strongest feeling in the dream?"

While this may seem like an easy undertaking, it isn't always straightforward to get at the subtlety and complexity of a feeling. Even if you are able to name it, it may not be obvious how to relate that feeling back to waking-life.

Because we use the word "feel" in such a range of ways, it's important to clarify that when we say "I feel warm" or "I feel tingly," we are describing physical sensations. When we say "This decision feels right," we are likely speaking from intuition. And when we say "This policy feels unjust," we are stating an opinion. But any of these experiences may also carry underlying emotion. When we have unexpected bursts of panic, fear, sadness, anger, or joy, we call them "feelings." However, in their raw, unconscious form, they are more accurately called emotions. Feelings are when we are able to bring these emotions to the surface to name and evaluate them consciously.

Emotions are involuntary, psychophysical responses, like when you're about to speak publicly and your throat tightens and your heart begins to race. Or when someone cuts in front of you in line and your temperature starts rising and your muscles clench up. You can also have a rush of emotions when triggered by an inner complex. Though Jung coined the term "complex," I think Jungian analyst James Hollis defined it best as, "a cluster of energy in the unconscious, charged by historic events ... generating a programmed response and an implicit set of expectations."[3] Jung described the complexes as "splinter psyches" because their origin is frequently a trauma or shock that causes us to split off a part of our psyche.[4] That split-off part can possess us in unexpected moments and act autonomously in ways we don't always under-stand. When you say "I was so angry I couldn't see straight," it's usually because one of these complexes took over, causing you to feel a lack of control. After some time, you may calm down and see the situation with greater clarity. Emotions always have something valuable to say, but it usually isn't until the storm passes that we can properly evaluate what that might be. This is where feelings are forged. Feelings are the conscious evaluations of your emotional experiences.

Considering how the dominant culture devalues emotion, it isn't hard to understand why so many people have difficulty knowing what they are feeling, or why. Since feeling is essential in our capacity to relate, this impairment hobbles us in many ways, extending harm into the world around us. But feeling is a competency that can be rehabilitated, developed, and finessed. Though we don't always recognize where it is coming from, following the emotions in our dream will draw us deeper into intimacy with ourselves and the world.

In order to rehabilitate our capacity for feeling, we have to challenge our basic assumption that feeling, thinking, intuition, sensation, imagination, and instinct are discrete functions within human cognition. While it's incredibly useful to have language that differentiates between them—and helps us know what our dominant strengths are—none of these abilities work alone. They are wholly interdependent, like organs in a body, and none can complete their task without the help of the others. The word "cognition" has its roots in the Latin words *co* (the prefix for together, mutually, in common) and *gno* (knowing). So cognition is the act or process of knowing through our integrated system of perceptive faculties. We tend to think of cognition as a purely mental process. But to know anything, we engage a complexity of intelligences including the acumen of our body in space, our ancient, inherited instincts, the subtle valuations of feeling, the capacity of our imagination, and yes, the analytical intelligence of our thinking, too.

We cannot have emotions without physical sensations any more than we can know what we are feeling without thinking about it. We have instincts that lead to sensations, sensations that produce feelings, thoughts about those feelings, and a limitless imagination in which to reassemble all the pieces into new ideas or stories. It's a wonderful jumble of intersecting systems, all of which happen as automatically as breathing or circulation. The notion that one can be "purely objective" is an abstract concept that doesn't exist in actuality. There is no such thing as objectivity when you live in a body because we are shaping the world in the very act of experiencing it.

Humanity's devotion to rationalism knows no bounds, but we must learn to restrain it in dreamwork. Rationality is the part of us that thinks mechanistically and logically, analyzing and explaining things in linear terms. There is no room for flexibility, nuance, or paradox in rationalism. It surgically dissects matters with either/or thinking in an attempt to provide evidence for certainty as its end goal. It is this precise faculty that has allowed humanity to develop incredible advancements in every field. But when rationality isn't guided and tempered by feeling and relatedness, it marches on pathologically. Without considering the larger, embodied context perceived by the other faculties, it tends to be parasitic and destructive toward its own ecosystem.

People are especially distrustful of their feeling life when they've been told that emotions are irrational, useless, and need to be managed or controlled. I worked with a man in his late seventies who had grown up during wartime in Europe whose father beat him if he ever showed signs of emotion. He hadn't cried since he was a child, but he was now having repetitive dreams of being lost. In the dreams, this man was desperate to find his way home. Every other day he woke up with his heart racing from these dreams but he couldn't relate the panic to his waking-life. There was such a backlog of unfelt feelings that he'd lost a sense of location in his own life.

When engaged consciously, feeling is a mighty and essential faculty that shows us what we value. It is the anchor of knowing how we feel that locates us in the world. It allows us to harmonize with our environment and make connections with others. Feeling is a relational instrument that shows the distance, texture, quality, and tone between us and the rest of our living system. Like invisible arteries across which we give and receive, feeling is what draws things into our orbit, and pulls us into theirs. Feeling is also the part of us that considers the impact of our decisions on the whole and it's reciprocal impact on us.

Thanks to its unapologetically disclosing manner, dreamwork is a powerful way to revive this capacity. This restorative process begins to serve you immediately: as you work with your dreams, it puts you back into a respectful relationship with your feelings. I use the word "respectful" because we are so often dismissive of our feelings, overriding them with conventional behaviour. A good example of a wounded feeling-function is the person who is pathologically nice and accommodating, even when they are secretly seething or harbouring resentment. They may dream of anger and aggression until they are able to give expression to their waking-life disagreements in a productive way. On the other end of the spectrum, someone who overreacts to benign situations will also need to calibrate. As an example, someone who was bullied by a parent might themselves become a bully because they've never given themselves room to unpack and acknowledge those original wounds. It may seem counterintuitive but in both cases, each must learn to value feeling so they can draw upon its guidance. Feeling has a locating nature—it shows us where we stand. Not where we'd *like* to stand or where we *don't want* to stand, but on the ground of truth in this embodied moment.

When you are working with emotion in a dream, the goal should be to validate your response, no matter what it is. Whether you are frightened, angry, sad, guilty, or elated, you are having the appropriate response to the conditions of your perspective at that moment. Only then can you begin to understand the larger context of what contributed to your feeling and why. So if you dream an intruder is trying to get into your house, and your response is to try to shove him out with physical force, the first step is to name the emotions you are having. If you feel shock and anger, it's important to validate those responses as appropriate for the dream situation.

Because the dream is a living system, we are holding multiple perspectives at once. The next step is to look at some of the other elements in the dream, especially the intruder himself. As you go deeper into the dream, you might discover that your feeling toward him (and his feeling toward you) changes. Following the feeling means allowing this change to take place. Let's say you describe the intruder as "an opportunist who will do anything to further his own ends." Maybe you think of yourself as someone who is generous and calm by comparison but now that you've articulated those shadow qualities, you have to ask yourself: "Why are they intruding on your world?"

In Chapter 10 we'll explore shadow work in depth but for now let's assume your intruder has something to teach you. You describe him as a scoundrel who takes risks and does improper things to get ahead in life. As someone who is always concerned with doing what's proper, it occurs to you that you could stand to take more risks, grabbing opportunities in life even if they seem "improper." Now when you return to your feelings of shock and anger, you can relate to moments when you've felt shocked by your own aggression, pushing those emotions away with anger in the same way you tried to combat the intruder. The intruder takes on a more sympathetic quality as you recognize his appearance as an unacknowledged aspect of yourself. Your feelings toward each other have now changed. He can relax his urge to attack you because you've dropped some of your resistance to considering his value. Maybe you even experiment with integrating a small dose of his risk-taking or assertiveness into your own personality.

The emotions you experience in a dream tend to mirror, exaggerate, or compensate for waking-life attitudes. Your dream-feelings might match quite closely to feelings that you experience in waking-life, even though the context of the dream is entirely different. This allows you to consider your feelings in that new context and look at them from a different angle. Exaggeration is when you don't feel strongly about something in waking-life but the dream expresses an intensity of feeling about the matter. Sometimes the overcorrection allows you to consider the possibility that you may be minimizing your waking feelings. Compensation happens when you're not at all conscious of feeling some way in daily life. Using the home invasion example above, the dreamer was trying to "rise above" intrusive thoughts of aggression but then dreamed of the kind of scary confrontation they wanted to avoid. The dream isn't suggesting you fly into a rage or grab whatever you want, but it is showing an important impulse in the psyche. Acknowledging the validity and full spectrum of your feelings as the intelligent responses that they are doesn't mean you should express them thoughtlessly—it simply means there is an internal response to the situation that needs recognition.

More than any other element, feelings behave as a quick bridge from the dream back to waking-life experiences. More often than not, naming and understanding your responses is in and of itself the healing process. By bringing feelings into the open through dreamwork, you can more consciously evaluate your inner experience and make well-rounded decisions about how to navigate life and relationships inclusive of those feelings. Over time, you will develop your feeling instrument and be able to draw upon its wisdom in the moment.

Paradoxically, the act of becoming more intimate with your feelings is what gives you distance from their intensity. It is only through the lifelong work of developing kinship with our feelings that we can put them to conscious use. It is also what allows us to fully realize who we are. As we grow increasingly comfortable with our own values, we learn what distinguishes us from the crowd and how living those distinctions puts us in harmony with our environment.

ACTIONS

Just as in waking-life, actions in dreams are what drive the story forward, for better or worse. They are decisions to act in response to the given situation, often driven by emotion and instinct, such as deciding to *run* from a shadowy figure or *snuggling* with a polar bear who appears in your bedroom. Actions are easily discoverable by circling the verbs in your dreams. Whether your own actions, or those of another figure in our dream, these moments are catalysts that put a cascade of events into motion. They rarely occur in isolation and always have an effect on what happens next. Actions may meet with resistance or momentum, or bring about sudden change, depending on the other elements in your dream ecology.

The actions taken in a dream are also symbols. Whether *running* is a metaphor for avoidance, or *snuggling* is symbolic of embracing something unusual, actions show you what movements, decisions, and strategies are at play in the issue at hand. Let's look at a dream from a woman named Adrienne, and pay special attention to how actions drive the movement of her story.

Abducted Woman: Adrienne's Dream

*I am with my brother **travelling** in a place I'm unfamiliar with. We end up in a room with a man who has **abducted** a woman and is **interrogating** and **torturing** her. She **is wounded** but **we stay out** of their affairs. I get the sense that she's **done something harmful** to them, but it's unclear what, so I **stay out of it**. Then I am **riding** a crowded bus when **I realize I've lost** my brother. I **make a snap decision** to **get off** the bus. I'm somewhere unfamiliar and am **attempting to use** my smartphone to **locate myself** and **get in touch** with him but am **unable to text**. Finally I **ask for help** from a fellow who turns out to be the abductor from earlier. He has **recognized** the error of his ways and **asks** me why*

*I didn't **step in** to **set him straight**. I realize now that I should have **intervened**.*

I've bolded the important action words and statements so you can see how effective it is to illuminate the ways in which Adrienne is actively handling the situation in the dream. It shows us where the energy is moving (and not moving). When she is travelling and making decisions, we feel motion and discovery, but when she's unable to text, and not stepping in, we feel contraction.

At the time of this dream, Adrienne had been estranged from her brother Greg for a number of years after a falling out. In the days before the dream, a family matter brought them together again and they were beginning to heal their relationship. Though they had been very close throughout their younger lives, Greg had drifted away after he was married. As a response to feeling hurt, Adrienne became increasingly withholding, until they eventually stopped talking altogether.

The dream begins with travelling together in an unfamiliar place. There is already a sense of movement in this first action. Travelling is a good metaphor for being in psychological transition: you have departed your first location and not yet arrived at the next. So while the siblings had been estranged for a number of years, at the time of this dream Adrienne had gotten back in touch with her brother to share some important life updates. We can feel something shifting in the action of travelling as the relationship begins to move into new and unfamiliar territory.

In the first scene, we learn that a woman has been abducted, interrogated, and tortured. Adrienne immediately associated this with an audiobook she'd been listening to the previous day on the topic of how needlessly we torture ourselves. The author suggested that the second half of life can be about liberating ourselves from the obstacles we place in our own way, so we can learn to cherish and love who we are. That idea resonated with Adrienne, who was in midlife. Like the abducted woman, she said she had been "holding herself hostage" from her brother, hoping he would apologize for something he'd done. But she was secretly torturing herself about the part she played in their estrangement. Though she hadn't done anything to deserve it, she described her internal dialogue as an endless interrogation of her guilt.

Though the woman is wounded, "staying out of it" is an important action in the dream. It's easy to miss because it is an act of refraining, but it is what generates the feeling of impotence and loss in the dream. In the next scene, Adrienne is on a crowded bus and has lost her brother. Since a bus travels in an endless loop, starting and ending in the same place, it is a fitting symbol for Adrienne's repetitive strategy for dealing with hurt. Indeed, in working with this image, she recognized her habit of withdrawing in relationships when she felt hurt, which rarely created the connection she longed for.

In what she described as a snap decision, dream-Adrienne gets off the bus. This is a turning action in the dream. She decides in a flash to dismount from that endless behavioural loop. Symbolically, she is stepping out of the established dynamic in which one person pulls away, the other pulls away further, and they drift into mutual distance. Getting off the bus echoed a decision she'd made a few days before the dream—to suddenly reach out to Greg and share some important milestones in her life.

In the dream she doesn't recognize the place where she dismounts. She attempts to locate herself and her brother but the cellphone won't cooperate. Having made this bold and different decision, Adrienne is now in a brand-new place psychologically, which for her is both disorienting and frustrating. The cellphone is symbolic of her desire to connect and communicate, but it doesn't appear to be working as it should. Indeed, so much had gone unsaid between the siblings that the relationship still felt awkward and stilted.

Amazingly, she asks for help from the abductor! Looking at the dynamic as a whole, we have three main actors: the punishing abductor, the wounded victim, and the witness who "stays out of it." The abductor has recognized the error of his ways, knows he was wrong to punish the woman, and is now asking why the witness didn't intervene. It's fascinating to consider this internal threesome as aspects of one psyche. While one part of Adrienne felt wounded, another part of her was convinced she'd done something wrong and was torturously scrutinizing her actions and motives. It was the avoidant witness (or the "I" in the dream) that needed to intervene and confront the abductor. We could perhaps take this intervention as the symbolic impulse to consciously arbitrate between those other two aspects.

This dream gave Adrienne deep insight into how to heal the outer relationship. After the dream, she decided to speak openly with her brother about how hurt she felt by his past behaviour. In this act of disclosure, she interrupted the internal dynamic of silently torturing herself and feeling hurt. As fate would have it, he was genuinely apologetic and the two siblings went on to repair their relationship together.

To see the symbolism of an action in your dream, remember to look beyond *what* it means to *how* it means. Does it have motion in it that is expansive and new, or does it contract the narrative with tension and reluctance? For example, imagine that you are eating in a dream. We know that eating is what we do to resolve hunger. It is the process of taking something into your body, chewing it into digestible pieces, and internally converting it to fuel. Eating in a dream may be about trying to satisfy a symbolic hunger or about nourishment, but it may also be a metaphor for experiences or ideas you are chewing on or digesting, as part of an "integration" process. In what way are you eating? Does it feel satisfying? Is it sensual, paltry, repulsive? Instead of just landing on "nourishing" consider the surrounding elements of the dream to get at the particular way the dream moves or doesn't move from this action. Conversely, vomiting is your body rejecting something you ingested. Symbolically, you might think this is an adverse image.

But I worked with a young man who had a powerful negative mother complex, and dreamed repetitively of vomiting a bitter substance as he worked to dislodge her toxic ideas from his psyche. Though these dreams were deeply unsettling for him, their purgative motion was a positive sign of healing.

The actions in our dreams describe the motion of our life force. How we use our energy is what determines the unfolding of our story. Our actions may move us toward connection, creativity, and healing, or they may be destructive, limiting, or regressive. In any given week, we occupy all the points on this spectrum. Sometimes our actions are unconscious and, like Adrienne, keep us in destructive loops. Other times, we do as she did, and make a bold decision that leads to a dawning awareness. By studying the actions in our dreams, we grow more conscious of our hidden drives, so we can reclaim agency in the pivotal moments of our lives.

DYNAMICS

Just as we describe a "certain dynamic" between two people, dream dynamics describe the interplay between the actions and attitudes of everyone in the dream. Dynamics are what result in the overall atmosphere and movement of the dream.

We are always attempting to achieve harmony and symbiosis within the larger psychic field, even when we fail splendidly. But psyche is in a constant state of flux and becoming, like any ecosystem or community, so understanding some of its complex dynamics can be useful in discerning which way the energy wants to go. While actions are the individual acts we take, dynamics are the way our parts interact. Together they ultimately generate a system that moves as one complex body.

When we are in a generative part of the development cycle, the dynamics move outwards toward discovery, connection, and collaboration. But if the dynamics are depleted, stuck, or destructive, they may be moving toward collapse. So rather than looking at our dreams as "good dreams" or "bad dreams," we can see them as energy in varying stages of expansion and contraction.

Maybe in your dream you are being chased by a threatening figure and are trying to outrun it. Consider how we use the common metaphor of "running from your problems" to aptly describe this avoidant strategy. But while it is our habit to identify with the actions the "I" is taking in the dream, it's incredibly valuable to zoom out from that perspective to see the larger dynamics at play. Often in dreams something pursues you because it wants to get your attention, and you run from it because you're trying to escape facing it. But the act of running from it is exactly what intensifies the chase. Marion Woodman used to say, "It takes the hare to constellate the hounds." In other words, they are interdependent actions. You might have good reason to be running from a problem, but that problem might also have a reason to be pursuing you. The more you try to discount or suppress something essential, the louder and more insistent it becomes.

Looking at the whole gestalt will give you great insight into your own interpersonal and intrapsychic dynamics and may inspire you to try out different strategies to the problems you face. Broadly speaking, the pattern of a dynamic is: action —> reaction —> outcome. As Adrienne discovered, if we keep choosing the same action, we'll likely get the same outcome.

Let's say you wake from a dream of being chased by a tiger. While it's tempting to go right for the difficult moment in dreamwork, dreams respond better to being circled from a safe distance. The big dynamics often germinate in banal scenes so we start with the opening setting to see if we can find a clue as to what brought about the tiger in the first place.

Imagine that same dream begins as a house party. You are trying to go to the bathroom, but the washroom has no walls so you feel self-conscious and increasingly agitated. The next thing you know you are outdoors, aware that a tiger has escaped from captivity. The tiger has spotted you and it is powerful and hungry, so you run in terror of becoming its prey. You are running through yards and houses but it follows close at your heels. With your heart pounding, you wake suddenly from sleep, relieved to be safe and sound in your bed.

It's worth noting here that dream scenes can switch dramatically like this with "jump cuts" making them seem like entirely different dreams. It's our habit to pay more attention to the more "charged" parts of the dream (a tiger is chasing me!) but when we take a closer look, we usually find connections between the discordant scenes in the dynamics. In other words, whatever prompted the jump cut gave rise to the tiger. This dream begins in a house that is overrun with people. Crowds in dreams usually have to do with our relationship to the larger social world. The action in the beginning of the dream is "trying to go to the bathroom" (an all-too-common problem in dreams) coupled with being "unable to find privacy." There are no walls in a place that is normally the most private room in the house, so it's evident that some necessary boundaries are missing. We could say the opening dynamic is: trying to find privacy —> intruding crowd —> agitation. Though the jump cut felt out of the blue with a tiger suddenly appearing, we notice that agitation was the precursor to its escape from captivity. Unlikely as it may seem, what gives rise to the tiger can be traced back to that unmet need for privacy.

The next section explores animals in dreams, but let's say the qualities you associate with the tiger are "fierce" and "territorial." Reflecting on the tiger's fierce territoriality, you suddenly remember how the day before you felt overwhelmed by social demands on your time. You wanted to ask your partner to give you some space, but were afraid to say it out loud because you didn't want to hurt her. Instead, you became angry and territorial and that feeling pursued you throughout the day. Now you can see the correspondence between the dynamics of the dream and your day. In both places you felt a longing for privacy, a growing sense of agitation from social intrusions, and hints of your "tiger nature," which frightened you.

You know your dreamwork is successful when a tension releases in both places at once, freeing up a new perspective. The bathroom is a place of privacy and release, often the most intimate and bodily part of your day. But you were unable to find even that small respite from intrusions. Your walls were missing in this most private refuge. Knowing the tiger was held captive makes you wonder if there might be power in its release. Maybe those instinctual qualities of fierceness and territoriality are something worth integrating into your toolkit. When you don't assert your boundaries because you're afraid of hurting your partner, you instead become silently angry about not getting what you need. So the tiger turns on you, pursuing you like an unmet instinct, full of hunger for acknowledgement. Maybe asserting your needs in relationships would stop them from developing into a fearsome dynamic.

The psychologist Rollo May wrote, "Between stimulus and response there is a space."[5] Power lives in that space where we are free to choose how we respond. The actions in dreams are symbolic responses to stimuli. So while you may not be literally running away from a tiger, you are trying to outrun your own fierceness, even though it's a valid response to feeling overwhelmed. The space that dreamwork provides allows us to consider what our deepest self wants—and to choose a different response. If we can imagine a better outcome for the dream, we can enact a corresponding choice in waking-life. That might look like asking everyone to leave the dream-party. So in waking-life you put an automatic responder on your email and say no to new engagements. Maybe you decide the solution is to fix the walls in your dream-bathroom, so you resolve to hold boundaries around your personal time. Or maybe you decide the tiger shouldn't be in captivity in the first place, so you experiment with what it's like to give that fierceness some free expression.

One of the most exciting things about dreamwork is that after enacting different choices in waking-life as an offering to psyche, you may receive follow-up dreams to affirm (or correct) your responses. Like a conversation that deepens when both parties feel understood, our symbols become richer and deeply affirming when we enact the teachings of our dreams in waking-life.

CHARACTERS

You've probably heard it said that every character in your dream represents an aspect of yourself. This is a great starting point for anyone beginning to work with dreams, but I also want to encourage you to stretch your concept of "self" to become a living plurality. This holds true in two ways: you contain multitudes and you are contained within a diverse ecosystem from which you are indivisible.

Family and friends, foes and strangers, hybrids and shapeshifters, angels and animals—even disembodied voices, talking plants, and ancient archetypal figures—are all relations in our dreaming community. I like to think of psyche as a meadow in which a thousand encounters are taking place at once. Grasshoppers, butterflies, dandelions, bees, herbs, and the soil they grow in are all in a living process of collaboration and exchange. Similarly, the dreaming is a habitat full of characters that exist in degrees of kinship with us and each other.

The characters in our dreams are personifications of what you might call "life forms" in the bustling ecology of consciousness. You might dream of walking with your beloved teacher, getting up to antics with your best friend, or fighting with a parent. Each of these figures are representations of the inner and outer others you are encountering in the psychic landscape. While your beloved teacher exists in waking-life, they may also awaken a similarly-shaped being in you that, at certain times, accompanies you as an internal ally. Conversely, fighting with a parent in your dreams may depict your struggle for independence from your internal enmeshment. Like living in a village, we don't get along with all beings equally. We keep some allies in our closest circle while others we hold at a distance. Some cause trouble, some are bullies, and many are yet strangers to us. As vast and unknowable as the world itself, our inner village is a dynamic enterprise, with many residents cohabitating, interacting, or just passing through.

Psyche conjures characters like a casting director chooses the perfect actor to convey a part based on the way they look, what qualities they exude, and how they make the audience feel. Everything about each figure will be perfect for the dream role they play. If you know the figure in your dream from waking-life, you can ask yourself, "What are their most defining qualities?" If you don't know them, ask yourself, "Who do they remind me of?" or "What do I like or dislike about them?" Even if they are totally unfamiliar, you will still have collected impressions of them. Take a moment to describe their persona, age, appearance, and the vibe they project. Even if you dream about someone repeatedly, it's important to make new associations with each dream, because your perspective is always evolving. Once you've come up with a robust description, you'll be better able to make correlations between the dreaming and waking realities.

Psyche is not a closed system housed in the individual mind, any more than we are physically sovereign bodies. Yes, we are unique individuals *and* we live in an interdependent ecosystem. Likewise, I propose a broader conception of psyche as a dreaming body that has complex internal processes, but one that also interacts with the larger psychic field inhabited by us all. Dreams give symbolic form to that broad range of energetic relationships.

Just as in waking-life, we are in a constant discourse with both external and internal energies. While you may interact every day with a colleague in your workplace, you also form an internal relationship with the person you *interpret* them to be. While the former is about two soulbodies interacting, the latter is more reflective of your own thoughts and feelings about that person. Dreams may depict "intrapsychic" phenomena. This is the psychological term used to describe dynamics existing or occurring within psyche, between aspects or parts of yourself. Or they may be "interpsychic" dynamics, which is how we describe a psychic exchange or encounter between individuals, like an invisible dance taking place beneath the conversation being had in the open. How do we tell the difference between a dream character representing our subjective (intrapsychic) experience and one representing an objective (interpsychic) exchange? In most cases, as we see in the dream example below, we don't have to choose.

I try to approach every dream character as having something valuable to teach me on three levels. I begin by considering them in their own context as a dream-being who is responding to their dream-reality. Then I'll reflect on the dream objectively, considering if it may be speaking to my waking-life relationships. Finally, I ask myself if that character mirrors an internal relationship (or intrapsychic) dynamic that I'm experiencing. This might sound like a lot of processing, but those jumps can happen quite naturally and even simultaneously.

To give you an example of how to approach a dream character on three levels, here is a brief dream of a woman in her thirties named Cora.

Corporate Drones: Cora's Dream

I dream of getting a new job in a huge corporation run by a powerful woman. It's a kind of private academy for competitive learning. Everyone must dress the same and work long hours. Without notice, we have to pass math tests for which I am unprepared. I realize I don't want to work for this woman anymore, but she could be the kind of person I'd like to keep as a friend.

I asked Cora to describe the powerful woman in her dream reality first. Cora replied, "She isn't someone I know, but she reminds me of women in high-level positions in the corporate world. She is very put together and somewhat rigid. I get the impression that she is tightly wound, a perfectionist who pushes everyone in the company beyond our limitations, expecting us to perform like robots." Once we had this robust description, I asked Cora, "Is there anyone in your waking-life that has a similar rigidity, who is placing high demands on you and others?" She thought about it for a moment but couldn't relate to anyone in her life with similar qualities. She did, however, mention that she worked in academia, which she described as an extremely rigid and formal field.

Next I asked her, "Can you relate to an internal rigidity, a pressure you feel to perform perfectly, even at the expense of your own limitations?" She had a strong aha! moment in response to this question. She was working on a big educational project that, because of its public nature, made her extremely anxious about how it would be received. She shared how difficult it was to take even a small step forward creatively because she was internally scrutinizing every fine detail.

The part that was especially illuminating for Cora was the dream's strong mirror of her own perfectionism as an uncompromising ruler. It struck her that there was no room for originality under that kind of leadership and that she would benefit from engaging other parts of herself in the creative process. It's true that she was up against some powerful expectations in her institution, but she was also upholding impossible standards for herself internally. Is this pressure and oppression external or internal? The quandary of distinguishing what is objective versus subjective in the dream falls away, because "yes" is often the answer to either/or questions.

Intriguingly, the ending of the dream seemed to suggest that Cora could make friends with this CEO instead of being subordinate to her. Reflecting on it in this light made Cora realize that she needn't pathologize that part of herself. While she didn't want the

CEO to be in control anymore, someone so capable and devoted would make an excellent ally in her work. Going forward, Cora played with shifting their dynamic to be on equal, collaborative footing. Whenever she felt that exacting perfectionism was starting to take control of her work, she would remind herself that there would be a time and place for that scrutiny. She remembered that she needed to invoke more warmth and flexibility in the creative process.

Whether they are a celebrity, mythic figure, or family member, each character in a dream has qualities and responses that are unique to them that also intersect with your own life. Though it's tempting to think of dream characters as literal embodiments of their waking-life counterparts, these figures are usually symbols for a similar cluster of traits that are active in your psychic field. The tricky part is not getting fooled into thinking the dream is objectively about a person, but rather a set of gestures that have taken the form of someone distinctive. This allows you to visualize how their qualities are playing out internally. Describing your honest impression of the character is the key to understanding their significance in your dream.

As you become conscious of why a character is appearing to you in a dream, maybe even across a series of dreams, your relationship with them will change. The deeper into the core the issue resides, the longer it will take to shift. But when it does, once you've broken a holding pattern, it can move quite dramatically from something that hinders you to something that empowers you. What began as a stifling, imperious, and domineering energy in Cora's dream became a powerful ally who could be called upon in times of need. Once you understand what's giving rise to a character, you gain insight into how to free up that energy for conscious use. Even though these "energy clusters" might appear frightening or painful, the energy behind them is neutral. In the same way that tension in the body drains your energy, and only releases when the tension does, vitality is hidden within shadow dream figures.

Sometimes a character will embody something that's been passed down to you through many generations, like an ethic or attitude that has been shaping your family tree. Or it may have formed like scar tissue out of your own life's experience. It may also have taken shape out of a set of ideas handed to you from your culture. Sometimes, though, characters and other symbols in your dreams are expressing an emergent dynamic sprouting in the places you've already pruned to make room. In Cora's dream, for instance, the idea that she could make friends with that controlling energy was an entirely new perspective. She'd been working with dominant characters in her dreams for some time, becoming increasingly conscious of how that complex expressed itself in her work and life. This emergent idea was like a spring of new energy from psyche after all her tending to the issue. As a habit, I look for these emergent springs in every dream, no matter how small they may be at first.

Sometimes characters in your dreams are composites of more than one person. For example, you might wake from a dream and say, "She looked like my first girlfriend, but she was also my sister." The dream may even morph between two-or-more figures to convey a fusion of their attributes, or to draw a correlation between the two. Try writing down each of those character's top five traits to discover what, if anything, they have in common. What you may find is that they symbolize a recurring pattern or dynamic appearing in both relationships. Sometimes composite characters speak to an intermingling of qualities in your psyche as you integrate new ideas into your existing imaginal forms. For instance, Cora might see her CEO in a new dream, but this time she looks like her best friend in her college art class.

Sometimes characters appear in groups. The important difference between an individual and a group is that while an individual can be considered for their distinctive traits, a group must be thought of as having a particular thing in common. Usually dreams of groups have to do with our relationship to the "group-mind," the thing they represent as a collective. Some examples would be a clique from high school, people from church, the police, an army, etc. So in making associations to that group, you would consider how you feel in relation to that social context. Do you feel belonging or pressure to conform? Do they possess attributes that you admire, or a belief system you reject? Together are they a power that you feel overwhelmed or empowered by? What makes you distinct from the group?

As a natural symmetry of inner character work, your outer relationships will also deepen. When you dethrone your inner tyrants, you become less tolerant of imbalanced power structures in waking-life. The more you stand up to your inner bullies, the braver you become in the world. The more you distinguish yourself from the crowds in your dreams, the more original and creative you become in waking-life. Perhaps most wonderfully, as you tend to your inner plurality, you grow your relational capacity in the world. You become increasingly perceptive of the world of connections around you.

ANIMALS

Some of the world's oldest known animal depictions were drawn on the cave walls in Lascaux, France, more than 17,000 years ago. Our palaeolithic ancestors used mineral pigments to paint over 6,000 detailed figures of aurochs, stags, bears, bulls, deer, ibex, felines, horses, rhinoceroses, and even what appears to be a mythical bird-man on the walls and ceilings of deep underground channels. Given there would have been no light in the tunnels, some archaeologists hypothesize that they lit torches, which diminished the oxygen in the deep reaches of the cave and put them into altered states of consciousness. The art created in these hidden places is believed to be ritualistic in nature, evidence of our ancestors communing with the otherworld.

In his book *Wisdom of the Mythtellers*, Sean Kane describes how in ancient societies and myths it was understood that there were boundaries between humans and the otherworld. These threshold places like "the forest-edge, the sea-surface, the sky, the holes and caves in the earth" mark the end of where ordinary thinking can go.[6] Beyond that, one must move from the deeper instincts—become more animal.

There is an energy field struck between humans and animals that, like a mirror into our own true nature, switches on the dreaming attention. As James Hillman put it, "Animals wake up the imagination … the imagination is itself a great animal."[7] Perhaps because we are mammals, yet live so distantly from our wild origins, when we see an animal in life (and in dream) the encounter crackles with recognition of our own true nature. One of my tricks for remembering a disappearing dream is to conjure an animal in my imagination. As I envision the presence of an eagle or a wolf, it often brings back the images of the last night's dream—especially if an animal was present in the dream. As Hillman said in his Eranos lecture in 1982, "[The imagination] is the place where the psyche opens into forms, beings of mystery and beauty who are creatures as we are and yet remain 'other.' The animal is that strange other I wish most to evoke … and from which, or whom, I hope further imagination will actively initiate."[8]

Most of us have a story we can tell about a time we were struck with awe upon spotting a whale surfacing on the sea, a wild buck poised on a ridge at dusk, a bobcat appearing in the moonlight, or an owl swooping down to land on a low branch. When they appear in our dreams, we have an even more heightened response to these encounters. It's as if the world stands still and an aperture opens between us and the animal. We are filled with the sense that something important is happening.

Throughout history, animals have been revered and respected

in mythological traditions around the world. In Egyptian culture, the gods themselves were portrayed as animals, like the feline deity Bastet, or Anubuis, the canine god of the dead. In the Iroquois and Yoruba creation myths, animals helped create the earth. Many myths depict animals as helpers, guiding the protagonist's way through great dangers or collaborating with them to complete a complex task. Sometimes they are seen as mediators or guardians between two worlds, like a witch's familiar, or the snake helper of Asclepius, the Greek god of medicine. Snakes were said to travel between worlds to retrieve healing wisdom and are still used in medical symbols today. Many myths tell the story of a transmutation between human and animal, like the Celtic selkie-woman and the frog who becomes a prince. There are many Greek and Roman legends about gods who turned mortals into animals as punishment. In shamanic cultures, medicine people were said to voluntarily shapeshift into their animal forms.

It has always been the way of humans to stay in close communion with our animal brethren. Whether through storytelling, altered states, art-making, or dreaming, our relationship to animals connects us to the primordial power of the physical world and the mystical wisdom hidden within it. Sadly, our reverence for the world of wild animals has died out in modern culture and, as a symmetrical result, many species are extinct or endangered. I'd like you to consider that when you dream of an animal, something of that endangered world is trying to reach out from within your own nature.

One of the ways in which dreaming has shaped me is to make me aware of my own plurality. Instead of the self as the centre of one's universe, dreaming shows us how there are infinite centres. Isn't the rabbit's knowing as valid as my dream ego? Just as I identify as the protagonist, maybe the same could be said for each of the figures I meet in my dream. One of the great gifts of dreams is that they invite us to inhabit different perspectives. When we see through the eyes of our dream characters, we can better understand the multitude of influences that operate in us unconsciously. This is a skill that we carry into the world to become more capable of diverse thinking.

When you wake up from an animal dream, you may have a strong impulse to interpret the encounter. But I want to encourage you not to consult dream dictionaries or animal totem books. Because we are habitually after *what* an image means, we quickly grab on to cultural memes, like interpreting Owl as, say, wisdom. But when we do this, we flatten the symbol into an abstraction, as if all owls were alike and reduced to that one thing. From this flattened abstraction, we may be able to acquire some quick-but-shallow meaning, but we miss *how* Owl means—how it carries authority in the strength of its spine and danger in its yellow gaze; how it embodies precision with its finely attuned and coordinated senses; how it uses its own body as a weapon, with 500 pounds of crushing power in its talons; how it tears flesh away in the hook of its razor sharp beak; how it sees in the night and has panoramic vision, eliminating barriers of darkness and blind spots; and how it flies silently and folds its throaty song into the low hum of our sleep. If we reduce Owl to a "what," we miss the *how*, which is where the real exchange of ideas and power takes place.

Not unlike people, animals have characteristics they exude with their bodies and behaviours. Consider the turtle who is slow and often shy, has a hard exterior but a soft underside, dwells in both water and on land, and is often blessed with extreme longevity. Notice how different a turtle is from, say, a rabbit who is fast and nervous, extremely fertile, and dwells in family dens. Whatever animal shows up in your dream, consider how it might be appearing as a messenger of the instinctual traits that are needed by you at this time.

When an agent of nature is luring us toward that internal wildness, we must step into its world of meaning. Dream animals are often interpreted as symbols of human instincts that have been blunted by the enterprise of civilization. But we must be cautious in this approach not to capture animals in the cages of a psychological context, when what's really being required of us is to *become* more animal. The harder and more rewarding path is to learn what your animals know and what they need. Let the animal elaborate itself, by way of your own curiosity, through its own embodied language. Let it draw you deeper into its context, into the betweenness that you share. Acknowledge the invisible field between you, the communications of its body in your space, and yours in its habitat. Inhabit the sensations and awarenesses that come alive in each other's company. Notice what silent transmissions are being exchanged.

This isn't to say that drawing on the studies of an animal's mythological or biological profiles won't yield important discoveries—just that written information shouldn't be your first or only way of making an encounter. Your experience is the greatest authority in this space. For a wolf, there are no words for hunger or territory, there is only what its body knows in smells of blood and fur, the delicious sounds of small scurrying, or the urge to protect its den from flickers of movement in the dark. When animals show up in our dreams, we are being called down into the instincts of our own bodies. One of my teachers was fond of saying, "Always follow the cats in your dreams," because animals live with a sophisticated attunement to nature that we humans can barely fathom.

In the endeavour to become more advanced, human animals have built an elaborate society to satisfy all our desires and comforts—but the great project has also distanced us from our own aptitudes in relationship with nature. With the development of social codes of behaviour, we have lost much of our animality. In our creation of a complex language to map the world of things, we have abstracted ourselves above it. With enough distance from the wild playground of life, we barely recognize the communications of our bodies. Instinct is that part of us that knows what and when to do something, which way to go, and how to respond. We can also call it "right responsiveness." It is the anger when your boundaries are trespassed, the vigilance that alerts you when a threat is near, the sourness in your belly when something doesn't feel right, and the hunger when it's time to feed. It is also the rush of pleasure that warms you when something resonates, and the electrical impulse to create something new. These inborn impulses don't require thinking—you just know what you know when you know it. But over the course of generations of neglect and refusal, our instinctual guidance system can languish and deteriorate.

Living in a culture that is alienated from feeling, body, and nature has taught us to diminish the validity of our intuition and experiences. We ignore our basic impulses, question and discount our feelings, override our honest responses, and are unable to recognize passions or violations until long after the fact (if at all). In the same way that we encroach upon and maraud the habitats of animals in the wild, our own animal nature is growing extinct.

When you disregard or dismiss your instincts, you might have dreams of wounded or neglected animals. This can happen during times when you are so busy that you aren't looking after your basic needs like sleeping and eating properly. But they may also speak to your longing for joy, connection, and physical affection. If the starved animal is a beloved pet, consider the nature of your relationship with them. Do you run and play with them outdoors? Do they inhabit unbridled joy? Are they deeply compassionate toward you when you're sad or ill? Do they love you unconditionally? Do you feel a bond with them in which you can be entirely yourself? Dreams of wounded animals are an invitation to empathize with your own body and soul in a way our world rarely encourages. Dreams understand that in order to even approach empathy for your own self, they must bring you a wounded animal to show you that something precious is in peril.

Other times, you may dream of being chased or attacked by a ferocious animal. To work with these dreams, you need to ask yourself: What part of your instinctual life are you trying to escape or outrun? You will find clues in the animal itself, whose dispositions are specific and unique to them. A bear, for instance, will be aroused by feelings of anger or protectiveness. Sometimes we say "Don't poke the bear!" to warn someone that a powerful animal within us might awaken if they confront it. An alligator has an ancient, cold-blooded energy. It lurks in the deep and attacks when we least expect it, pulling us into the underworld. Combine what you've learned about actions, feelings, and the setting of a dream to get a well-rounded idea of the nature of this danger in your psychic field.

One of the greatest quandaries when working with an aggressive dream figure is to discern whether they ultimately mean us harm or good. For example, a bear chasing you might be trying to reunite us with some aspect of ourselves we've lost. There are times when anger is the right response to being poked. On the other hand, if the alligator can be traced back to a cold-blooded complex that wants to "drag you down," the last thing you should do is integrate that energy. What might be needed instead is the inner fortitude to stand up to that alligator and refuse to let yourself be devoured by your fears.

People make the mistake of thinking that to feel belonging means accepting everyone and everything as if "we are all one." But a huge requirement of dreamwork is the practice of discernment and the creation of boundaries. In his book *Radical Ecopsychology*, Andy Fisher describes humans' relationship to nature as existing on a "kinship continuum."[9] On one end of the spectrum lies the attitude that nature is inert, separate—objects without life-force. On the other end we find the "blissed-out mystic" who experiences no separations from anything. But somewhere in the middle exists reality, a paradox between the extremes. It is our unique plight as humans to be both distinct from, and in kinship with, all of nature. It is upon this threshold that dreamwork takes place.

Some of the characters and animals in our dreams, like the alligator above, are destructive by nature. If we try to embrace or befriend those things, we will do more damage to our instincts. What's needed instead is curiosity from a distance, like standing back from a painting so you can see it in its totality and not get lost in the details. But you don't want to be so distant that you can't also perceive subtlety. There is a just-right space we need in order to both "see" the character as they are, and identify what we have in common with them. Far enough to see the other in their *suchness*, or essential nature, but close enough to see ourselves in them too. It's like enacting a boundary while opening a door at the same time.

In working with the alligator, you might come to recognize negative energy lurking in your own psyche, like a deep fear you're unable to confront, or a malicious thought that attacks when you least expect it. That sharp-toothed, relentless aggression might describe a complex developed in trauma. Or you might correlate the dream to a treacherous relationship or situation in your waking-life. Making this connection between the dream animal and the fears that are trying to possess or overwhelm you is, in and of itself, all that needs to be done. The work of correlating is already setting a process of change in motion. Once you see the form an energy takes, you have made your first step toward making it conscious. It can no longer operate as stealthily in the unconscious. Though it may persist in trying to undermine you, knowing its true face means you'll be more savvy to its approach in the future, making it less able to function autonomously. Before the dream, you may have been overwhelmed by a storm of distressing feelings, but now you have begun the process of differentiating between alligator and self. Freeing it from the tangle of your identity allows you to recognize it as *other*. Yes, alligator energy lives in you, but as you develop your awareness of what activates it, how it operates, and what resources are needed to wrestle from its jaws, it will grow less powerful and eventually become benign.

With particularly deep complexes, often from childhood

trauma, progress can be arduous and slow. We never get rid of these complexes, but we can learn to live with them. As much as we want to push these things far away from us, healing a complex means entering more deeply into the wound. As Jung said, "A complex can be really overcome only if it is lived out to the full. We have to draw to us and drink down to the very dregs what [...] we have held at a distance."[10] Best done with the support of a skilled mental/somatic health professional, healing means taking our attention down into the wound, exposing it to the light and oxygen of consciousness, grieving what harm has been caused, and slowly gaining distance from it.

Sometimes dream animals will transform into other animals or even into human forms, and vice versa. The fluid nature of form is one of the dreaming's great capabilities. Nothing is fixed. Unlike physical reality, the dream is flexible and instantly responsive to its ecosystem. It's the habit of the rational mind to be certain, to choose one form or the other, but dreaming teaches us to become skilled with ambiguity—to tolerate a *bothness* or even a multiplicity. So if you dream of a shark that becomes a whale, look at both of their dispositions and ask yourself what might have brought about a transformation from one to the other. Do your feelings shift with the animal, for example, between fear and awe? Are you in the midst of embodying a whole new perspective? Is your animal body experiencing a shift in countenance? What is the emerging animal way?

When I am working with someone who is having a hard time making associations to a dream animal because they are too threatening, strange, or unlikeable in some way, I ask them to play an imagination game with me. I have them close their eyes and inhabit the dream from the animal's perspective. We then explore what it is like to be in that body, to notice what feelings or sensations they experience, and how it feels to be in the dream's location. Then I might ask them what motivates them in the dream— why they are chasing the dreamer, or what they are after. We get the most surprising results! What often happens is that by empathizing with the other's perspective, the dreamer suddenly recognizes that wild part in themselves: how angry and devouring they may have gotten in an argument, how intensely they feel they need to control their world, or how defensive they are of their territory.

Try playing this game on your own to better understand a dream animal, especially if you feel stuck. It can be especially powerful to do this as a physical exercise where you inhabit the bodily experience, movements, and sensations of your animal. Or you can do this through journaling, telling the dream experience from the character's perspective instead of your dream ego. Start with the physical and feel what it's like to be in their body. Feel how it moves, where it holds tension, what it sees through its eyes. Then move (or write) with those motivations and feelings. Try not to judge what arises as being "made up," because this is exactly the creative space you want to inhabit. Somatic exploration of this kind is often a direct and honest way to evoke the dream's wisdom.

Keeping in mind that the *anima mundi* is dreaming through us, it's worth considering that animals and other living beings may sometimes come into our dreams to ask for our help. They might warn us of dangers they are facing that we too need to face. They may be asking for us to bring our attention out of human context into their wild world, which is in tatters. To put us in better touch with the ecosystem from which we feel so removed, so we may see how desperate matters are. I think it's inevitable—a natural evolution of our work with dreams—that the more you embody the wilderness within, removing hindrances to your own instinctual nature, the closer you become to the rest of nature. As you become more imaginative, you become more animal. And as you become more animal, your intimacy with the natural world also grows.

OBJECTS

Though they may not move or speak, a symbolic object can hold the key to a dream's significance. But because there can be infinite objects in a single dream, it has to have special properties to get our attention. Whether it's a stolen journal that feels important to a writer, a broken guitar for a musician, a door that keeps something hidden behind it, or a fence beyond which a wolf lives, objects worth exploring will convey a special significance to the dreamer within the dream.

Someone once shared a dream with me that was full of characters, dynamics, and feelings, but no matter how many associations she made, she couldn't understand why she was driving with a famous comedian. Though it seemed like an odd detail, the comedian was wearing a particular sweater that she described in detail. When I asked her if she recognized that sweater, she instantly remembered that her husband wore a sweater just like it. Suddenly, she could see that her husband and the comedian had many characteristics in common and the dream began to flower. That one object illuminated all the other symbols in the dream.

Clothing in dreams is very common and generally has to do with identity. Just as in waking-life, clothes cover the most vulnerable version of ourselves and present an image to the world. What we wear, the colour, style, fit, and origin of our clothing represents the values we want to convey. Consider how your personal style has changed over the course of your life and how that reflects an evolution in your values and personality. If the clothing (or lack of clothing) feels important in a dream, notice what the item's primary use is first. A hat will have a very different purpose than a pair of shoes. Then notice if the style or condition of the item feels like a match for how you want to present yourself to others. If there is an issue with the clothing, is it a problem of fit, colour, style? Maybe you are wearing an outdated identity or conveying a mood that is unlike your true feelings. Or maybe it feels awkward because you are trying on a new and exciting way of showing up in the world. It can help to ask yourself, "What kind of person wears a dress (hat, belt, shoes, etc.) like this?"

Sometimes an object holds particular religious or cultural importance for the dreamer, such as a rosary, kippah, or a sajjāda. To understand an object's significance, you can begin by defining its most basic properties: a set of beads to count one's prayers, a sign of respect for God, a carpet which designates a sacred place to pray. Next you can explore your personal associations to that object. Do you or someone you know have one of these objects? How does the discipline or orthodoxy of prayer fit into your life? Are these traditions comforting to you, or do you experience them as oppressive? Once you have a detailed description, you can begin to reflect on how the associations you've made relate to your spiritual practice in waking-life.

Most objects, whether it's money, a wallet, a key, or a ladder, will have basic properties that you recognize: money is a currency that denotes value and worth, a wallet is a container for money and identification, a key opens locks, a ladder is a tool for climbing a height. Always begin with the object's primary purpose, then consider the context in which the object is being used in the dream. If your money has been stolen, for example, try replacing the object's name with its basic purpose in your question. Instead of asking, "Why am I being deprived of money?" Ask, "Where do I feel like I'm losing or being deprived of *my value*?" If your wallet is lost, ask, "Where is my *identity and worth* feeling lost?" If a key is found, have you recently discovered a way to *unlock* a problem? If you've fallen off a ladder, where do you feel you've fallen from a *height you climbed*?

There are occasions when a dream gives you an inexplicable object, shape, symbol, or even a word that you have no immediate associations to that feels important nonetheless. In cases like this, I find it most helpful to draw or paint the shape. Sometimes depicting it as best you can opens a dialogue between you and the object. As you draw its curves and lines, or shade in its colours, ideas can sprout in your process and offer you insights into the object's mysteries.

Colours have very specific personal, cultural, and archetypal associations embedded in them. Following this thread alone can reveal so much. You'll know when a colour is important when it has a particular presence in a dream. Sometimes a dream might be entirely coloured in a scheme from another era, like a black-and-white TV show from the 1950s or the vibrant psychedelic hues of the 1970s. This could lead you to a set of associations you have about that time in history and how those colours (or absence of colours) make you feel.

A woman I once worked with dreamed of her mother-in-law dressed in a taffy pink Victorian dress with an excess of ruffles. She stood stiffly against a backdrop of pink roses and pink decor. The dreamer immediately associated that colour to "performative femininity," a pressure that she was often under from her mother-in-law. While pink may be an empowering or pretty colour to one person, it brought up very different feelings for this radical artist. If you give yourself a moment to feel into the colours in your dream, you'll notice that you have very specific feelings and associations to them. They might intrigue you, repulse you, or make you think immediately of people, places, and times. You can tend to the colours in your dreams as you would any other element by asking yourself what feelings and responses they arouse in you.

EVERYTHING IS EVERYTHING

The categories we erect to give ourselves a sense of orientation in the imaginal world can be helpful, but they can also dissolve as we discover exceptions and contradictions. When you wade deep enough into the mysterious realms of psyche, everything gives way to everything else. It's all interconnected and the boundaries between elements often prove themselves to be illusory. Objects become animals, pretty things mask dangers, endings are hidden beginnings, order descends into chaos, and even ancient patterns can be advanced with the right melodies. The Dreaming Way challenges us with increasing complexity until we relent and say, "this too belongs." We can allow for paradox and multiple layers of meaning in a dream—even complete reversals—as time gives us new perspectives. Dreaming is energy in flux made visible and linear thinking tends to be inadequate to navigate this fluid reality. But if we enter into dreamwork with a voluntary attitude toward our own not-knowing, we get remarkable glimpses into the relational field of meaning that is holding our world, and the universe itself, together.

CHAPTER 8

Forgetting and Remembering

WHETHER WE REMEMBER our dreams or not, researchers estimate that by the end of our lives we will have spent about seven years dreaming. This is based on the assumption that we mostly dream during REM sleep, which is two hours a night on average. But I believe dreaming extends far beyond that. There is a sort of "dreaming channel" that is continually receiving and broadcasting, even while we're awake. We simply don't notice it because our daytime attention is focused on the waking world around us.

This outward focus is what Carlos Castaneda called "first attention."[1] First attention notices the surface activity of things. It is what allows us to function in consensus reality day to day: going to work, paying our bills, grocery shopping, socialising, and so on. But there is a "second attention" whose primary relationship is with the unseen depth below the surface. Its language is one of symbols, intuition, feelings, symptoms, and unbidden thoughts or ideas. It communicates with us all day long, through our own body and in the world around us. When I describe the Dreaming Way, I am referring not only to our nocturnal dreams, but to this unseen dimension we interact with constantly. These two streams of attention—surface and depth—are always running simultaneously and, at any given moment, we can choose to focus on either or both.

You've probably noticed that when things get really busy in your outer life, dreams tend to recede. In times of quietude and contemplation, you are more likely to have an abundance of dream material. Rather than thinking of this as an involuntary condition, know that it is possible to rekindle the flow of dreams through certain basic practices like good sleep hygiene, psychic and physical boundaries, and a devoted practice. It's possible to create a more balanced and reciprocal way of living between the outer and inner life.

It is normal to go through ebbs and cycles with your dream recall. For instance, when you're launching a big project you might jump out of bed in the morning with a big list of to-dos. Or if you have a new baby, you are likely not getting as much deep REM sleep. Taking certain medications can also cause a lapse in remembering your dreams. It's also possible that after doing a lot of inner work, you need a break from the mental and emotional intensity; you may need to balance yourself by focusing on the practicalities of living. Only you can decide whether you're experiencing a normal ebb in your dreaming life or if it's a dream drought from neglect or avoidance. But if you are missing and longing for your dreams, know that it will take very little practice to get them flowing again.

When people who usually dream vividly report losing their relationship to dreaming, they describe a nebulous grief or depression that arises from the disconnection. If this has happened to you, you might recognize that feeling of dislocation, as if you're lacking an important anchor. Or it may show up as anxiety or confusion about your overall direction in life or about where you belong. When you consider that dreams are like an internal compass that is always attuned to where we need to go—they give us guidance and connect us to our ancestral wisdom and they offer physical and emotional healing—it isn't hard to imagine how deeply we can miss them. When you're in an active relationship with your dreams, you feel a rekindling sense of magic and connectedness.

As always with loss, our starting point has to be with our deep longing for reconnection. See if you can articulate for yourself why you long to remember your dreams. Is there a particular quality they bring within your reach? Do they remind you of a time in your life when you were more connected? Do they give you something you feel is missing? Please know that even in asking these questions, you are closer than you realize to rekindling your relationship with your dreams. Dreams are like lovers; they'll blossom if you pay attention to them and abscond if you ignore or invalidate them. If we can create a welcoming, non-judgemental space for the dreams to express themselves, it generally takes very little to recover them. But it's important to consider the ways in which you may have contributed to your drifting apart.

Every day I am approached by people who say they never dream or rarely remember their dreams. With so few examples in our midst of powerful and skilled dreamers, people can spend a lifetime thinking that they just don't dream or that "remembering" is an ability that doesn't come naturally to them. Remembering is a skill that can be practised, and forgetting is a choice. It's a passive choice, but a choice nonetheless. When we wake up from a dream that appears as a jumble of nonsense, or it has threatening and uncomfortable images, we often set about forgetting it.

The more we forget our dreams, the more they forget us. We may, even by default, choose to forget because we are deeply acculturated to believe that our dreams are nonsense. But somewhere deep in our bones we also know that remembering is an act of rebellion—one that might push us into the fringes of consensus reality. It is a choice that carries responsibility. Remembering means looking at that which cannot be unseen and offering our service to its redemption and resurrection. But like learning a new language, or mastering a craft, the Dreaming Way has to be cultivated and practised. The truth is, it takes very little to get your dreams flowing, but the starting point must be to value your dreams. This may seem like an easy shift but when you consider the dominant culture's dismissal of dreams it isn't difficult to imagine how deeply this devaluation may run in your personal psyche.

Let's begin by taking a broader look at some of the reasons we become disconnected from our dreams in the first place. Whether influenced by the culture's emphasis on outer-world values, a natural exhale in your dreaming cycle, or your own fears and resistance to tough dreams, it's valuable to understand the underlying reasons for your forgetting so you can successfully tend to your inner guidance system.

One of the biggest reasons why people don't remember their dreams is because they don't want to. At a very basic level, especially when the dreams are difficult, ugly, or terrifying, the first instinct is to push them away. But of course, the more you push the dreams away, the more reluctant they are to return. Or they return in more terrifying forms. It's important to shift your attitude around so-called nightmares or difficult dreams to understand that your dreams are there to support you on a fundamental level. Nightmares are an opportunity to resolve hindrances that are undermining your creative well-being. It may seem counterintuitive to value a dream that is full of anxiety or seems to be replaying a traumatic theme, but we have to understand that they are simply turning up the volume to get our attention.

When you lean in with curiosity to a dark dream, it often reveals a concealed medicine. Even when a full resolution is not ready to be reached, it will offer you breadcrumbs on the path toward that redemption. Dreams are always in service to our wholeness. We often focus on the negative or difficult part of the dream and we become unable to distance ourselves from the charge of emotions wrapped up in those images. However, if you can trust that the dream is there to support you and is in service to your healing, you create the neutrality needed to see other images in the dream as glimmers of a new attitude, symbols of insight, or novel sources of support.

Remembering is really a choice to make room in your life for your dreams. You can open an inviting space in your home, your day, and in your heart to care for and converse with the flow of symbols naturing through you. Especially when those images disturb you, choosing to show up for your dreams is a commitment to the beauty and fullness of who you came here to be.

SEVEN STEPS TO DREAM RECOVERY

If you don't already have a dream journal, take yourself on a special date to buy one that you can dedicate to dream recording. You may prefer to record your dreams with a voice recorder, but it can be harder to review and work with your dreams unless they are written down, so consider transcribing them afterwards. If you are taking a smartphone to be, be sure to put your device in "airplane mode" so you aren't tempted to check your notifications. It is your inner notifications we're after here.

Before going to bed, reflect on the day you've had, acknowledging and accepting any thoughts or feelings that may have lingered with you. Notice the day's highlights and if anything feels unresolved. My favourite place to do this is in the bath or shower but it might also be in conversation with a beloved, on a solo evening walk, or in your journal. The important thing is to acknowledge your experiences and to let them go. Trust that whatever remains unresolved will be more approachable tomorrow.

Step 1: Set Your Intention

Setting intent is more than casually wanting something to happen—it is the conscious willing behind every creation made manifest. Allow yourself to connect deeply with your longing for a dream. Throughout the day and into the evening, remind yourself of your intention. Say to yourself, "Tonight I am open to receiving and remembering a dream." If you want your intention to be powerful, take some time to clear both your mental and physical space. Nowadays we fill every unstructured moment we have with devices and distractions, taking in so much information that we rarely leave room for our own creativity to arise. So before going to bed, consider turning off or unplugging all digital devices for at least an hour. Think of this time as the opening courtship of your dreams. Open your dream journal to a blank page near your bed and put a pen in its crease, poised to write the dream you receive upon waking.

Step 2: Let Go and Trust

As you lay yourself down to sleep, take five minutes to silently repeat and deeply feel your mantra: "I am open to receiving and remembering a dream." Then, as the Hebrew phrase *abracadabra* ("it came to pass as it was spoken") suggests, trust that the future dream is assured and nothing more is needed. It's important that you not go into sleep with a vigilance that prohibits you from getting genuine rest. Trust that your intention has been heard, and your dreams have been set in motion. Let go of your attachment to the outcome.

Step 3: Wake Up Slowly

Avoid using an alarm clock. The sudden sound jars the body awake rather than allowing a gradual awakening that dream recall requires. If you have to be up at a certain hour, prepare a week or so in advance by training your body to wake you up at a specific hour. You'll be amazed by how accurate the body clock can be. So if you have to be up at 6 a.m., ask your body to wake you up at 5:45 a.m. You can keep an alarm set as backup in case it fails to work. But with enough practice, you should be able to dispense with the alarm altogether. When you awaken, keep your eyes closed and remain in your waking-body position. Dreams can easily be dislodged if you open your eyes, change positions, reach to check your email, or start thinking of your to-do list. Stay present with the dream, as if carrying a fragile creature across a rickety bridge.

Step 4: Mentally Rehearse It

If you only remember a fragment of a dream, try not to judge or interpret it. Oftentimes we wake up with just a wisp of a dream, an image, a word, or a feeling—and our instinct is to dismiss it. We think it isn't substantial enough, or that it's too chaotic or nonsensical. Sometimes we think we already know what that dream means because it contains a familiar scenario. But this urge to dismiss the dream comes out of left-brain thinking, which doesn't understand the non-linear, symbolic language of the unconscious. One of the most difficult things to master with dreamwork is to overcome that urge to dismiss the dream long enough for you to write it down. Once you do, you'll be amazed at the details that can emerge from one fragment. Trust that what you have received is more than enough to start with. Without judging the dream, hold that scene, image, character or feeling, and "rehearse" it in your mind's eye. Play it back in your memory from beginning to end, noticing any new details that emerge. Include these details in your next rehearsal. If you find your thoughts drifting, just come back to the dream. Do this four to five times until the dream feels solid in your recall.

Step 5: Write Down Your Dream

This act is key because it is a physical honouring of your dream. By writing down or recording what you remember, you are bringing the ineffable, as best you can, into materiality. Some people are daunted by the task of trying to describe the impossible in words, and certainly dreams often defy logic and vocabulary. But even if you fail to capture it in all its glory or ambiguity, try anyway. Go slowly and enjoy the process of combing the slipstream for the right descriptors to represent your dream. Allow for the confusion and ambiguity to be included in your writing. For instance, if you dream of a well that opens into an ocean, though it won't make sense to your logic, it's important not to edit out that detail to make it more rational. Similarly, if you aren't told anything directly in the dream, but you just "know" what you're meant to do, you can say, "I understand that I am supposed to descend into the well and out into the ocean."

If there's anything you can't describe in words, you can always try drawing it instead. It can be delicious to flip back through your dream journal to find splashes of colour and shape amongst the words. Jung's *The Red Book*, which was written during a years-long "creative illness," took dream journaling to another level.[2] More like an illuminated manuscript, it was a leather-bound folio filled with calligraphy on parchment, flanked by luscious drawings of mythical characters and psychedelic geometry.

Always write your dream in present tense. Instead of "I was in my childhood home" use "I am in my childhood home." Writing in the present tense has a transportive effect, taking you right back into the immediate, sensual environment of the dream, as if you were experiencing it vividly for the first time. Magically, many people report gaining new memories from the dream as they are writing it in the present. When you're done writing down your dream, give it a headline like a news story. Keep it simple and concise, using only 3–5 words if possible, and try to capture the most memorable event, action, or character in your title. Not only will the title act as a mnemonic device for you to recognize your dream when you're flipping through your journal later, but it will act as a mini-interpretation. Just as glancing at a headline will give you a condensed version of what you'll find in an article, a dream title should give you a glimpse into the heart of the dream's mission or events.

Step 6: Love the Dream You Are Given

I can't emphasize enough how important it is to honour the fragment dreams you receive. So often people think things like, "My dream isn't interesting enough," "It doesn't have a narrative," or "It's just replaying images or experiences from the previous day, it's meaningless." This is a huge mistake. Dreaming is a little like gardening in that you have to tend to new sprouts with a special kind of tenderness if you want them to grow. You must love the dream you are given. Even if you remember a fragment, those little ones tend to be the most powerful dreams of all. Fragment dreams are like a hologram in that the genius of the entire dream can be contained in a single image. If you receive a dream fragment, trust that it is the beginning of more to come, and honour it as you would any heralding.

Step 7: Exploration and Playwork

Once the dream is recorded, find enjoyable ways to explore its message in greater depth. You can reflect on the dreams you received in your journal, using the "Courtship Keys" discussed in the next chapter, or try painting your symbols. If you're more research-oriented, Google the behaviours and habitats of a dream animal on a quiet morning, or consult a fairy-tale database for similar themes or archetypes. You can also take the dream into your yoga or movement practice, and let it speak to you through bodily sensations and other insights. I love going on what I call "integrative walks" where I simply walk in nature with my dream and let it work on me. You may decide to share your dream with a trusted friend or even start a dream group. In Chapter 12: Rituals and Enactments, we will explore other ways to engage and participate with Wisdom. And in Chapter 13: Dreaming as a Village, we will dive deeply into the value of dreamsharing to foster intimacy and connection in our families and communities.

DREAM INCUBATION

One way to enhance your practice is to explore dream incubation, the practice of posing an intentional question to your dreams on a specific topic. Whether it is a question regarding your health, relationships, vocation, or other decisions, dream incubation is a way of asking the divine to meet you halfway with solutions. Guidance may come in the form of follow-up dreams, intuitive "hits," or synchronicity in your waking-life. Dreams naturally respond to what's most precious to our hearts—the questions we are obsessed with. Instead of letting this happen unconsciously, dream incubation is simply "getting behind the creative wheel" by setting an intention to dream on a topic important to you.

Similar to a vision quest, the more intentional your incubation, the deeper the wisdom you'll receive. There are many questions you might use to frame your inquiry, but the most successful incubations are well thought out and deeply held. In other words, the more imprinted your question is, the clearer the guidance will be. Asking for a yes or no answer will only frustrate you because dreams speak in paradoxical layers of metaphors and symbolic language. So to get the most out of the process, your question should leave room for input. An example question could be, "What do I most need to know in this situation?" Or, "Will this decision I have made bring about the most benevolent outcome?"

Spend some time really crafting your question so it's clear and simple. Hold your question in your heart and mind throughout the day (or previous days). When you're ready, write it down on a blank journal page and leave it by your bed. Set the intention to write down the dream you receive below it.

Sit quietly before bed with your question in mind, genuinely asking for guidance. As you drift off to sleep, trust that the exercise will be successful. It's important to let your focus soften as you fall asleep or you might be too vigilant to dream. If you've focused throughout the day, trust that your question is secure in your heart and mind, and *abracadabra*.

Follow the seven steps above to record the dreams you receive. If you don't feel like your question has been answered, your process will have helped you fine tune your query. It's also possible that you simply need more time to incubate. Be open to, and write down, any insights you receive in the following days. If you don't receive a dream, try again the next night and throughout the week. Practising gratitude for any guidance you receive will always bring greater revelations, so consider adding something to your dream altar to represent your incubation.

If you do receive helpful guidance, be sure to put it into practice. This might look like experimenting with new relationship strategies, starting a new creative project, or following a lead toward your purpose. Risk is often involved wherever we need big change. While it's not always necessary to take a big leap, taking even small risks toward your next becoming will inspire deeper dreams to support you.

CHAPTER 9

Courting the Dream

THE FIRST TIME I heard the word "courtship" in a context other than old-timey dating rituals, I was sitting in ceremony with author and Mayan Shaman Martín Prechtel. He was explaining to a group of us how to approach the Holy in Nature. He said, "Courtship is to sit next to someone and discover what they love." As sometimes happens with great teachers, Martín's eloquent use of the word shifted my perception into a new configuration regarding my own work. Suddenly I could see that approaching the symbols in my dreams wasn't about getting what I want, but about discovering how I can be of service to that which I love.

Though we don't value courtship in modernity, it was origi-nally a circling process that people engaged in when they admired each other. Struck with an affection for someone, you couldn't just swipe right and know instantly if they accepted you. Instead you slowly circled their sphere, approaching them (or their relatives) from a respectful distance to learn about what they valued, who they loved, what they longed for. You aspired to one day be of service in helping them reach those dreams.

The great hope of traditional courtship is marriage. In the context of dreamwork, we can think of this marriage as the union between our inner and outer life. Like an ideal marriage, it should be a reciprocal and mutually supportive relationship that is also in harmony with its village or ecosystem. But in order to have a chance at this kind of belonging, you must first prove yourself trustworthy. In dreamwork, this is a process of refining the quality of your approach so that the soul feels safe enough to open its mysterious depths to you. If you're able to convey your reliability, honesty, and absence of judgement, your symbols will share their secrets with you—telling you how they ache, what is missing for them, and what they love more than anything. In sharing these secret things across the arteries of your connection, your body begins to fall in sync with the soul's rhythms. You begin to respond with a sense of purpose. You show up with greater presence in your life, guided by the clarity of your own knowing. As this happens, the mysterious Other will naturally become receptive to (and curious about) you in return. The soul will respond to your attentions in the form of affirming dreams, a wellspring of originality, and a quickening of synchronicity in your day-world.

There's a wonderful documentary called *My Octopus Teacher* by a filmmaker named Craig Foster, who makes a radical decision to leave his profession to return to his childhood passion for snorkelling under the sea.[1]

One day, in the tangle of a kelp forest, Foster makes eye contact with one very special octopus. Intrigued and enamoured with her, he makes a vow to return every single day to see if he can learn more about her. After weeks of watching him watch her, she extends one tentacle to touch his hand, keeping the rest of her body firmly tucked in her den of rocks and shells. It is a numinous experience for Foster. Though he can only hold his breath for so long, an eternity is held in that first contact. He goes back the next day, excited to deepen their relationship, but makes two fatal errors. He drops one of his camera lenses into the sand between them, and it's enough to frighten her away. The next time, he approaches her too quickly and, in a whoosh of inky clouds, she leaves her compromised den for good, never to return.

In the following weeks, Foster returns every day, mapping out the kelp forest, learning its topography and discovering the many inhabitants that live there in harmony. He decides to see if he can track her. He observes the small traces creatures leave behind on the seafloor. Still, she is a master of cunning and disguise, eluding his best efforts. One day, he finds the evidence of prey she has eaten and he focuses his search into a two-metre radius until suddenly he sees her, impersonating a white sea sponge. He knows he'll have to earn her trust. He comes back every day, approaching from a respectful distance, even backing away slightly when she finally reaches out again.

Over the course of a year, the two become friends. They touch each other, cuddling, swimming in unison, playing with commuting schools of fish. After a terrible run-in with a shark, Foster even feeds and cares for the octopus while she's unwell. When he is back on land, he thinks of her, worries about her, researches her needs and habits. And he imagines that she thinks of him, too, experiencing octopus joy in his friendship as he does in hers.

He becomes deeply involved in her life. When he comes home, he tells his young son of these encounters. As the boy grows up, he swims with his dad in the same sea forest, carrying the knowledge passed down from his father. And in poetic symmetry, he even befriends one of her babies. Foster goes on to be the founder of the Sea Change Project, an organization dedicated to protecting African sea life through education and storytelling.

This story illustrates so well what we are doing in the courtship process with our dreams … tracking the symbol's almost imperceptible traces as it moves in and out of hiding; approaching in an invitational way that, over time, makes you trustworthy; showing up every day without your "lenses" of perception; and allowing yourself to be amazed by the dream's intricate disguises and strategies. Instead of dragging the dream onto your shore—demanding it adjust to your language and culture—following it deeper into its native world of images. Interfering as little as possible, allowing yourself to regulate its climate and habitat. In return, you will always be fed by its beauty and friendship.

Courtship reverses the idea that we are trying to get something from our dreams. Instead we are trying to discover what *they* want and to attempt, with our lives, to fulfil that longing. A good marriage is kept alive by seeing the other in a constantly changing light rather than settling into a single impression. If you're doing it right, you never reach "the bottom" of a dream, because there is no end to the depths of the unconscious. Instead, every turn around the spiral is another opportunity to be more deeply engaged with its mystery. And as we learn to appreciate their ambiguity and complexity, our symbols continue to feed us with their concealed wisdom over time.

With the intent of making dreamwork accessible to all, I've narrowed down what I think are five essential keys to coaxing a dream to open like a flower in blossom. I call them "keys" because they have the effect of opening undiscovered rooms in the imagination and body. But as a musician, I also love the word keys for how, unlike steps that move in a linear direction, keys can be layered and interchanged. The first "Courtship Key" can be combined with the third, or after the fourth, and even all five can be embodied in one layered movement.

We can get a feel for this way of layering in the fugues of Johann Sebastian Bach. The music begins with the introduction of a melody. In dreamwork, this is the dream itself. Then a second voice or instrument chimes in with a response, using different notes. In musical terms, this is called the "answer." Your answer to a dream might look like writing it down in your journal, painting one of its symbols, or recording it in some other way. Now the conversation has been struck! Your answer is a way of acknowledging the value of a dream, contributing your own voice to what will become a deepening conversation.

From there, a classical fugue may expand upon the original melody, growing more complex. In dreamwork, this new material might be your own associations to the original images, but it might also be in synchronicities around the dream's symbols, or the introduction of myths or fairy tales with similar motifs. As each new voice responds, it gives the composition more complexity. In order to join all of these voices into one smooth composition, fugues have codettas—brief resolutions—connecting the original melody with its variations. In dreamwork we create bridges between the dream and waking-life; moments of correlation between the two worlds.

Finally, when every voice has had its say, the fugue ends with a passage that brings it all together. This is a synthesis of all that's gone before. Synthesis in dreamwork is a process of summarizing the most important revelations, integrating any expanded perspectives, and enacting the Dreaming Way. Like how a great piece of music can transform us, when the work is finished, the change begins. Your imagination is enlivened with all that you've discovered in the dream, and you begin to move your life in response to its music.

In this chapter, I will be going into subtle detail for each of the five Courtship Keys. But once you've integrated these concepts, dreamwork should come quickly and naturally to you. Like a skilled musician can improvise once they've mastered their instrument, with practice you will be able to use the Keys in a fluid and organic way. In Chapter 13: Dreaming as a Village, you'll find an example of how to use these Keys in a group dreamwork process.

Perhaps most miraculously, the skills you are learning in dreamwork are fundamental capacities for being human. By courting your dreams, you are honouring the sacred, awakening your creative originality, embodying your true values, and discovering how to thrive in diverse relationships.

KEY 1: EMBODIED PRESENCE

Whether you are witnessing someone else's dream or working with your own, you must begin by listening with embodied presence to the dream's original statement. This means preparing your body and space for the encounter by putting all distractions away. Make sure you (and the other) feel focused, comfortable, and safe, so that you can listen to the dream with curiosity and an open heart.

There's an old alchemical phrase, *prima materia*, that translates to "original matter" and, in our context, refers to the raw material of psyche that appears in our dreams. It is the *prima materia* that we want to represent accurately in our journal because all future movements will respond to this foundational statement. It's vital that you receive or record the dream as it presents itself, not as you would like it to be. Even when images seem irrelevant, weird, off-putting, or disjointed, practise accepting the dream with all of its knobbly bits. While acknowledging your waking-life feelings and responses is essential, they must be put carefully aside until later. The first Key is all about being present for the dream itself. I love the term "active receptivity" because it suggests that you aren't passive in the process of listening to or writing down a dream, you are actively engaged in your reception of it.

A thousand processes are taking place in the soulbody when you listen to a dream. You may experience sensations, like a tightening in your chest at a stressful juncture in the dream, or a welling up of emotion during a conflict, or the opening of a small crack into awe at the appearance of a dream helper. You might feel discomfort at the content of the dream or toward the ambiguity of the process itself. You may begin having associations to the dream's images; memories of similar dynamics or situations you've experienced in waking-life. Your analytical brain might get involved by beginning to interpret or project upon the dream. You may also have instincts and intuitions rising up out of nowhere. If you are listening to a friend's dream, there may even be dynamics in your relationship and environment that emerge while you listen. All of these responses are valuable and belong in the dream-work process, but initially, they need to be acknowledged and set aside—because nothing is more important than receiving the dream as it presents itself. Active receptivity requires you to expand your awareness to include all these phenomena while simultaneously suspending any judgement or input so you can make a true encounter with the dream.

Your presence is essential to the process. If you're writing down your dream but also checking your phone or composing your day's to-do list, the dream will be less likely to yield its sumptuous details. To show up half-way for a dream unconsciously communicates your disinterest. Like a friend who interrupts you during a vulnerable share, or listens with only cursory attention, you may find that a distance eventually develops between you.

If at any point during the courtship process you find yourself drifting or losing interest, circle back to remember that you are wooing the mystery. When you are witnessing a dream, you are in the presence of something Holy. Like the octopus in the documentary, we are not seeking to teach it our language or to see through our lenses of perception but rather descending into *its* world to learn *its* ways from *its* body of knowing. What really makes someone feel seen and loved is when you listen with the fullness of your presence. Can you remember the last time you felt deeply seen by someone when you were feeling vulnerable? Was it because the other held a focused and accepting, loving presence? This Key, all on its own, is magical in that it opens a field of safety between you and the other. It is that moment when the diver realizes that he can't approach too hastily—that even backing off a little can draw the other closer. It says: "I am paying attention. I'm in no hurry." This field is a kind of offering in that it gives the other a desperately needed invitation: to know what it already knows.

Along the same lines, when listening to someone else's dream, you may find your own mind wandering. This is usually for one of two reasons. The first is that its language will feel foreign until you develop familiarity with dreams. The sequences between scenes don't seem to be connected. The events that take place in dreams are so out of the ordinary that they are hard to follow in any rational way. You may find yourself feeling bored or irritated as you struggle to follow the plot. But as you improve your capacity to think symbolically, dreams start to make the only kind of sense that matters, and you'll be riveted to see how they unfold.

The second reason you might drift is that your own dreaming gets activated when listening to another's dream. When someone shares a dream with us, or even speaks generally about dreams, it opens a space of permission for valuing the imaginal. Like being called up after a long wait on the bench, this part of you jumps alive at the chance to play. You may slip into a daydream, get a flash of a recent dream, or even feel your creative imagination getting enchanted by symbols and moods. This symbiosis is one of the great powers of dreamsharing! But the art of this Key is to make your presence is an offering; to invite the other to come into their deepest knowing.

Much like creating an invitational field with children, when we refrain from imposing our wants or desires onto them, they often surprise us by coming to their own good conclusions. The same is true of dreamwork. When I work with a dreamer, I hold the perspective that they are the expert—if I ask the right questions, leave enough silence, and tolerate my own discomfort with not having the answers, the dreamer's own knowing always emerges. When you are courting your own dream, do your best to listen as carefully as you can to the *prima materia*, to discover what it knows rather than following your waking responses to it. This means noticing the feelings you have *in the dream* as distinct from the feelings you have *about it* after you wake up. Often images or scenarios that might shock or embarrass you in waking-life don't hold the same impact inside the dream reality.

Active receptivity, by its very nature, requires you to get comfortable not knowing where the dream will lead. Instead, you are practising at allowing yourself to be led. The most skilled dreamworkers are successful not because they have encyclopedic knowledge but because they are comfortable with this groundlessness. Even after twenty years of doing dreamwork, I still experience the discomfort of not knowing where the dream will lead— but I am comfortable with that discomfort. I trust that the dream will allow me to know some of its mystery if I show up with embodied presence. But even when I am left with confusion or a lack of connection, I trust that there's a reason it remains in its den. This not-knowing prepares me to be surprised and humbled when the dream's wisdom decides to emerge.

You can see how valuable this Key is, not just for the dreamwork process but for life. The invitational field we are creating is a form of prayer—it is the starting point for all sacred connection. You can think of it as clearing an emptiness for magic to descend into your life, a sacred enclosure for the holy to enter. Whether you are listening to an elder's story, comforting a person in grief, learning how to track an octopus, or courting your dreams, this humble gesture of emptying the self to be attentive to the Other opens a doorway into the Imaginal World.

Beginning this work is like suddenly turning off the lights and having to fumble through the dark so don't be surprised if you feel afraid, anxious, and insecure as you step foot into this territory of unknowing. Every artist, writer, and innovator experiences waves of fear and doubt that anything of value will appear in the emptiness. But as it is with music, art, or architecture, negative spaces are what draw you in closer. They allow you to slow down, to pay attention to what might otherwise be missed. In active receptivity, you are engaging your subtle senses, so you can track communications from the world behind this one.

KEY 2: WONDER

You dream you are riding on the back of a great blue whale. You feel an emotional bond the great animal that is unspoken, but understood, as it drives you deep under the water to the ocean floor. You don't have any difficulty breathing underwater, or holding on to its back, because your body is an extension of this magical creature. You are flooded with exhilaration and the privilege of allying with the most powerful, ancient animal on earth. When you reach the bottom of the ocean, it swoops up toward the surface with one push of its muscular tail. You breach together, out into the sparkle of sunlight, airborne for a moment before diving headlong back into the ocean. When you wake up, you are in a breathless state of awe knowing you've been graced by the miraculous.

Every dream deserves to be met with this degree of wonder. Even dreams that appear mundane at first glance have something miraculous to offer you. The fact is dreams are innovative by nature. They don't tell us what we already know, but provide us with new perspectives to draw us into our own development. If we want to be led anywhere new, we have to meet it with *wonder*. Wonder is a transformative human capacity that behaves as a door through which one can discover a whole new world.

The Oxford English Dictionary defines wonder as "a feeling of surprise mingled with admiration, caused by something beautiful, unexpected, unfamiliar, or inexplicable."[2] It comes from the German *wundrōnq* meaning of "unknown ultimate origin." But it is a verb as well as a noun. To be in a state of wonder is to be actively curious, to suspend the urge to explain things away, and to be willing to be surprised. This is the countenance we want to inhabit as we move through a dream. We are, after all, visitors in this unfamiliar land. Like explorers, our greatest passport to discovery is a natural curiosity. In asking artful questions, the dream will draw us deeper into its landscape, and we will be changed by the adventure. As the poet David Whyte proposes, "a beautiful question starts to shape your identity as much by asking it as it does by having it answered."[3]

While the Key of Embodied Presence opens you to the imaginal, the Wonder Key is all about engaging your curiosity. Curiosity is what draws us into relationship with our surroundings. It looks around and under the dream's surface into its hidden depths. Like a toddler putting dirt into its mouth for the taste, or chasing after snakes and frogs to see how and where they live, curiosity is the mechanism behind how you learn about yourself and your environment. It is how you locate your body in relation to the many other bodies around you.

Working with a dream is not unlike getting to know your physical environment. There is a whole ecosystem to explore. The first step in entering into a relationship with any other is learning their unique communication style and wondering what, if anything, they might have to say. When I step out of my house, my own body is immediately in relationship with other bodies. At the bottom of my front steps, a little too close for my own comfort, a cranky buck we call Jack is resting his huge body under the shade of the lilac tree's body. I scurry past the hedge bodies who, in the morning dew, reveal a hundred spider bodies in their tent webs. I try not to step on the pinecone bodies under my feet who have a mission I don't want to crush. I notice the grass bodies are deeply entwined with the body of soil, and a cool body of wind enters my own lungs. Each of these bodies is in varying degrees of communication with me if I slow down to notice them. Jack's communication style is hard to miss. He snorts aggressively to let me know he is only tolerating me living on *his* land. For a short few weeks in summer, the lilac tree communicates in glorious flowers and a heady perfume, but the rest of the year she speaks in tones of shade and shelter.

If you've ever had someone offer you their authentic curiosity, saying "Tell me more...," you know how precious these simple words can be. It is the question everyone needs to hear. Our symbols are no different. Each has a story to tell and our curiosity is what draws it into the open. Rather than giving unwanted advice, interpreting too early, or offering a fix to a conundrum, the simple act of expressing wonder communicates that what the other has to share is valuable to you.

I find it most helpful to work with a dream in chronological order, tending to each symbol as it appears in sequence, until I feel oriented within its landscape. While it's tempting to jump to the climax or conflict of a dream, it's best not to rush intimacy. We all know the sensation of closing up protectively when someone is a bit too nosy or hasty with our hearts. Dreams respond best to a slow and steady approach. The chronology of a dream, as best you can remember it, is important because each moment gives birth to the next. If you want to know why a conflict has happened or a transformation has taken place, look to the moments that led up to it.

The biggest clues are often held in less dramatic scenes and transitions. Returning to our universal dream elements, always begin by locating yourself in the opening setting of the dream, which sets the stage for the unfolding events. What is the environment and mood of the moment? Who are the figures appearing here? What is the mission at hand? By gentling your way into a dream, you are preparing yourself for its revelations. If you have a complex dream with many scenes and characters, this process may feel overwhelming. If that's the case, try zeroing in on the most potent symbols in the dream. Otherwise, I recommend going into as much subtle inquiry as you have time for.

My intention when asking questions about another's dream is to put myself in their shoes. I want to locate myself in their dreamscape as viscerally as possible. I want to know how the dreamer feels in every interaction or scene, who the characters are to them and how they are perceived. I want to know about the environments and history of the places we move in and out of and how the moods shift and weather changes. This process is the same when working with your own dreams—but in addition to asking these questions, you are also answering them.

Begin with the most basic descriptions of each symbol in the dream. For instance, say you dream of being in a car that has broken down. You might start by asking yourself, "What is a car?" Asking about the basic function of a familiar object like a car might seem silly, but defining it can be incredibly illuminating. All words are symbols, not the thing itself. So to make the shift from thinking literally to thinking symbolically, we must attempt to get at the idea that the word or image is representing. Let's say, for instance, you respond, "A car is a mechanical vehicle that moves me to destinations at high speeds." Suddenly we have an evocative and personal description of how the car means *for you*. It means in a mechanical way, moving you toward goals, and with speed. Once you have this basic association, you can start wondering with more complexity, asking questions like, "Why did it break down?" or "Where was I going?" At this early point in the process, choose questions that are located within the dream context itself so you can get as robust a description as possible.

The art of asking good questions takes some time to master, but if you're having trouble coming up with the next line of inquiry here are a few examples to get you started:

- What sort of person is [name of character]?
- If you don't know [name of character], what's your first impression of them?
- Are you familiar with this [feeling, place, person]?
- What do you associate with [name of place, person, object]?
- Use three words to describe [name of place, person, object].
- Describe how you felt when [event or action] happened.

- Why do you think [name of character] did what they did?

While it may be tempting to Google a dream symbol or look up an animal totem, you will only ever get vague and arbitrary results that borrow on cultural beliefs that are irrelevant to you. Everything you need to know about your symbols is contained within your own imagination, and the Wonder Key is how you access that knowing. No professional, no expert in mythology, not even the entire internet knows more about your dream than you. All you have to do is follow your curiosity and allow the dream's responses to unfold. When you think about it, it's relaxing to know that you aren't expected to know anything about a dream without first engaging in this simple process. As you receive responses, more questions will be generated from those answers. We can call this a refinement of your inquiry.

As the questions reveal memories, associations, sensations, feelings, and ideas, remember not to stray too far from the dream. If you start feeling overwhelmed or off-track, return to the *prima materia*. The images in the dream will anchor you with their inherent order.

As you wonder deeper into the dream, you might start forming a hypothesis about what it all means. But rather than setting up camp in any specific theory, the art of this Key is in turning that hypothesis into a question. Perhaps you dream that your house is burning down. You only have a moment to decide if you can rescue your cat. Your knee-jerk reaction may be to think, "Cats are symbolic of the feminine, and the cat must be saved." You form a hypothesis that the dream is about saving your "instinctual feminine" from a destructive force in your life. But if you remain curious and ask instead, "What qualities do I associate with fire?" you may find that your answer is surprising: "Fire is a destructive element, but also transformative in that it burns away debris and nourishes the soil for new life to grow from its ashes." Suddenly, the fire is a paradoxical symbol and can no longer be written off as good or bad.

Holding this new knowledge, you decide to explore your dream cat in more detail. After all, not all cats are the same. Maybe she was an actual barn cat you adopted in your twenties, who had a distinctly feral streak and never quite adapted to domestication. When you reflect on her particular personality, you realize, "She embodies qualities that mirror an old identity for me." Maybe, like her, you resisted being tamed, but are now in a phase of your life when you're ready to put down roots. Putting these two descriptions together helps you arrive at a very different conclusion about your dream: that while the loss of an old version of yourself can be painful, you no longer identify with that feral aspect. You are transforming in the fires of change and ready to root down and start a family. Sometimes in the dream courtship process, the answers to your questions confirm your original hypothesis. But by remaining curious you are also willing to be taken in a totally different direction.

With the Wonder Key, we are attempting to get a depth perspective on each of the elements in the dream. We are plumbing below the surface of our images that appear to be one thing at face value but reveal hidden dimensions. That subtle dimension might include how you perceive a figure, what personality traits you associate with them, what properties and uses an object might possess, who owns the space you're in, or how a place has shaped you and makes you feel. It's also important to notice if you have any strong emotions welling up, sensations in your body, or memories surfacing. Take note of these responses too, because they will often be guideposts in your process.

You will know you're on the right path when you experience resonance, like recognizing an aspect of yourself in the symbol's mirror. This mirror may reveal a situation or quality you are dimly aware of but have been reluctant to look at directly. Or perhaps you only knew it intellectually, but the dream reorganizes the ideas for you to know it somatically. When meaning is generated from this process, it will almost always have a flood of feeling accompanying it. As Jan Zwicky says of an effective metaphor, there is an "arc of energy released when one context, laid across another, coincides."[4]

As you feel this arc of release, you will say to yourself, "Oh! Yes. A-ha!" Or, if it's a harder mirror to look at, "Cringe" or even "Ooof," but there is still an accompanying sense of the fit. It will feel like something falling into place, breaking free, or finally being seen. I call this an anchor in the dreamwork process, because it serves as a locating truth that we can keep coming back to throughout the process. To be certain you're on the right track, check your anchor against the other symbols in the dream. So in the case of the house-fire dream above, the fire as a transformative element may not have been enough to stand on its own. But once the cat was understood as an old but beloved identity, it behaved as an anchor for the rest of the dream's images to resonate with.

As you *wonder* through the dream, eliciting associations to memories, feelings, and descriptions, you will begin to feel located; you will begin to realize the dream's correspondence with your life. This sense of location is often accompanied by a strong revelation, like the arc of release described above. There may be a sudden recognition of a situation in waking-life that correlates with the dream, a familiar dynamic in your inner dialogue, or a spiritual question that's been weighing on your heart. Once you have this locating experience, you will know your Wonder Key has worked. You can now circle back to central symbols in the dream and see them in this new light.

Once you've moved through the dream in its entirety, a new batch of questions may emerge as you deepen your dialogue. You can ask yourself, "Have I captured the dream's description well? Is there anything I missed?" Or you may feel satisfied that you now have a wealth of associations and are ready to move to the next

Key, which is to reflect on all you've gathered to see what patterns and connections emerge.

Similar to meeting a fascinating stranger on a park bench and striking up a life-changing conversation, the quality of our curiosity is what leads another to entrust us with their life story. Suspending our assumptions and judgements about someone or something long enough for their essence to emerge. To wonder about another is to communicate an invitation to their emergent self. It offers room, where it's too-rarely given, for the other to be heard, recognized, and come into belonging. But the intimacy that is struck through wonder serves both parties—in seeing well, one also has the chance at being seen. As the other surprises us with something unfamiliar, we meet the unknown in ourselves. This small sacrifice of our own agenda opens the field in which true reciprocity takes place. Our work with this Key is near constant because psyche innovates and expresses just beyond our capacity to grasp it. We are perpetually not-knowing, which is appropriately humbling for the ego. After all, wonder is a befitting gesture to extend to the unknowable mystery.

KEY 3: REFLECTION

After exploring a dream in the Key of Wonder, it can be tempting to drive deeper into analysis. You may feel the urge to pick things apart in a methodical way with the goal of acquiring insight. With that sort of analytical approach, you might be successful in reaching intellectual conclusions about your dream but wisdom is not generated by reason, it is arrived at through reflection. The difference between these two methods is as stark as the sun and the moon. While the sun's light is outward, directed, and scrutinizing, the moon's light is inward, receptive, and reflective. It remains in darkness and allows itself to be illumined when the timing is right. Reflection requires us to take a step back from the details so we can see the larger picture. In this Key, we are taking stock of our own language, motivations, and responses in the dream to allow insight and perspective to dawn on us. The discipline of the Reflection Key is to become as clear and neutral as a mirror.

There's a wonderful passage in the essay "Notes on Poetry and Philosophy" by the poet Charles Simic in which he writes, "My poems (in the beginning) are like a table on which one places interesting things one has found on one's walks: a pebble, a rusty nail, a strangely shaped root, the corner of a torn photograph, etc., ... where after months of looking at them and thinking about them daily, certain surprising relationships, which hint at meanings, begin to appear."[5]

What he is describing here is a wonderful analogy for our Reflection Key. While the full significance of some dreams can take months or even years to dawn on us, more often than not, meaningful connections begin to reveal themselves in the simple act of gathering and reflecting on our associations. The Reflection Key is an invitation to give yourself the contemplative room it takes for those connections to appear. Reflection is a kind of active spaciousness that allows the minutiae to fall away so meaning can reveal itself.

In the previous two Keys, our intent was to put ourselves as viscerally as possible in the objective dream reality to gather its many details. But in the Reflection Key we are intentionally standing outside the dream experience to see it with waking eyes. From this new distance, we can spot the metaphors, observe the story arc as a whole, and check in with our body for any resonance or resistance. It is from this vantage point that we will also look for an entryway into meaning—that undeniable bridge into the dream's significance where the most resonance is gathered.

Connections between your dream and waking-life can and will occur spontaneously at any point in the dreamwork process. But more often than not, we need to take a beat to reflect on what we've gathered in the previous stages. Here we can recombine the dream with the associations to create coherence. The Reflection

Key is like picking up each symbol to feel its weight, now heavy with the associations made in the Key of Wonder, turning it over in our mind's eye to behold it through a metaphorical lens. If you've already had a revelation about a metaphor, ask yourself how it connects to its companions. Notice how the scenes of your dream sit in relation to each other. In the dream of riding a whale, let's say you associate the ocean with *the depth of the unconscious*, and the whale as a *huge and ancient intelligence*. Now you reflect on how those symbols fit and flow together, recombining your metaphors with the feelings and actions of the dream. So if you were restating it, your dream would now become, "*I am in an exhilarating symbiosis with an ancient intelligence, in which I dive into the depths of the unconscious, breaching back into consciousness with my underworld experience.*" This example was actually one of my own favourite dreams from when I was starting out on the Dreaming Way.

One fantastic tool for self-reflection is to rewrite the dream in short form, as I've done above, swapping out the central images with their metaphorical definitions, and/or your most resonant associations. To illustrate, let's take a look at how this process worked for an artist named Francis. We will start with her original dream, followed by a list of her new symbols and their associations. Then we can see how she replaces the original words with those new insights in a rewrite of the dream.

Buying a Hotel: Francis' Dream

I dream I am considering buying a former hotel. It only has two or three individual rooms, but huge amounts of unusable collective space, like a giant ballroom for events and conventions. I wonder what to do with these huge spaces. I think the only way I can make this work is to find a roommate who is quiet and creative, so I begin to interview people. One woman shows up and decides she loves it and just begins to claim space there. I feel defensive because I haven't even accepted her yet! Similarly, the

*less-than-trustworthy vendor says, "Congratulations!" and sticks
out his hand for a handshake. It's all feeling a bit fast and out of
my control. I decide I have to confront the woman who's moving
in without my consent. She attacks my character, saying I am not
nice or spiritual enough.*

After writing this down, the first thing Francis did with the
Wonder Key was pull out the biggest themes and symbols to make
the following associations by asking herself basic questions:

Buying: *Investing value in something, and taking ownership of it.*

Converted Hotel: *A temporary accommodation for someone who
is passing through, now being made permanent.*

Unusable Collective Space: *Decommissioned spaces for gathering
in groups.*

Roommate: *Reminds me of a character on a TV show who is bold,
domineering, dynamic, pushy. She feels like an interloper.*

Consent: *Something I haven't agreed to is happening anyway.*

Vendor: *Seems like someone who has made bad investments,*

Fast and Out of My Control: *Reminds me of being diagnosed
with Multiple Sclerosis (MS), which has altered my life dramatically in a short period of time.*

Confront: *The action of facing something, asserting boundaries
against an interloper.*

Nice and Spiritual: *These are words that I've been rejecting
recently, because I associate them with people from my old*

community who have a "love and light" persona but haven't integrated their shadow.

Then swapping out her symbols with the associations, Francis rewrote her dream like this so she could reflect on its meaning:

I am considering taking ownership of a temporary situation to make it permanent. To make this transition, I would have to figure out how to make use of the decommissioned spaces in my life that were once used for gathering in groups. It seems a quiet ally could make it work. But the force that takes up residence is bold, domineering, dynamic, pushy and feels like an interloper. This relationship is one I haven't agreed to, but it's happening anyway. Like MS, which my husband and I call "the roommate," my life has been altered dramatically in a short period of time. Part of me feels unprepared and out of my depth. I am trying to assert boundaries, but I am being attacked for not having a "nice and spiritual" persona. I associate this criticism with people who haven't integrated their shadow and tend to bypass things like grief, suffering, and pain.

Can you see how Francis has stayed true to the dream's chronology and images, but woven her associations into the language? Reading through this rewrite, where the symbols have been swapped out by her most resonant associations, I imagine you are already making some pretty strong connections between the dream and her waking-life. As you become more skilled with this in your own work, you may find you don't need to rewrite the dream but can simply read it back to yourself and reflect on the symbols now enhanced by your associations.

The transition we are making in Reflection is from our literal experience of the dream to its symbolic appreciation. As we have learned, the dream is psyche's experience of events, spoken in metaphor. Imagine the dream as an impressionistic drawing traced on a transparency, which, when laid upon your waking-life reality, echoes its shapes and gestures. The two may be drawn in different styles—one realistic, the other impressionistic—but they map a shared territory. When held together, they tell a more complete story of our total experience. Neither reality or impression are lost in bringing them together but are enhanced by one another.

By swapping out the name of the object, character, or place with its nuanced description or association, we are holding these two gestures against each other—but instead of a visual overlay, we are doing it with language. We stay with the dream's objective reality, "I am buying a hotel" but replace the literal language with the substance of our associations to say, "I am taking ownership of a situation that used to be temporary."

If you begin to feel resonance, you have likely found your anchor of the dream. It's important, however, to check that resonance against the other elements in the dream. Francis makes an association to her disease in both the "roommate" character and the feeling of being "fast and out of my control." This is likely the direction for finding meaning in the dream but she will need to test that hypothesis against the other symbols to see if they all make sense in that context.

As you proceed along the dream's edges to see if the rest of the symbols correspond, you may come up against images that don't feel like they fit. You must be willing to either revisit your associations or toss out your hypothesis and approach other elements anew. It's also important to acknowledge that some issues are reluctant to come into the open. This may be because you're approaching a sensitive or core issue too directly. So when you encounter resistance or rejection of an idea, consider pivoting to a different element, and another; but if, after you've done your diligence, resonance never comes, do leave the dream alone. Let yourself walk in nature with it, or simply sit quietly with it. Let your body wander with the images to see what wisdom emerges. If you're a more sensory-oriented person, you can close your eyes and re-embody a physical position from the dream and let your imagination speak from your embodied experience.*

Reflection is also when those sensations, intuitions, and feelings you put aside to respect the *prima materia* can be invited back to have their say. How does what you discovered in the process now fit with your somatic experience? Maybe you felt enchanted by a certain figure that, through the Key of Wonder, proved to be revelatory. Or maybe during the process, tension gathered in a part of your body that acts as a clue for a wound that needs tending to. For instance, when confronted by certain triggers in waking-life, you might find your throat habitually closing up with anxiety. Maybe the dream uses this explicit sensation to teach you something about when and where that occurs, offering up potential solutions in the surrounding dream. Did you have an intuition at the outset of the dreamwork that is now ringing true after making associations? Sometimes our feelings about the dream change after exploring them in more depth. Take a moment to acknowledge where your perspective may have shifted.

It is often when you least expect it that a realization will hit you all at once: in the shower, on the yoga mat, in a moment of synchronicity out on an errand. Whether in a quiet pause to let your imagination sift through what you've collected in the Wonder Key or in a creative or somatic exploration with our dream, Reflection is what enables us to witness and evaluate our own unconscious behaviours. For some people, Reflection is most engaged when moving the body and exploring dream sensations and feelings; for others it's when they are meditating or soaking in a bath. For many, the act of writing or painting is inherently reflective. What each of these methods have in common is the capacity for turning inward and listening for what's resonating. While analysis involves a scrutiny of data, being reflective is a

---

* *See Chapter 12: Rituals and Enactments for a step-by-step somatic dreamwork exercise called Move Your Symbol.*

diffuse awareness that connects us to our body's felt experience. We drop the focused attention of the Wonder Key to allow the two worlds—temporal and symbolic—to show us what they have in common. Reflection opens a portal through which bridges form so we can cross between the worlds.

If, after reflecting on your associations swapped into the dream story, you still aren't making strong connections, you can try reflecting on the larger patterns and subtle dynamics in your dream. Here are some example questions to consider:

Themes: What are the broader themes in my dream? Do I recognize any patterns or motifs from my previous dreams?

Feelings: Where is the highest concentration of feeling? Did this feeling arise before or during key events or interactions in the dream? How did my emotions influence my actions?

Plot: By what threads are my dream scenes connected? Can I identify external or internal dream dynamics that caused the scene to shift?

Motivations: What motivations were underpinning my (or another's) choices or actions? What was driving me (or others)?

Strategy: If there was a threat or problem in the dream, what strategy did I use to navigate it? Was it successful? If not, what strategy might have been preferable?

Allies: What were the supportive elements, symbols, or figures in my dream? Were there any glimmers of affirmation?

Another powerful exercise is to imagine yourself in another dream-figure's shoes. Reflect on how the dream feels from their perspective. Dreams often cast us (the dreamer) in the most sympathetic role so we can learn to see ourselves with compassion. But the real bravery of dreamwork is then stepping into our adversaries' shoes so we can see what drives the unconscious forces in our psyche. In the dream example above, Francis might ask herself how the dream feels from the vendor's perspective, or what the roommate's feelings and motivations are. You may feel as if you are "making it up," but you can trust your imagination to reflect your true impressions of the dream and its inhabitants. *

Always check in with your body as you're deepening your courtship and listening for resonances and resistances. Resonance usually points us in the right direction, while resistance may be a signal to approach from a different angle. But if you're left feeling overwhelmed or anxious by the process, it's always a good idea to give yourself some breathing room. Close your journal, nourish your body, and let yourself be a moon in the dark who isn't rushing a reveal.

This Key works differently for self-reflection than it does with another person. In relationship, we are trying to provide a clear reflection of the dreamer's own associations back to them to make sure they feel seen and heard. It offers them an opportunity to make any corrections or additions to what we're mirroring. In order to do this, you have to be able to put your own assumptions, projections, and language aside so you can reflect the true nature of the dream. This is harder than you might think. Even psychology professionals, with their extensive training and knowledge, can project their fixed ideas on to a dream. A dreamer once came to me after twenty years with an analyst who kept referring to the figures in her dreams as her "animus" or "negative mother complex," which left the dreamer feeling pathologized and unable to move forward.

When someone tells me a dream, I listen to the entire story once using the first Embodied Presence Key. If they've read it from their journal rather than telling it from memory, I'll ask them to share it a second time from memory so I can hear the more casual, embodied version. This often results in new details emerging that weren't written down. Once I feel I have heard the dream well enough (Embodied Presence), I will restate it (Reflection) to them in as clear a way as I can remember, using their own language and

---

* See Chapter 12: Rituals and Enactments for more on Active Imagination.

references. I may interrupt myself as we go, asking if I have that particular detail right, or if I missed anything, asking for descriptions and associations (Wonder) to images and characters as I walk through the dream chronologically.

As you become more experienced, the Wonder and Reflection Keys are often intertwined, asking questions about the environment of the dream at the same time as reflecting the dreamer's language to them. But in the beginning, you may want to gather all your associations first (Wonder) and then restate the dream in sections, mirroring their own language and associations (Reflection). In the above example, you would say, "So you are buying a hotel, which you describe as a process of taking ownership of something that used to be temporary. Do I have that right?" And the dreamer might respond, "Yes! But I would add that I am also reluctant in the process." Helping this important detail to emerge sets you up to ask an artful question in the next Key of Relating.

When I retell the dream to the dreamer as I've heard it, using the associations and language they've shared with me, it has a dual purpose. First, it ensures that we both understand the perspective the dream is presenting. Second, hearing their own words and associations strung together often triggers an "aha!" moment for the dreamer. As I mentioned, this resonance will act as an anchor for the next two Keys. For example, Francis had two strong associations to her disease. This knowledge will act as the starting point for not only how the other symbols relate to each other but how the dream relates to her waking-life. If a dreamer and I still haven't found this sense of location, I will pivot and reflect other symbols back to the dreamer or return to the Wonder Key and ask for more associations before continuing. Reflecting someone else's dream takes time to master. The art is in learning to be as neutral as possible in the process of listening, holding your own projections back long enough to represent the dream as purely as it's been told to you.

This skill, learned in dreamwork, develops within us a

powerful capacity for empathy. Mirroring is the basis of diplo-macy and intimacy—it is what allows us to build trust and under-standing in relationships. More effective than giving advice or offering solutions, reflecting someone as they truly are is paradox-ically what allows them to step into their own potential. In being seen and heard deeply, the other can begin to stretch into new creative territory. Though you may be doing the mirroring, the wisdom comes from the depths of their own knowing. It reflects their unconscious attitudes in a non-threatening way. Instead of repressing or projecting these qualities, they are now given the opportunity to own or overcome them. Reflecting is the greatest service we can offer in drawing out a person's potential.

As helpful as it is to have another person mirroring for us, we can also engage this process on our own. Being self-reflective is what builds emotional intelligence. As we understand our own motivations, they can no longer govern us autonomously or behave destructively in our relationships. In reflecting on psyche's experience of events, we learn to live richer, more nuanced lives. We grow more perceptive, judicious, and empathetic with others. It enhances our creative thinking by adding diversity and depth to our one-sided perspectives, and brings our two worlds—symbolic and literal—into symbiosis, like two wings of a bird finally taking flight.

KEY 4: RELATING

Now that we have listened to the dream with Embodied Presence, opened a dialogue with the otherworld through genuine Wonder, and Reflected on what we've learned, it is time to Relate what's happening in our dream to what's going on for us in waking-life. There is almost always a relationship between our nighttime dreams and what's happening in the daytime. Occasionally a dream comes out of nowhere, but more often than not there is a direct correlation between our worlds that will reveal itself if we've successfully used the previous Keys. When we make that connection between the two realms, it gives us a sense of direction in the mythic unfolding of our lives. It may not answer the question "Which way should I go?" but by firmly locating us where we are, we may instinctively know what the next step should be.

Recall that metaphor provides a relational bridge between dream and waking worlds. In this way, metaphor is inherently connective in that it brings spirit and matter into relationship with each other. It's profound to consider that this primordial language serves as a form of joinery between the worlds. Embedded in the deepest structures of our own biology is this homeostatic impulse to connect our realities. In the Relating Key, we cross this kinship bridge. By seeking to understand how psyche experiences waking events, we begin to move out of our literal, rational perception of the world into meaning. If meaninglessness is the enduring belief that what we are going through isn't connected to or impacting anything else, then meaning is generated when we lay bare the web of pre-existing connections between our life and the archetypal realm.

Relating can happen spontaneously during previous Keys in the form of an "aha!" moment or when a deep resonance rings like a bell being struck. You will know you've correctly found the parallels between the two worlds when you experience that arc of release. Like a surge of energy that frees you from being bound solely to the temporal situation, tears may spring to your eyes in the process of working with the dream—as if a part of you that needed acknowledgement finally got the recognition it deserved. Relating can also happen when you're telling the dream to a friend. The simple act of sharing with a receptive listener can allow you to recognize the symbolic dimension of your own words and feelings as you speak them out loud for the first time.

If a spontaneous bridge doesn't appear, or if you're seeking connections for other symbols in your dream, there are a number of Relating questions that you can ponder. These questions are often crafted around three "R" words: relate, remind, or recognize. They always reiterate the descriptors from the dreamer's own associations, discovered in the Key of Wonder. For instance, we might ask the dreamer, "Can you *relate* to that dynamic that you described as 'frenzied and impatient?'"; "Do you *recognize* that feeling you described as 'relief after a long battle?'"; or "Does that treatment you described as 'a cold dismissal' *remind* you of anything you've experienced?" These questions almost always trigger an instant relationship to something in waking-life. When you're working with your own dream, you are looking for the same parallels between the language of your associations and inner or outer experiences during the day.

Here are a few general examples of Relating questions. When working with your own dream, simply swap out "you" for "I" or "me":

1. Does [name character], who you describe as (repeat description), remind you of anyone in waking-life?
2. Can you relate to [name character]? In what way are you similar/different from [name character]?
3. Does this setting, which you describe as [mirror description], remind you of anything in waking-life?
4. Does this [name action or dynamic] remind you of a dynamic you're navigating in waking-life?
5. Can you relate to feeling [name feeling] recently? Or when was the last time you felt [name feeling]?

Keeping in mind Francis' anchor, which was her strong association to her disease, here are some of the Relating questions and responses she journalled:

In what way can I relate to reluctantly taking permanent ownership of a temporary situation?

For years I thought I might be able to beat this disease or avoid the worst symptoms. But because I was experiencing more pain and muscle weakness, I saw my doctor yesterday and had an MRI and other tests; they confirmed the irreversible progression of my MS. I am no longer passing through like a traveller, but faced with having to accept the decline of my abilities.

Does this quandary of transitioning decommissioned spaces that were once used for gathering in groups remind me of anything?

Definitely. Before becoming ill, my career and personal life was full of public events. Now I have to say no to these invitations because I am physically unable to participate in them. It has left a giant hole in my life.

In the dream I describe how "a quiet, creative ally could make it work." Can I relate to those qualities?

Yes. I've always wanted to sculpt and write. Having such a quiet-and-spacious life is perhaps the only thing that would work with my condition.

I describe the roommate that takes up residence as an interloper who is bold, domineering, dynamic, and pushy. Do those qualities remind me of anything?

Yes, she reminds me of a character on a TV show I watched recently. Everyone regarded her as cool and savvy because she was an activist but she was always calling people out on their privileges in a mean way, making others feel inadequate. Now that I write this, this reminds of the invalidations I face when I begin to work with clay. I am constantly battling the shame of my own privileges, and the fear of not having anything relevant to offer.

Can I relate to it as a "relationship I haven't agreed to, but is happening anyway?"

Certainly. It feels automatic, like an inner bully that's taken up residence in my thoughts without my consent.

Do I recognize those qualities of the Vendor, who I described as "unprepared and out of his depth?"

I am imagining what the dream situation would be like from his perspective and selling the hotel feels a bit desperate. It reminds me of how many businesses in tourism collapsed during the pandemic because they were no longer viable. I think the Vendor wants to offload this hotel, like a bad investment. Making this transition from a busy public life to one that is quiet and painterly definitely brings up my fears around money. I do feel out of my depth and I am concerned that I'm not prepared for this transition.

In the dream, I try to assert boundaries but am criticised for not having a "nice and spiritual" persona. Does this remind me of anything?

This is exactly what I've been going through. Since I got sick, so many people in my community distanced themselves from me because I was open about my suffering. They kept expecting me to "feel better soon" even though MS is a degenerative disease, or they would try to fix me with suggestions like, "Have you tried yoga, acupuncture, reiki, gluten free diets, etc.?" I spent years trying all these suggestions, believing I could "heal naturally" but it only sped up the progression of the MS. After a while I started pushing back and asserting my boundaries by explaining that my disease was incurable, so it's unsupportive to keep suggesting I am not doing enough to heal myself. I ruffled a lot of feathers and lost a lot of friends who felt I wasn't the "nice and spiritual" person I used to be. It's true that my spirituality is having to undergo reno- vation, maturing to include grief, pain, and suffering as part of life. I feel like this dynamic of shunning these things is one I am trying to confront internally.

So you see, a great number of connections have been made for Francis as she moved from image to image, in the dream's chrono- logical order, to relate each of the symbols to her waking-life. Perhaps you can even feel her two worlds now layering to enhance each other, giving her physical life more dimension and her dream experience more context. The dream helped give a voice to her innermost feelings that were previously obscured even from her own view.

Once you have established relationships between your dream and waking-life, and feel you have a handle on what a dream is about, it's always a good idea to test your hypothesis out against the other elements in the dream. Does the setting make sense symbolically to your issue? Are there any unexplored facets in the dynamics at play? Does the ending of the dream present you with a solution? Is it an effective one?

If you aren't making any immediate connections to something happening in your waking-life, consider whether the dynamic is strictly an internal one. Just as Francis discovered her interloper was an unconscious judgement, it often happens that our dreams give form to internal complexes and dynamics. To give you another example, a woman came to me with incessant dreams of not being able to find a private toilet. She described herself in those dreams as feeling utterly self-conscious, as if she was always being watched and unable to find relief. But when I asked her if she related to that experience of "always being watched" she said no—she lived alone and rarely socialized. So we returned to her other associations and I asked her, "Where in your life do you feel 'utterly self-conscious?'" In a flood of recognition, she said she felt that way chronically. She described carrying around the judgements of her family and church, even in her most private moments. It generated a terrible anxiety in her from which she rarely found relief. Realizing that this crowd of onlookers were actually internal critics empowered her to begin asserting boundaries with those inner invalidations.

When two people are working on a dream together, you will both feel resonance when you're on the right track. When you've made a successful bridge, you will get a rush of feeling, glow of warmth, shivers, or a sense of awe at the genius of the dream. I often have the experience of everything falling into place, like finding a familiar constellation in the galaxy. And in Sophia's mysterious way, the dream often has medicine for both people. We are not only revealing bonds between waking and dreaming but fostering connections between the people who share them.

When we consciously participate with Sophia through dreamwork and other imaginal practices, we experience catalyzing movement within. By relating our temporal situation to the eternal truths of nature, we also inherit its maps and ways of going. New ways of approaching our predicaments move us out of our calcified attitudes. As Zwicky writes, "Metaphor is always an act of overcoming."[6] The skill we are developing in this part of the work is our relational capacity. Simply put, it is the ability to discover our life's relationship to the great ecology of things. It grows in us the capacity for holding multiple perspectives at once, a core competency for navigating complex and divisive times.

KEY 5: SYNTHESIS

We always want to feel deepened and energized at the end of a dreamwork session. While not all dreams provide us with rosy teachings, they always take us into the heart of something that is ready to be seen and healed. This readiness is inherently vitalizing because it catalyzes our growth when we follow it. Sometimes vitality in dreamwork looks like a big release of tension, a total shift in outlook, or a surge of healing emotions or ideas. Other times, vitality is as modest as a faint twinkle in a depression or a hairline crack in an old perspective. But it's essential to value these unassuming moments as the tiny triumphs that they are, because in giving them relevance, we guarantee their vigour.

Synthesis is about finding a new coherence from the dream-work process. In this Key, we gather everything we've learned in one place, giving special relevance to those supportive elements that generate new energy and commit to an enactment of the dream's prompting in our waking-lives. To Synthesize a dream, I use a three-step process. The first step is to retell the story of the dream in a connected chain of insights. The second is to discover from that story what the dream longs for. The third and final step is to come up with an action of some kind that puts the dream's longing into ritual, practice, or enactment of some kind.

The first step in Synthesis is to gather all your insights into one cohesive story so you can see how the energy is moving (or not moving) in the psyche. This exercise can help to clarify the overall mission of the dream, how you are attempting to achieve it, what blocks or impediments you are coming up against, and which way the energy wants to go next. At this point in the process, I try to focus on the central connections in the dream as discovered in the Relating Key rather than going back into the weeds with details.

To give an example of how I might string together a chain of insights from the Relating Key, let's return to Francis' dream. Upon reading her metaphors, I might say, "You are in the process of moving into a more permanent ownership of your disease. Of course you are reluctant, because to do so also means accepting all the losses you've sustained on every level: bodily, financially, socially, and spiritually. Some of these losses have left huge swaths of emptiness especially in your professional life and former community. But despite all of that, you are looking for a way to adapt and find a creative way forward. And you have a wonderful idea for how to make it work: a quiet and creative life. You summon this inner artist but instead are confronted with the interloper of invalidations that say you aren't artistic, talented, or relevant enough. It strikes me as quite archetypal to meet a shadowy gatekeeper just as you're entering the unknown creative depths. But what I love about your dream is that you are willing to bravely confront it. While it tries to convince you that you aren't being nice or spiritual enough, you are quite clear upon waking that your are shedding this old paradigm. You want to live a life and create from a place that is inclusive of suffering, grief, and pain."

So you'll notice that, with the exception of my comment about shadow as gatekeeper, everything in this Synthesis came out of Francis' own dreamwork. The language, insights, and connections are just gathered together to restore cohesion after the expansions generated by the previous Keys. Following the dream's own path, I am restating it chronologically, but instead of using the symbols to tell the story, I am using Francis' core insights from her Courtship process. You may also notice that I am affirming the validity of her feelings, such as reluctance and grief, and celebrating those moments of creativity, adaptiveness, bravery, and clarity.

To do this for yourself, I recommend starting by looking for any clues in the dream that suggest a new way of looking at your waking-life situation. I like to scan the dream for any healing or catalyzing moments or symbols in which the energy of the dream shifts, or tries to shift, as the dreamer attempts to realize their mission. These moments may appear like an opening or possibility, a new voice in the matter, a longing or desire for things to be different, an inkling of an idea, a mysterious power embodied by a figure or symbol, or even an unacknowledged feeling rising to the surface. Once you have these redemptive moments in mind, they behave as pivotal hinges—turning points—in the process of finding meaning.

The moment that gave Francis the most energy was this one

sentence: "I think the only way I can make this work is to find roommate who is a quiet artist." Indeed, it was this creative idea about how to repurpose her overwhelming emptiness that was essential in accepting the realities of her disease. I also thought the confrontation with the interloper (which ended with a harsh attack on the dreamer's character) was brave and full of vitality, so I chose to include it as a triumph of this dream. This is a good example of how vitality can take the form of a big release of tension, even if it's uncomfortable. Confronting these inner invalidations means that they can no longer operate without consent in Francis' unconscious. She forced that aspect to say out loud what it thought of her and in her conscious analysis, they were qualities she no longer aspired to. The confrontation was like drawing poison from a wound so she could begin to heal.

Incidentally, it often happens that insights continue to arise after the initial Synthesis process. The day after doing this work, Francis remembered a moment before the dream when she was working on a series of sculptures about her changing body and kept getting hounded by an inner voice that said her art wasn't original. She got so sick of it jamming up her thoughts that she actually spoke out loud to the invalidation and said, "Listen! How can I discover anything beautiful if you don't be quiet and give me some space to sculpt!?" She couldn't believe she'd forgotten this moment, which felt silly at the time but was remarkably effective. Now she could see how the dream replayed that exchange and gave form to those intrapsychic dynamics. She saw the hotel in a new way too, not just as an intellectual concept of "a space I'm reluctant to own" but as the literal space she was trying to occupy creatively every day as she put her hands on the clay.

In Francis' case, it was important for her to recognize the value of summoning that quiet, artistic nature. While it did constellate painful invalidations, that only speaks to its hidden power. Often a new attitude will threaten the old guard—the thing that keeps us stuck and is invested in maintaining its status in the psyche. Seeing it raise its hackles is a validation in and of itself that Francis is onto something more powerful.

If someone is wrestling with a particularly tricky decision in their life, at the end of a dreamwork session they often ask, "But what should I do?" It is important to remember that dreams rarely provide us with these kinds of black-and-white solutions. I think this is because all decisions are valid in that they ultimately lead to more life experience. Becoming aware of a dynamic is more than enough to change how we respond to it in the future. Given this perspective, the capacity to read and integrate the unseen dynamics in your life will strengthen your inner knowing and this is more potent than any situational bottom line. It is this unassailable capacity for Wisdom that will serve you on every decision threshold.

Keeping in the spirit of courtship, I prefer to reframe the question from "What should I do?" to "How can I serve the dream?" Every dream has a secret longing and to work well with a dream we must discover what that is. Longing is the vital impulse at the centre of every living being that inclines it to wholeness. Our job is to come into conversation with that desire, uncomfortable as it may be.

In the Sufi way of seeing it, longing is a divine inclination, drawing us toward the Beloved. Just as lover and beloved long to be in each other's arms, so too is it between us and the life that is meant for us. Like a plant growing toward the sun, longing is nature inclining us toward the light we need in order to be fruitful. But also, as Rumi writes, "that which you seek is seeking you." So longing is not only the quality of seeking reunion, but the sound of something in search of us: the calling homeward.

When I asked Francis what the secret longing was of her dream she said, "To claim that spaciousness as my own. To not be intimidated by the emptiness that is no longer filled with events and activities, but to truly embrace the opportunity I now have to create. Especially now that I know how to stand up to my inner bullies, I think the dream longs to make art that comes out of my experience with hardship."

Once you have discovered the secret longing of the dream during the courtship process, it is important to take a symbolic step in the direction of the dream's prompting. This might look like altering your own behaviour in a relationship dynamic, or taking a chance with your creativity, or simply enacting a small ritual that acknowledges the wisdom you've received. Dreams make the inner life substantial, giving our feelings and instincts dimensionality, colour, and form. Ritual is a way of feeding that which is nourishing us so that our living conversation with the holy in nature grows in strength and vocabulary.

Deciding on an enactment or ritual doesn't have to be anything elaborate. In fact, it's better if it is simple to accomplish so that you don't skip this step. I can't emphasize enough how powerful this part of the process is. This action will generate the most magical results in the form of colourful and potent dream responses, synchronicities erupting into waking-life, and various kinds of support for your new becoming. What's so awe-striking about these responses is that it's confirmation of Sophia acknowledging you, acknowledging her, remembering you. Your life has purpose. There is a way, and you're on it.

To give you a few examples of how we might create ritual, let's say you have a dream of a softball game where you can't move your legs, and the overwhelming pressure to hit a home run makes you feel stuck. Maybe your ritual response is to write out every small step in a manageable project so you can walk one "base" at a time. Your list helps you remember that follow-through is about putting one foot in front of the other which is more achievable than making a splashy home run.

I asked Francis to come up with a ritual or enactment to acknowledge the wisdom she'd received from her dream. She reported back, "It's a small-but-significant ritual that I don't look at email or social media in the morning anymore. Instead, I sit down to sketch or write and I feel the hugeness and wealth of the former hotel around me. I've noticed the negative voices have subsided for now and I've been extremely productive. Internally, I guess I'm defending that space as my own now."

One woman I worked with dreamed of bones buried in her yard. As we worked with the dream, it emerged that there was some ancestral healing that needed to be addressed in her life. As a ritual response to her dream, she planted a linden tree in the spot the dream had shown her. Every time she passed it and smelled its intoxicating blossoms, she remembered and honoured her ancestors. Another person dreamed of a sensual woman dressed in a Grecian blue dress. As he worked with the dream, it became clear that she was an emissary of his soul's deepest longing. To remember and keep her alive in his waking-life, he bought himself a scarf in the same colour and wore it everywhere he went.

Another way to give thanks for the dream you've been given is to create a dream altar. Simply find a space in your home where you have privacy and quiet. Using any surface—a mantlepiece, a window ledge, or a small table—begin by laying a lovely scarf or fabric. Then collect and arrange a few elements from the outdoors that are symbolic of the season you're in. For instance, winter greens (cedar, pine, and fir), colourful berries (holly, hawthorn, callicarpa), or pinecones. In summer, it might be a vase of wildflowers. These elements help to position your dreaming as occurring in the context of nature, enabling you to see how your inner cycles are unfolding within an ecosystem. Add a candle and a box of matches nearby so you can light the flame as you contemplate your own seasonal shifts.

If you already have an image or object that has come through your dreams, place it on your altar. If you are wanting to summon dreams about a certain question or longing you have in your life, start by articulating for yourself what you are most missing or aching for and find or create an object symbolic of that longing.

Don't be afraid to leave your altar empty until you find the right symbolic objects to include. Emptiness can act as a powerful invitation. Symbolic objects may be a feather you found on the day you woke up from a dream about an owl. Or it may be a printed or painted image of a mountain lion after you dreamt of caged lions. Or it may be simply a word, drawn on a piece of paper or painted on a stone. Try to remember that this is a living altar and it's best not to let it remain static and gather dust. You can keep it full of vitality by removing things when they no longer hold potency for you, or adding new offerings to it. Perhaps you gather something from your integrative dream walks, some fruit that wants to be there to remind you of your ripening, or a particularly beautiful leaf that taught you about release when it fell at your feet. Keep adding to the altar so that it is creating a living conversation with Wisdom.

The purpose of a dream altar is to continue the conversation with your dreams in daily life. If you carry those symbols and reminders with you throughout the day, it helps to stimulate your relationship with them. So spend a few moments every morning, lighting your candle and sitting at your altar, holding your dream in your mind's eye and letting it work on you. Pay attention to the ways your symbols change, offer new insights, or communicate with you through your body. As symbolic objects become obsolete to you, remove them from your altar.

Synthesis is a powerful skill set in life as well as dreamwork. It offers a layered way of gathering lessons learned, giving relevance to healing and supportive allies, and enacting new ways of advancing. It places our focus on the living edge of our own evolution. It shows us where we are bravely working to overcome the things that challenge and hinder us, even if it's in small steps. It also helps us to focus on what is supportive and what generates well-being in our lives. By giving those things gratitude, especially in physical ways, we are substantiating them. We are making them more apparent—which, like the sun shining on a small sprout, encourages their growth. Gratitude causes life's generosity to multiply as we seek it out.

* * *

As we conclude our courtship, it's helpful to acknowledge that there is always more to be done, always more we've forgotten, always more than we have the capacity yet to know. One of the greatest challenges in approaching dreams is to simply allow mystery to work upon us. In that way, dreaming is an echo of our relationship with the earth itself. There are certain questions that, as the poet David Whyte puts it, "have no right to go away."[7] There is a delicate alchemy brewing in our not-knowing that is essential to our becoming worthy of revelation. So if you are left with more questions than answers, allow them to work on you. Sleep on it, ask for a new dream, and leave room for your questions to ripen. We can always begin again, by remembering that which remembers us, like a conversation that deepens across our lifetime. Not only will this courtship bring meaning to our personal lives, it is also an act of restoring Sophia to the world.

CHAPTER 10

Poison is the Medicine

YOU WAKE UP WITH A START. Your heart is pounding and you're covered in sweat. Adrenaline is racing through your veins. As you will yourself to breathe normally again, you're flooded with relief that whatever horrific thing was happening in your dream isn't really real. But it feels real to your body and you're afraid to go back to sleep. Part of you doesn't trust your dreams because how could they put you in that situation? What good could possibly come out of experiencing that horror? How do you know it won't happen again? You'll do just about anything to rid your mind of the terrifying and repulsive things you experienced, but another part of you is unable to look away. The dream haunts you the next day (or even for weeks afterwards), but you can't talk to anyone about it because you feel ashamed. You think there must be something seriously wrong with you to have conjured up this ugly, scary scenario.

At some point in our lives, we've all had terrifying nightmares. We've all dreamed of violent, cruel, and repulsive things, but rarely do we talk about this in the open. We feel shame and fear that others won't understand. It's true—most people don't know how to tend to the dark power of a nightmare. But the truth is, these dreams are radical agents of change. The dream we most want to hide, run away from, or bury deep in the soil of our forgetting is the one with the most potential to heal. If we are brave enough to metabolize it through shadow work, there is always a medicine in the poison.

For those who experience chronic nightmares, dreaming can feel almost adversarial. If you wake up day after day not feeling rested because your dreams have been full of anxiety, violence, and fear, it is understandable that you might begin to believe they are working against you. Some people even develop insomnia because they are afraid of going to sleep only to have another bad dream. So it can be extremely liberating to learn that your dreams are always in service to your healing, even if they need to raise the volume to get your attention.

When every instinct in our body wants to push the dream away, to shake off the terrible imagery, it feels counterintuitive that these awful nightmares would be supportive or healing in any way. But it's helpful to think of a nightmare like a wound that is trying to heal. At first the wound becomes red and swollen as our body pushes the infection or debris to the surface. Then there is a weeping, which cleanses the wound. Only after that can new tissue regenerate. In this metaphor, the wound may have occurred long ago but something in the present has allowed it to finally break through the surface of your unconscious in the form of a nightmare. Maybe the conditions of your life have become supportive enough to meet with this challenge, or perhaps something has been put in your path to draw out the old pain but the very fact that you have been startled from sleep to face this difficulty is a validation of your readiness to heal.

Instead of pushing them away, it's important to cultivate a small measure of curiosity toward troubling dreams. By giving form to our turmoil, our dreams are actually doing us a service. Instead of leaving us to experience indistinguishable waves of emotion and other physiological disturbances, our dreams show us the face of our complexes for the first time. By personifying them, our dreams help us to look directly at what may be trying to undermine us. Though it is rarely comfortable to see what destructive characters live in our psyches, this begins the process of being able to differentiate between what is you and what is not you. This is the first step of shadow work. From there, you can begin to confront those forces that are hindering you and reclaim the power that is clustered in the fear they command. With enough practice, you can eventually free up that energy for more creative and conscious use.

In *Belonging*, I wrote a chapter called "The Dark Guests" about the importance of inhabiting the full spectrum of our feelings and experiences.[1] The title was inspired by the thirteenth-century Sufi poet Rumi, who described being human as a guest house upon whose doorstep all sorts of characters arrive: sometimes joy, other times meanness, depression, sorrow, violence, shame, etc. Though we are taught to distance ourselves from our so-called negative emotions and dreams, they are foundational to creating belonging in our lives. As Rumi advises, we should invite them in because they've been sent as guides from beyond.

I love the guest house as a metaphor for dreamwork. If we want those miraculous, numinous dreams, we have to pass through the gates that are guarded by our shadows. Though our encounters with them are often humbling and deflating, they tend to conceal a trove of wisdom and energy that we can only claim once we've faced them. But our tendency to distance ourselves from what feels weird, unfamiliar, unlikeable, or unacceptable seems to be human nature. As a result, there are two versions of us: the one we display in the open, and the other who comes out under the cover of darkness. Jung described these split-apart aspects as ego and shadow.

Colloquially, we use the word "ego" to describe a person's pride or arrogance but it's just the Latin word for "I." The ego is really the conscious hub of our mind. It is where we organize our identity, thoughts, and beliefs, and it is where we become aware of our feelings, intuitions, and sensations. It's the executive part of every individual that mediates between ourselves and the world around us. If someone is egotistical, it usually means they haven't ventured far out of their own perspective yet, or haven't begun to make friends with their shadow.

From the ego, we create a persona to help display our ideals and values to others. From the Latin, meaning mask or character, our "persona" is like a set of clothes we wear to present an image to the world. That image may be to look cool, generous, fit, or productive. Or it may be to come across as successful, likeable, or witty. A persona may be preoccupied with looking respectable or being seen as bold, rebellious, cynical, and so on. Sometimes we even have several masks to switch out for different situations. One function of the mask is to conceal that which is deemed inappropriate or unacceptable in ourselves and in social life. The real trouble begins when we start conflating our persona with the true self, believing the mask that we wear is our real face.

Underneath the mask we hide our shortcomings, dislikes, fears, and neuroses ... but also the extent of our vibrancy, genius, and latent potential. Jung called this concealed part of ourselves the shadow. The shadow is all that we unconsciously reject in others and within, the biases we overlook, that which we devalue, and everything we have yet to discover in ourselves. Aptly named because it follows us around everywhere we go, the shadow is as indistinct to us as darkness. We don't know what we don't know. But as ephemeral as it may seem, the shadow is substantial. It is the total accumulation of what we, our families, churches, schools, and culture at large shun, dismiss, and ignore. And there is only so long the shadow will tolerate living in exile.

This split between persona and shadow is chillingly illustrated in the classic novel *The Strange Case of Dr. Jekyll and Mr. Hyde.*[2] During the day, the mild-mannered and upstanding Dr. Jekyll is a pillar of his community. But in secret, he indulges in unnamed vices, over which he suffers great shame. So Jekyll develops a serum that allows him to act out his impulses without detection. Under its influence, he becomes Mr. Hyde, a shadowy figure who terrorizes London with acts of violence. One day, Jekyll runs out of serum and vows to give up Hyde completely but the shadow refuses to be caged and begins to act autonomously. Eventually, Jekyll loses all control of the transformations and only Hyde remains to face his crimes.

While most people's shadow selves are more benign than Dr. Jekyll's, the story offers a powerful illustration of how the failure to recognize and integrate one's shadow can result in terrible internal strife and, when acted out, can have devastating consequences. The unaddressed shadow is at the root of most interpersonal conflicts. It is also what fuels prejudice, wars, and inequality in the world.

The rejected aspects of ourselves don't cease to exist when we try to rise above them, they just express themselves in thwarted and indirect ways. With all the force they gathered in exclusion, the estranged "inner others" never stop seeking to re-belong with us. When they can't reach us through our dreams, they begin to manifest as conflict in our relationships, friction in the workplace, and discord between groups and even states. When we aren't yet ready to admit that we possess these shadowy tendencies, we see them more readily in the people who aggravate, disgust, and annoy us. But shadow can also turn its harm inward and take the form of chronic self-loathing and criticism, anxiety, or depression. Entrenched shadow can even result in illness or other crises. We can be grateful for nightmares because they offer us a safe place in which to meet our shadow self before it wreaks too much havoc.

HOW SHADOW FORMS

Learning to work with the shadow figures in our dreams begins with understanding how this pernicious part of our nature develops. The shadow accumulates at three levels: personal, cultural, and ancestral. All three levels are connected and indivisible but it helps to distinguish them so we can acknowledge the scale of challenges and limitations we face in this work.

The personal shadow usually begins forming in the family home where we are taught overtly or indirectly to reject parts of ourselves and others. It's in those formative years when we first learn what is bad and good, what is acceptable behaviour, and what is off limits (or even considered dangerous). Every home has a unique culture that celebrates and encourages certain traits and accomplishments and devalues others. For example, in one person's family, a strong work ethic may have been the most-prized characteristic while an artistic or sensitive nature might have been ridiculed or criticized. In order to maintain a sense of belonging in our family of origin, most of us develop qualities we know will be praised and distance ourselves from those traits that might make us a target. Even if those attributes are central to who we are, if they continue to live in exile, in the shadows of our consciousness, they can eventually become like strangers to us. These rejected, disowned, and unexplored aspects of ourselves live on in what the poet Robert Bly evocatively describes as the "long, black bag we drag behind us."[3]

So if someone tells you in early life that little boys don't cry, showing weakness goes into the bag. If you heard that expressing sexuality is sinful, into the bag it goes. If you learn that creativity is for the lazy and unproductive, your artistic nature goes in the bag. By the time you reach adulthood, you already have a giant, invisible sack that is weighing you down and demanding in nefarious ways to be unpacked.

Sometimes shadow also develops in reverse, where the young person rebels against the parent's values to become their opposite, but doing so enshadows the positive aspect of those traits. For example, if you were raised by an adult who was unreliable, you might become hyper-responsible as a way of creating stability in your life. But shadow always thrives in those places that we neglect. In being too organized, you might then struggle with spontaneity and letting loose. The problem with developing any one-sided bias, in that even a small measure of its devalued shadow traits might be essential to your healthy development.

Trauma is a huge contributor to creating personal shadow because psyche will splinter off our most difficult experiences to help us survive them. We may carry harmful judgements against ourselves as a learned response from being harmed and even small triggers can flare up a defensive response to these core wounds. When it comes to working with traumatic dreams, which tend to replay the violations you sustained, it's always best to work with a trusted therapist who can create a container of safety for you to enter these dangerous-feeling places. So much of the trauma we carry as individuals also stems from cultural shadow.

The cultural shadow is harder to overcome because its values are reinforced in the systems that comprise our daily lives. If the personal shadow is hard to see because it lives in our blind spots, the cultural shadow is that much harder because its values are so broadly accepted and built into our societal infrastructure. Everything the culture rejects and condemns, including the events of its own historical past, is stored in our collective unconscious. Racism, sexism, ableism, ageism, and homophobia are just a few examples of what it looks like when shadow accumulates at the level of culture. Everyone who doesn't fall into its narrow band of what is acceptable is "othered" into the shadows, where they are likely to be marginalized and persecuted. Each of us unconsciously internalizes some degree of that shadow because we are embedded in, conditioned by, and dependent on the culture. In this way, shadow work is inherently rebellious. We each have within our power the ability to dismantle and overcome these biases in ourselves which, combined with many others' efforts, can change collective consciousness.

The untended cultural shadow can also metastasize through

generations. The old wounds, unmetabolized grief, rage, and legacies of power over others are all part of our ancestral shadow. While we receive many priceless legacies from our ancestors, we also inherit unresolved trauma. We have for some time understood that children must work out their parents' unintegrated shadow, but we now know through the field of epigenetics that trauma can be passed down through generations. Holocaust survivors, for instance, sustained unthinkable violence and cultural loss in the Nazi genocide of Jews in World War II. This trauma was too great to process by a single generation, so it persists in the lives of survivors' children and grandchildren, manifesting as illness, anxiety, depression, and addiction. While our ancestors' memories may not be directly accessible to us, their trauma expresses itself in our genetic and psychic make-up.

To understand how ancestral shadow manifests in your life, it's helpful to learn about your family's history and culture of origin so that you can grapple with the context in which those wounds originally formed. Without context, there is a danger in believing the effects of trauma and the inheritance of resilience began with you alone. While we can begin to address these complex wounds in the personal psyche, it's essential for shadow to also be addressed at the societal level. An individual can never heal so long as they are forced to keep living within a context of racial and gender violence, poverty, poor medical care, and other barriers to peaceful living and livelihood.

Whether personal, cultural, or ancestral, the disowned and shunned aspects of the shadow self are like strangers to us. They live beyond the fringes of our consciousness where they grow increasingly agitated and destructive, like calls for help that have gone unanswered for too long. Shadow has a way of possessing the individual, causing them to act out in uncontrollable and destructive ways—like the man who becomes as violent to his child as his father was to him because he's never healed the underlying powerlessness he felt as a small person. Or the person who procrastinates because they are deeply afraid of failing, only to miss out on opportunities for success. A woman who was taught to be accommodating might have a hard time asserting boundaries, so she seethes with irritability instead. If someone was made to believe they didn't have any talent, their shadow might be jealous or critical toward a friend who is succeeding in a way they wish they could.

Shadow is inevitable and one of the first places it manifests is in violent, disturbing, humiliating, or sad dreams. But we can learn to appreciate these terrible dreams because they show us exactly what we've been dragging behind us in the long, black bag. They give form to that which has been weighing us down, taking the wheel of our lives, and homogenizing our unique beauty. The very fact that these unwelcome guests are showing up at your doorstep means they are ready to come to consciousness. They are ready to be seen. They're ready to release their power to you. In this way, the most tyrannical, mean-spirited, invalidating, and shameful dreams can become our greatest and most important allies.

The word "heal" is from the Old English *hælan*, which literally means "to make whole." In the Dreaming Way, we are not trying to get rid of the shadow. We are learning to accept and show compassion for all our parts.

I worked with a wonderful woman named Molly. She suffered from social anxiety so severe that she had been hospitalized for several months, forcing her to leave college before graduating. After that, she went home to live with her parents for several years until she got married in her mid-twenties. Once she moved in with her husband, she was plagued with a number of health issues that prevented her from leaving the house. She began to have so many upsetting dreams that she was growing afraid to fall asleep. When she reached out to me, she was desperate for help and wanted to understand what her dreams were trying to tell her.

Molly was beside herself with shame to share the first dream she brought, but I encouraged her to share it and promised I wouldn't judge her. She dreamed a simple but shocking scene in which she was giving oral sex to an abandoned baby boy. She said he was turning blue and she instinctively thought the act would save him. I asked her if she felt shame in the dream itself and she said no—it was only when she woke up that she felt embarrassed and repulsed. Of course this image would upset anyone, but I reassured her that psyche is purposive and dreams about sex always have deeper symbolic meaning.

As we worked with the metaphor, Molly came to see how the baby was an aspect of her own nature that had been abandoned. Through her long withdrawal from the world, she watched her peers go on to have careers and make accomplishments, all of which was crushing to her confidence. Her own active side had been neglected for so long that, like the baby, it felt on the brink of death. She had sunk into a prolonged depression that drove her to think often of suicide. Molly described how afraid she was in the dream that the baby might die but something in her instinctively wanted to protect it and, as she kissed it, its skin began to turn pink again.

In women's dreams, the active/Yang side of our nature tends to show up in dreams as the masculine archetype. Like the dream-baby, Molly's inner masculine had never had a chance to mature but the dream put her in touch with her compassion for that side of her life. The symbol of fellatio in this context was about a deep longing to integrate the young masculine, to renew its life force. What began for Molly as a terrifying and shameful dream became a healing image of resuscitation and compassion. It inspired her over the next couple of years to get back into the world, set manageable goals for herself again, and move with nurturing discipline toward them.

It can take decades to learn who we really are in our totality, partly because we are always becoming new people. Like Molly, we outgrow versions of ourselves and must let the previous version go, so that we can step into new ranges of becoming. That means undergoing initiations at various thresholds in our lives where we are forced to dismantle the persona we've worked so hard to construct—to look in the shadows lurking behind our bright performances to see what is pulling our strings so we can reclaim that energy for new endeavours.

One of those first big transitions is in puberty when we begin to disidentify with family and discover what we're made of. Then there is the transition into adulthood, when many young people graduate and step into a career, start a family, and take on responsibility for the first time. Another strikes in what astrologers call our first Saturn Return (around age 28–33), when we must orient ourselves not by society's standards but on our soul's true path. Around midlife there is another big threshold, when we are asked to turn our attention away from the expectations of the outer world to more firmly stand in our power. Finally coming into elderhood, we begin facing mortality and big, existential questions. It's when we are asked to offer wisdom and guidance to others, to become a shelter where they can take refuge. But there are many unnamed transitions between each of these big chapters. There are times when we have to let go, in big and small ways, of an outdated way of life. These moments are often experienced as failure, defeat, and loss to the ego, but they are signs of the self coming into realization.

It takes real courage to accept these calls to change and not everyone has the inner and outer resources to do so. This is in large part due to a failure of the culture to provide acknowledgement, support, and ritual around big thresholds, making them so much harder to go through alone. But when we don't do the work to support the emergence of the Self from behind its armour, the shadow is forced to manifest in more disruptive ways to make itself known.

PROJECTIONS AND INTROJECTIONS

If we don't do the work to reflect on our shadow, the world becomes that mirror instead. We become fixated on the problems and faults of others, or the world at large, instead of looking at our own hindrances and shortcomings. This is what Freud first referred to as projection, when those shadow aspects we've splintered off are attributed to others. Projection is when we see the shadow self in others before we can see it in ourselves. This may look like being unreasonably irritated by, disapproving of, or repulsed by a person or group of people we dislike. We might find ourselves making accusations about others' behaviour but just can't see that we are doing the same thing. As an example, imagine a man who constantly complains that his father-in-law is controlling but can't see that he's just as brutish with his own son.

Fascinatingly, projection uses the same mechanism as empathy; it allows us to connect our own experience to that of another. But when it comes to shadow, projection behaves a bit more like psyche's defence mechanism. When the ego is afraid or in denial of its shadow qualities and impulses, it projects them onto others. The bully who attacks weaker or differently-presenting people is really trying to stamp out what he perceives as his own difference and weakness. The person who has a hard time talking about uncomfortable feelings habitually asks others, "What's wrong?" Someone who is chronically self-critical perceives others as criticizing them. Or someone who puts constant pressure on themselves to be productive judges others for being lazy or incompetent.

On the flipside, projection can also look like over-admiring others, even to the point of jealousy, when the other is successful in a way we yearn to be. We project "positive shadow" onto others because we aren't ready to acknowledge those attributes in ourselves. Perhaps you dream about a colleague who is rising through the ranks with great success. He may be symbolic of a capable part of yourself that holds the same potential. But if you're unable to recognize that star quality in yourself, you may see that colleague as superhuman or out of your league. Similarly, you may dream of your therapist as an infinitely kind and nurturing mother figure until you are able to give yourself the same unconditional love. Unlike negative shadow dreams, or nightmares, dreams of positive shadow often cast larger-than-life characters like gurus, authorities, celebrities, or even extremely tall people who symbolically *look down* on us. Projection doesn't mean that the other doesn't possess those attributes in actuality— only that they have just the right hook to activate our own shadow.

In his work on synchronicity, Jung shows how unaddressed shadow can also manifest in the physical world through crisis events like illness, accidents, and relationship conflicts. For this reason, when shadow gathers at the collective level it is arguably the most dangerous. When there is enough unmetabolized shadow in a culture, it can result in catastrophes such as ecocide and war. Shadow projection can have a devastating impact when combined with power and charismatic leadership. Hitler was able to rise to power by tapping the collective shadow of the German people, legitimizing a genocidal hatred of the Jews.

Collective projection is why we see so much corruption in religious institutions and spiritual communities. Any social system that observes a one-sided fundamentalism or moral and religious righteousness will cast a profound shadow. You can recognize these groups by how their structure is hierarchical and dogmatic, how they demand adherence to strict principles, or if the rhetoric focuses on ascension and purity. Any system of thought that denies the existence of shadow or claims to rise above evil and suffering is in a practice of repression and projection. These groups reject evolution and diversity in their traditions and will often increase control when they feel threatened by change. Anywhere the messy stuff of being alive is supplanted by a blissed-out image of goodness, you can be sure the shadow is coiled in hiding.

When we learn to work with shadow, projection serves an essential and important function. It is the first-and-prerequisite step to integrating split-off aspects back into our lives. One way to spot our unconscious projections is when we revile or admire someone in mythic proportions. There is usually some seed of truth that allows the projection to attach itself to the other, but it is our own shadow that casts them in the extreme. We may find ourselves obsessed with them, unable to drop whatever our gripe may be. Projections are helpful in that they allow us to first see the shadow outside of ourselves before we recognize it within. As Rumi's beloved teacher Shams Tabrizi taught, "We can't find the truth only listening to our own voice's echo. We can find ourselves only in someone's mirror."[4] As much as we need others to support and encourage the best in us, we need conflict in relationships to see our shadow selves more clearly. The next work, however, is in pulling back those projections to integrate the unacknowledged qualities in the self.

WITHDRAWING PROJECTIONS

In order to withdraw projections, we must go through what Marie Louise von Franz outlines as a five-stage process.[5] In the first stage, you believe the projection is real; you experience your unconscious projection as an outer fact. A perfect example of this is falling in love at first sight. Without knowing much about the other, you somehow believe them to be your ideal partner on every level. But in the second stage, you begin to notice chips in the armour, differences between your projection and the outer reality. You might see red flags or start experiencing conflicts when the other person doesn't behave as you expect them to. So many relationships end here, each going their separate ways, only to project their ideal onto a new, unsuspecting partner.

But if both people have the courage to move into the third stage, there is an opportunity for endless depth together. This is when you acknowledge the discrepancies you are seeing and begin to differentiate between what you're projecting and what is objectively real. Sometimes called the end of the honeymoon phase, this is when you see and accept your partner for who they are and not just who you want them to be. As an example, you might expect your husband to be strong all the time if you have an internalized image of masculinity as unflappable. So when he has an emotional breakdown, you may feel triggered about the veracity of his manhood. The task of this stage is to differentiate between the concrete reality and the image you are holding inside. Whether this happens through self-reflection or openly in the relationship process, it is like looking into a mirror to see your inner other for the first time.

In the fourth stage, you take responsibility for having projected your shadow. This is always humbling, because you must admit to yourself that which you'd rather not. In the example above, you would have to face how you've been carrying a heavily gendered notion of masculinity into your relationship. This process is humbling in the best sense of the word. You can now see things as their true size, neither enhanced or diminished by your projection. This softens the defences in you; it is what allows healing to begin.

Finally, in the fifth stage, you search internally for the origins of your projection. Maybe your own father concealed his vulnerabilities, which left your mother to do all the emotional heavy lifting for the family. You can now recognize this same pattern in your own relationships. You realize that withdrawing the projection of an impervious masculine will not only allow your partner to have his full spectrum of emotional diversity but gives you access to all those qualities you thought belonged only to men. Knowing where the shadow takes root is a kind of re-collecting, both in the sense of remembering and in gathering those precious shards that have been split off from you.

Whether it allows you to touch a hidden grief, dissolve some calcified trauma, or reclaim qualities you didn't believe you could embody, withdrawing a projection is always energizing. It also releases the other person from your projection. It allows them to be seen as they are and not as you wish they were (or weren't). Though it is often a painful process, the redemption of shadow generates tremendous creativity that is necessary for growth in long-term relationships. Marion Woodman once said that she and her husband Ross had three distinct marriages as they integrated their projections to become new people. "I saw my husband without projection for the first time," she recounted, "after we'd been married twenty-five years."[6]

It's also possible to be the target of someone else's projection. To describe this phenomenon, Von Franz used the analogy of the arrow found in many old myths, most recognizable as Cupid's weapon of choice. She wrote, "One of the oldest ways of symbolizing projection is by means of projectiles, especially the magic arrow or shot that harms other people."[7] She explains how when one becomes the target of another person's negative projection, "one often experiences that hatred almost physically as a projectile."[8] Most people can relate to feeling the impact of a mean-spirited comment fired in your direction. The arrows may only be words but the body responds as if it had physical impact. You may even dream of being shot, or having darts thrown at you.

If that person isn't aware or concerned with withdrawing their projection, it is up to you to pull out the barb on your own. This generally isn't an issue unless on some level you believe the falseness to be true. Even when you know better intellectually, if the projection matches a vulnerability in your own psyche, the barb will stick. In psychoanalysis, adopting a projection is called introjection. It's when you identify so strongly with another person, or what they're saying, that you lose the ability to discern between their voice and your own.

Introjection happens most commonly in early development

when we adopt the ideas of our parents and other influential people in our lives. If those ideas are positive, coming from a parent who is compassionate, generous, and kind, then introjection can reinforce a healthy self-image. But if you've been exposed to negative parenting, with enough reinforcement you will also internalize their judgements, beliefs, or ideologies without running them through the filter of your own critical thinking or integrity. Adopting someone else's projection as your own is like taking on someone else's shadow as your own. It might sound like an inner voice that repeats things like "I'm doomed to fail" or "I am irresponsible" or "I'm not very smart."

Like characters in fairy tales, we can fall under the dark spells or enchantments of those more powerful than us. So if your father repeatedly told you you were incompetent, you might harbour a secret conviction that you aren't as capable as other people. Even when you work hard to overcome that internal block, the moment someone projects incompetence onto you, it will trigger the original complex, causing you to believe it to be true. You may even shy away from opportunities out of the inherited fear of your own failure.

To break these spells, you must first become aware of them. With the help of your dreams, you can expose the narratives that are operating compulsively in your life and bring consciousness into the places they are keeping you trapped or stuck. While we can't get rid of our complexes, we can learn to recognize them. And in doing so, we gain the presence of mind to adopt a counter narrative.

A young man I worked with named Matthew had a recurring dream of being in jail, punished for something that was always vague or inconsequential in the dream. In the course of dreamwork, it came out that he thought of himself as irresponsible. But nothing in his life proved that to be true. So I asked him where he got the idea that he was blameworthy. He said, "My whole family always says I'm the irresponsible one." Starting around the age of nine, Matthew had memories of being shamed by his father in front of the rest of his family for being unreliable. Though he couldn't think of any concrete examples to have earned that reputation, his father repeatedly told him he was untrustworthy. He'd internalized his father's distorted projection and believed it to be true his whole life. He always felt at some deep level that he was bad and had to make up for something he was guilty of. He said he couldn't even trust himself.

After having worked with Matthew for some time, I was able to reflect back to him all the ways in which he was acting responsibly in his life, more so even than his peers. One day, I challenged him to find any evidence that the introjection was factual but he was unable to anything to corrorborate these negative ideas. It was like a spell was broken that day, having spat out the poisoned apple of inherited shadow, and he was able to see clearly how the judgements he carried all his life belonged squarely with his father's own shadow.

ENCOUNTERING THE INNER OTHER

Paradoxically, the things we most want to hide are also the things we long to reveal. Like the tornado that sweeps Dorothy Gale out of Kansas and into the Land of Oz, the shadow can take us on an odyssey that is both scary and necessary to our psychological growth and maturity. While we may not be conscious of wanting change, sometimes change is what we need. A storm may leave your garden full of debris to be cleaned up but it also sows seeds for the next season. So too can shadow introduce a generative element into a stale or outdated situation. While these shadow storms are inevitable, we can minimize their destructive nature by entering into a willing relationship with our inner others.

Shadow work is less a rational process than it is an encounter. The word "encounter" is vastly different from an ordinary "meeting." Not only is an encounter unexpected, but within it an embodied exchange takes place. Two beings come abruptly nose to nose and, if they are able to hold the tension between them, a transaction of unique energies is exchanged. The dark figures in our dreams may not be friendly or inviting, but that's only because they've been forced into displacement for so long that they've grown ornery. What they really crave is our attention. More than anything they want to be known, which is why they've raised their hackles to be heard. If we are successful in discovering what they have to teach us, a transfer of power takes place. The energy it once took to keep the shadow hidden is released in the encounter and we feel the buoyancy of reclaimed knowing that we can be more wholly ourselves.

The process of naming and accepting our dark guests may involve dreamwork, ritual, creativity, and the use of active imagination—but integration of a shadow aspect is rarely completed within a single dreamwork session. Often these figures have to appear in multiple dream disguises to get us to recognize their pattern in our lives, helping us to become conscious of the moments in waking-life where the shadow is active.

For instance, a person who discovers a dream figure symbolic of their combativeness will need to grow aware of waking moments where they unconsciously switch into fight mode. This is a precursor to actually changing their behaviour. The dreamwork encounter is just the first stage in the process—it's when we can see for the first time how that hidden part of ourselves operates, out in the open. It's no longer repressed in a generalized anxiety, depression, or fear, but emerges as a figure or image with a shape. Then we have to make it conscious in waking-life so it can no longer operate without our consent. We recognise its energy, words, or attitude in our own behaviour. With enough practice, we grow familiar with and sometimes even affectionate toward our shadows. That said, it's not always appropriate to befriend all shadow figures. Some are downright antagonistic. Just as in life, any character that is hurting us or causing someone else harm should not be allowed to keep doing so. We may need to confront them with our own centre of power to stand them down. If we try to override our boundaries, rushing to accept what we don't understand, we may lose the opportunity to get in touch with a necessary anger, grief, or edginess that we've been missing.

When we make an authentic encounter with the shadow figures in our dreams, the result is a bestowal of meaning. We learn something about ourselves in the exchange that is substantiating. It allows us to accept more of who we are, flaws and all. But it is also differentiating in that we see ourselves in contrast to the other—the encounter also shows us who we are not.

Jaguar Encounter: Danielle's Dream

I am hiking in the mountains when I come face to face with a jaguar. My heart is pounding and I feel frozen in its dark, powerful gaze. I am terrified and unable to move. Just in the nick of time, I wake up to discover it was just a dream.

Before we began to work on this dream, Danielle shared with me that she looked up "jaguar" in a book of animal totems and the entry said, "Jaguar is a symbol of a powerful, strong, warrior." She was delighted by this and took the dream to mean she was meeting a part of herself that was a powerful warrior. While the totem book wasn't entirely wrong, it also wasn't entirely right. To make a true encounter with a shadow figure, we must be willing to go below the superficial layer of an image and enter into our body's physical and emotional responses, both within the dream and upon reflection.

I asked Danielle to inhabit the dream again, especially focusing on her feelings and bodily sensations. She said her predominant feeling was fear that made her heart pound, her breathing shallow, and her body feel otherwise paralyzed. I asked her when she'd last felt a similar cluster of feelings in waking-life, she immediately remembered an interaction she had with an older woman the day before the dream. "I was standing in line at a grocery store and was a bit distracted, looking at my phone, so I didn't see that it was my turn to approach the cashier. This cranky woman behind me said, 'You gonna wait for an invitation, princess?' It wasn't really a big deal, but my body got really upset and I felt frozen and unable to respond. I kept perseverating all day, replaying the moment back in mind, wishing I'd told her off." When I asked Danielle if she generally had a hard time expressing herself in conflict, she explained that this wasn't an unfamiliar feeling and went on to tell me how often she felt frozen with fear as a child when her mother was in a rage.

I asked her to then take a moment to play a little imaginative game with me and retell the dream from Jaguar's perspective. As she inhabited Jaguar, she described feeling powerful and territorial in her body. She said she "didn't like people encroaching on her domain." As Jaguar, she said she wanted to bite them with her sharp teeth or at least "take a good swipe at them." Coming back into her own perspective, I asked Danielle if she ever felt territorial, as if others were encroaching on her domain. She said she definitely felt that way in the grocery store, as if she was being shamed for taking up her rightful space. She related to the Jaguar through the surge of rage in that moment but remained silent instead of telling the cranky lady to back off.

Each of these layers of association are relevant to Danielle's dream: the trigger from the day before, when she perceived a Jaguar-like quality in the cranky woman and felt frozen; the childhood memory showing her the root of that dynamic with her mother's anger; and the somatic experience of inhabiting Jaguar. Each association helped reconnect the disembodied relationship to her own anger. While there certainly is power and strength in inhabiting the Jaguar archetype, it also has a destructive side and can't be safely embodied without first bringing its shadow qualities to consciousness.

This was the beginning of Danielle's process of learning how to give voice to her own anger. She needed to understand the complex created in childhood to do this. She unconsciously believed that anger was intrinsically damaging because her mother had used rage to control her and the rest of Danielle's family. Knowing how destructive it could be, she was unwilling to access any of its value and power. Her child-self believed her world would fall apart if she stood up to her mother. This was well-founded because when anyone confronted her, it made things much worse in the home—sometimes for days or weeks at a time. Danielle needed to acknowledge what she suffered as a young person, starting with how helpless and vulnerable she felt around the vicious power of her mother's rage. Danielle had developed an inverse persona as someone who was accommodating and compassionate—even when that wasn't her honest truth. She needed to become aware that suppressing her own anger was causing her inward harm, like anxiously perseverating for hours or days, and building resentment in her relationships.

Danielle began to practise asserting her boundaries in her relationships over the following months. It wasn't easy because her friends and family had come to expect her to be accommodating but she kept with the practice and eventually found that she was able to express her dislikes and disagreements without the world falling apart. Eventually, when anger bubbled up in her, she saw it not as something terrifying but extremely powerful and intelligent. Rather than using it in a harmful way (like her mother did), she took time alone to understand what the anger needed to say and then expressed it with authority and precision.

In the encounter with Jaguar, Danielle learned to become more substantial in herself, bringing those outcast traits back into belonging in her body and her life. But she also learned that she wasn't purely Jaguar. Unlike a wild, instinctual creature, she could use the power of her anger consciously. She began to have many dreams of wild cats. Rather than fear, she felt awe and exhilaration in their presence. Once she even trusted a lion to come close enough to sniff and nuzzle her and though she felt its over-whelming power, it was also gentle because they now shared trust in one another. There is the bestowal of meaning that comes from making an embodied encounter with the shadow. As Jung famously wrote, "One does not become enlightened by imagining figures of light, but by making the darkness conscious."[9]

Shadow work is the basis of all psychic integration—and the absence of this critical work is at the root of the world's greatest conflicts. The thing about dreamwork is that it isn't just an under-taking for one's personal growth; it is the training ground on which we learn to consciously evolve as a species. There is a symmetry between the aptitudes we develop from working with dreams and the competence we carry in the world. As we develop a curiosity toward our inner community, we feel greater solidarity with outer others. As we learn to turn toward the darkness, instead of running from it, we get to see how moving through conflict can deepen our relationships and generate wisdom. Can you imagine a society that entered consciously into conflict, knowing that if the tension between opposing perspectives was held long enough a middle way could be found?

When you dream of a shadow figure, whether despicable or admirable, consider journaling about their most pronounced qual-ities, as we do with all characters. But then reflect on that list to see if any of those qualities also describe *you*. Does the shadowy other possess attributes that you habitually struggle with in rela-tionship with others? Or, on the flipside, do they possess strengths that you're reluctant or afraid to embody? Is there something you could stand to express more directly? Might there be a way that the irritating quality could also be seen as a strength? Or in the case of introjection, maybe your shadow figure is symbolic of a distorted belief you've inherited?

Once you have a sense of the shadow you're contending with, consider the ways in which healing it might be contributing to the culture you want to change. If you are concerned about capitalism, notice where your inner "top dogs" profit from the less fortunate parts of yourself. When are you expected to be productive as a measure of worth? If you are concerned about encroachment onto nature, ask where you might be eroding your inner wilderness. Where are you ignoring the communications from your own body? Where does your drive for self-development end? Is any part of you left wild and free? If you are a champion for marginalized voices in the world, be sure to ask what inner truths you may also be silencing. If you take issue with the homogenizing culture we live in, explore how tolerant you are of your own uniqueness. When others seem closed-minded, ask how patient you are with your own ignorance? Do you allow yourself to make mistakes, to evolve new perspectives? When the world is divided, do you allow yourself to feel two ways at once?

This is where dreamwork and belonging almost become synonymous for me. In doing our own shadow work, we are symmetrically building resilience in our communities. As we grow less afraid of difference, embracing plurality within, we naturally embody an attitude of belonging and symbiosis in the world. Bringing light into the darkness is not only what leads to us living a more authentic version of ourselves but contributes to the evolution of human consciousness.

CHAPTER 11

Wisdom in Matter

THERE IS a famous story told by Zhuang Zhou, a Taoist philosopher who lived in fourth-century China, who dreamed of being a butterfly. In this vivid and vibrant dream, he was fluttering here and there, following his fancies, landing on colourful flowers and feeling the lightness in his wings. As a butterfly he knew nothing of the life of Zhuang Zhou the man. But when he woke up and found himself in his human body, he was left with the question: Am I a man who dreams of being a butterfly, or a butterfly now dreaming of being a man?

It inevitably happens to those of us who follow a passion for dreamwork: at some point, our inner and outer lives begin to overlap. You may find yourself dreaming within a dream, or interpreting the dreams of dream characters while still dreaming. You may become spontaneously lucid and know that you are awake within the dream. Similar overlaps may occur in waking-life as events seem to take on a dreamlike quality, or images and figures from your dreams begin to appear in the physical world. It can feel disorienting as you first adjust to the paradox Zhuang Zhou alluded to: it's all dreaming, and it's all real.

We tend to think of dreaming as a fantasy that unfolds in our imagination while we are asleep. But the version of you that is living in the dreamtime considers their life and experiences to be every bit as real as your own. Dream-you awakens to their life while day-you is asleep. But the same is true in reverse: dream-you sleeps while you live out the dream that is your waking life. Both versions of ourselves experience a stream of moments that at times seem utterly real, and other times, impossibly dream-like. Whether we are in one world or the other, we almost always consider our current experience the *real* reality. But what if we don't have to choose?

The belief that the physical world is separate from psyche is a relatively new phenomenon, and particular to the modern world-view. It was only in the seventeenth century that the French philosopher René Descartes advanced the idea that mind and matter were two distinct substances. To his observation, they behaved in such different ways as to be irreconcilable. Matter, he believed, obeyed deterministic laws, requiring force in order to be moved, whereas consciousness was subtle and quick and seemed to have no influence on matter. Descartes laid the groundwork for Western civilization to think of our inner and outer worlds as disconnected, now referred to as "Cartesian Dualism." But there was one problem with this worldview that, for centuries, scientists have been unable to solve: if they are separate, how does consciousness interact with matter?

We know that we are conscious because we experience it all day long, but we have no idea where it lives or how it interacts with our own bodies or the rest of the physical world. We know there's a connection between the two because when you find something funny, your body spontaneously laughs or when something strikes you as sad, tears spring to your eyes. We have many kinds of physical responses that arise from emotional or mental states, and our mental health can also change our physiology. For example, it's been shown that chronic stress can diminish our white blood cell response. Conversely, changing the chemistry of your body with nutrition, sleep, or pharmaceuticals, profoundly affects your cognitive and emotional state. Though the inner and outer worlds are in a constant dynamic interplay, there's a tiny miracle of connection between the two that no one yet understands.

The brain is the physical nerve centre for the rest of the body, sending and receiving information across a complex network we call the nervous system, but the true residence of the "mind" has never been found. Our thoughts, feelings, memories, perceptions, and will, all influence matter (and vice versa) in a way that science can not explain. Consider how your most memorable experiences in life were a confluence of inner and outer factors such as the landscape where events unfolded, the sounds and smells of that place, the impact of others around you, your feelings of love, or perception of beauty. Consciousness is the astounding synthesis of all these elements in your awareness. It is their coalescence that determines how you perceive, interact with, and shape the world around you. As theoretical physicist David Bohm once said, "Consciousness is an internal relationship to the whole."[1]

Consider how birds move together as one murmuration without any one individual coordinating with another. Animals of all kinds migrate across vast distances by land, sea, and air, generation after generation. Science can't explain how they know where to go, or when to leave, if they've never made the journey before. The simple act of picking up a glass of water instantly moves from a thought to a physical act involving trillions of cells, each with their own purpose, but we have no idea how they synchronize. In philosophy, this is called "the mind–body problem" and is nowhere closer to being solved than when Descartes first declared them two entities.

One of the reasons this problem has stumped scientists and philosophers is the foundational assumption of causality. Causality is the belief that the universe obeys strictly deterministic laws: that every event is caused by a prior event. You may have heard this in everyday language as "cause and effect." Science has been heavily based on determinism, searching for the causal chain of mechanics between all things in nature.

But in the early twentieth century, quantum mechanics discovered a number of wondrous things that fundamentally shifted this reductionist view of reality. While classical physics observes nature on a macroscopic scale, quantum mechanics looks into the subatomic world. Physicists set out to discover the elementary building blocks of matter, but over the course of a hundred years, what they found defied belief.

The word atom means indivisible, but in the 1930s it was discovered that every atom contained a nucleus that was composed of smaller particles called protons and neutrons, charged by orbiting electrons. But the deeper they looked, the more complexity and contradictions they discovered. Those particles have the ability to turn into other kinds of particles. Almost a hundred years later, scientists have detected over 200 subatomic particles that interact with one another in unique and inexplicable ways. It's plausible to consider that as the tools of science improve there will be infinite depths of discovery in the quantum world. Yet, as we explore this bottomless complexity, we can't help but wonder at the miracle of their coherence. What is the wholeness that governs the parts?

One of the most mind-boggling discoveries in quantum physics is that matter and energy are inextricably linked. At the atomic level, matter doesn't always behave in the causally expected way, like when you flick a marble and it rolls away taking the kinetic energy with it. Sometimes particles behave like waves: if you imagine dropping a pebble into a pond, the ripples it creates in the water travel a great distance, distributing that energy across space. It's been found that particles behave in both these ways. Depending on whether they are being observed or not, they might follow a simple trajectory, like a flicked marble, or surf along unseen waves. What we call particles are not inert at all, but have this wave-like nature until we observe them. Waves are the best metaphor we have to describe this organic landscape of intersecting peaks and valleys. But while a boat can be overturned in the ocean by a wave that travels from some distance, in the quantum world, the effects on related "particles" are instantaneous no matter the distance. This is a phenomenon called quantum entanglement.

So we can talk about sub-atomic particles in this abstract way, but they are indivisible from this organic field of interconnectivity we call "the whole." Just like a human heart has no independent existence from the rest of the body, we as individuals would cease to exist without the air, food, and water we depend on for survival. Every unique part of the universe - from the quantum world to the vast reaches of outer space - is an abstraction of this wholeness.

Like our murmuring starlings, some behaviours are emergent from that mutual whole, or what Bohm called the implicate order. Consider how the human body grows out of a single zygote. In this impossibly complex process called morphogenesis, (literally the "generation of form"), cells cooperatively decide what unique shape they'll each take, guided by some organising intelligence in the background. DNA alone can not explain why some cells become organs or tissues, and others become optic nerves or neurons. Similarly, metabolism, tissue regeneration, and the immune system are all cooperative systems that emerge from simple atoms and molecules. At the biological level, life is not causally or mechanically linked, but organic. Held together and governed by unseen patterns of the universe. Sound familiar? You'll remember how the sages of ancient Israel spoke of Wisdom as, "the divine order written into the very nature of things." Psyche and matter, it turns out, are two aspects of the same thing.

We have been taught to think of psyche as the inner life, as a subjective experience housed within the scaffolding of the human body. But psyche is more like a field that includes our own bodies and reaches everywhere into the animate world around us. Psyche is certainly within us, but we are also in psyche. It does not belong to us in the objectified sense, but extends into every aspect of the cosmos. Though being in a body allows us to access something akin to a node in its network, psyche is without any definite barriers. We cannot say where "our" psyche ends and another's begins. This is why if someone we love is suffering we experience their pain as our own, or why we feel grief upon encountering a clearcut, or why sometimes we know things that don't come out of our own experience.

Not only does psyche extend beyond our bodies but the physical world is inseparable from this energetic one. These two domains are not independent of one another, but are in dynamic, constant reciprocity. Our thoughts, dreams, and intentions take shape in the physical world—and the reverse is true as well: the material world can sometimes act upon *us* in moments of synchronicity.

Many years ago I was searching for a new place to live in the Kootenay mountains of British Columbia. I was flipping through a beautiful book at a friend's house called *Builders of the Pacific Coast* by Lloyd Khan, a curated collection of photos of owner-built homes from California up to B.C..[2] There were many gorgeous designs of wild homes built with sustainable materials, but one series of images had me spellbound.

The photos were of a magical caravan nestled in a forest. Masterfully built in the style of the Romani vardo wagons from the mid-nineteenth-century, it had a curved roof covered in cedar shingles that hugged it like scales of a fish. Inside was a platform bed covered with colourful pillows, a guitar propped up in the corner, and altars adorned with sacred things on hand-sanded ledges. At the kitchen end, there was a circular window so you could gaze out into the forest while cooking on the little gas range. Or you could sit in the rocking chair by the cast iron stove reading on a winter day. This way of living appealed so profoundly to me that it felt familiar, like an inner image. It had a numinous quality, embodying the solitude, creativity, and connection to nature that I was craving in a home. I picked up a napkin and drew it as best I could. And I carried that sketch around in my pocket as a talisman while I continued my search.

One day, I posted on social media that I was looking for a place to live and a friend reached out to me. She thought she might have something for me even though she lived a two-hour-drive away. When she said there was a vacant caravan in the woods behind her house, I couldn't believe it! I immediately made plans to travel up to see it. When I arrived, my jaw fell open. It was the exact same caravan from the book that I sketched just weeks before.

It was the first in a chain of synchronicities that spanned the next ten years of my life, but it all began with this miraculous event of an inner image spilling out into the physical world. The caravan first captured my imagination because it embodied an internal vision I had for the life I wanted. In other words, there was a resonance between my inner image and the outer one, which means something already existed within me to create this sympathetic resonance with the caravan. The ritual of sketching it out on a napkin and carrying it with me was a participatory act that further substantiated that resonance. And then the physical world responded to my ritual act by materializing the exact caravan!

SYNCHRONICITY

You dream of an owl and the next morning one swoops by your windshield. You are feeling grateful for a friend's support when the song, "You've Got a Friend" comes on the radio. You finally quit an unhappy job and are offered a great opportunity the same afternoon. When synchronicity strikes, our lives seem not random and chaotic, but purposeful. We are given a brief, rapturous glimpse into an awareness that everything is connected and life is like a waking dream.

We might think of synchronicity as something vaguely occultish, an obscure branch of Jung's work that few understand and many write off as "woo." But at the end of his life, Jung came to believe that the relationship between matter and psyche—a phenomenon he coined *synchronicity*—is the fundamental dynamic of life in the cosmos. We tend to use the word to describe extraordinarily rare events. But what if synchronicity, that meaningful connection between our waking and dreaming lives, is not an exception—but the rule?

A synchronicity is a dreamlike image or event within waking life that corresponds to your imaginal world. The word "synchronicity" comes from the Greek roots of *syn* (together) and *khronos* (time). But unlike the word "coincidence," which means two incidents occurring together, Jung emphasized that a synchronicity is a *meaningful* coinciding of the inner and outer worlds. Synchronicity is when the dreaming expresses itself in the physical world in some undeniably meaningful way.

What is meaningful to one person may not be to another, so this difference can only be measured internally. You may not be able to interpret that meaning right away, but you know that you've had a true moment of synchronicity when it fills you with a feeling of awe. You'll find it hard to dismiss these events as purely coincidental because they have a numinous quality. It is as if the rest of the world falls away for a moment while you stand in the magic of your worlds coordinating. Many people report feeling reassured by synchronicity, as if something is saying, "You're on the right path."

Synchronicity seems to say, "Keep going this way," but how is it that something knows better than we do what the way is? In as much as we find her patterns in the dreaming, Sophia speaks to us in our waking life. Synchronicity is a Wisdom event in the physical world that communicates your sacred story to you. We are coming back to the idea that Sophia is written into the nature of life, down to its very subatomic existence. Wisdom isn't just something inside us—it permeates the material world.

I believe we need to liberate our concept of synchronicity as those rarefied moments that break through ordinary consciousness in times of urgency. Perhaps it takes an event of magnitude to get our attention, because we are too guarded against the sensitivity necessary to perceive the symbolic world. But what if causality is just a subset of the greater dynamic of life, which moves in a synchronistic manner? What if synchronicity happens all the time on a spectrum and it is our own sensitivity to it that needs to be engaged? As Annie Dillard wrote, "Beauty and grace are performed whether or not we will sense them. The least we can do is try to be there."[3]

Jung had many experiences of synchronicity both in his personal life and in his consulting room. He spent much of his career trying to understand how the dream could express itself in the material world, and he had the hunch that there was a reciprocity between the physical world and psyche. But this perspective isolated him from the scientific community at the time, who dismissed this as a kind of "magical thinking."

As discussed earlier, the basis of classical physics is that the world of matter always follows the law of causality (cause and effect). So if you drop a sack of sand from a hot air balloon, the absence of weight *causes* the balloon to rise on thermal air. If you kick a stone, the force *causes* it to roll out in front of you. But synchronicity defies this rule because the connection between events occurs without a cause—it is *acausal*. So my napkin sketch of the caravan was clearly connected to the photograph I'd seen in the book, but no causal event could account for how it then appeared in reality. I never showed the caravan to anyone, and I never declared I was looking for a caravan. Some other, non-linear principle was connecting the two events.

Albert Einstein famously called those things that he couldn't explain—those that defy the fundamental laws of science—

"spooky actions." Not only does synchronicity defy the law of causality but it reverses the subject/object dynamic. The so-called objective physical world spookily seems to behave as the subject, acting upon us. It nudges us in a specific way with meaningful results. In other words, we are the stone being kicked or the balloon rising.

At the same time that Jung was wrestling with these questions, Austrian Nobel prize–winning physicist Wolfgang Pauli was asking similar questions within the field of quantum physics. When they met in 1932, Pauli was a professor at ETH, Zürich's Institute of Theoretical Physics. He was in a personal crisis when he decided to consult with Jung. He was binge-drinking and getting into bar fights on the heels of a failed marriage while still grieving his mother's suicide. Jung ended up referring him to another analyst but when Pauli was no longer a patient, the two men developed a collaborative friendship around the synchronicity question in a famous correspondence spanning decades. Their 200-or-so letters have been published in a book called *Atom and Archetype*.[4]

The letters written between the two men over twenty-five years (1932–1958) were filled with dream analysis, but they simultaneously wrestled with the question of synchronicity—a quandary shared by science and psychology. At the subatomic level, it had been discovered that electrons would "jump" between orbits in an unpredictable way when energized. These quantum leaps are acausal, meaning that—in defiance of determinism in classical physics—their path can not be predicted. This was the beginning of physicists understanding that particles also have a wave-like nature, referred to as quantum nonlocality. Similarly, Jung was beginning to expand his understanding of the unconscious not as something that only lived "inside" the individual's body, but as something that extended into the world around us. He wrote, "the collective unconscious cannot be fixed locally but is an ubiquitous existence ... it must not be seen in spatial terms and consequently, when projected onto space, is to be found every-where in that space."[5]

There, at the intersection of psychology and physics, the concept of synchronicity was born. Pauli and Jung worked together on an analogy between the nucleus of an atom and its orbiting electrons, and Jung's concept of the Self and its relation-ship to the archetypes in the unconscious. As Jung was extending his notion of psyche into the world of matter, Pauli was acknowl-edging a spiritual dimension at work within the material world. Pauli wrote, "After a careful and critical appraisal of the many experiences and arguments, I have come to accept the existence of deeper spiritual layers that cannot be adequately defined by the conventional concept of time."[6] He went on to say in 1947 that their collaboration generated, "serious evidence that what is devel-oping is indicative of a close fusion of psychology with the scien-tific experience of the processes in the material physical world."[7]

By 1948, Jung was using the term "synchronicity" to describe this acausal phenomenon of the world behaving like a dream. While it didn't appear as if something physical was connecting these events, Jung believed *meaning* was the ordering factor behind synchronicity. What distinguishes a coincidence from a synchronicity is the felt experience of the event as being meaningful.

Meaning is a relationship between two sorts of things. When we ask, "What does (any word) mean?" We are trying to under-stand the relationship between the assemblage of letters or mouth-sounds, and what they signify. The same is true of metaphors: meaning is revealed by discovering the connection between two different ideas. What we consider meaningful in life is also a rela-tionship between two contexts. For instance, one year my older brother gave me a packet of glow-in-the-dark stars for my 28th birthday, which instantly made me teary because we had them on our bedroom ceiling when we were little. It was meaningful because it drew a correspondence between then and now.

When we experience a synchronicity, we feel a sense of meaning because it reveals the relationship between our inner and outer worlds. For a moment, their unifying field becomes evident, as if it were breaking through ordinary reality. Whether it was brought about by engaging in dreamwork, imaginal play, or ritual, the outer world acts as if it is responsive to our tending to it. Wisdom is alive in matter and when we participate with it, it feeds us with meaning. As Mayan Shaman Martín Prechtel frames it, "You sit singing on a little rock in the middle of a pond, and your song makes a ripple that goes out to the shores where the spirits live. When it hits the shore, it sends an echo back toward you. That echo is spiritual nutrition."[8]

This reciprocity between the archetypal and temporal worlds was the central theme in Pauli's dreams, which were analyzed in depth by Jung himself. They were filled with imagery pointing to a necessary union of the opposites in his worldview, but he struggled to get the idea past his own rationality. Pauli wrote to Jung in one of his letters that their discovery could render the distinction between psyche and physics meaningless. But as a Nobel Laureate and Chair of Physics at ETH, the stakes of his worldly position were high and he was unable to bring this radical idea forward into the world of science before his death.

Jung struggled in a similar way. He wrote to Pauli, "It means a lot to me to see how our points of view are getting closer, for if you feel isolated from your contemporaries when grappling with the unconscious, it is also the same with me, in fact more so, since I am actually standing in the isolated area, striving somehow to bridge the gap that separates me from the others. After all, it is no pleasure for me always to be regarded as esoteric."[9]

Some seventy-odd years later, physics continues to grapple with the indivisibility of matter and energy. Everything in the universe—from planets, to water, and even light—behaves like a particle and a wave simultaneously. The paradox of how something can be both a wave (spread-out across space, like energy) and a tiny, localized particle—is the central mystery of quantum physics. Meanwhile, we have the analogous paradox contained in the concept of synchronicity, where the collective world of matter behaves as psyche, yet psyche is also concerned with the unique development of each person.

Though we think of ourselves as individuals, what drives us and gives us purpose may also be expressions of a unified field, or ecopsyche. When I remember that I may be a character in someone else's dream, I think, "I better be as weird, lovely, and unpredictable a protagonist as possible!"

THE WORLD IS A SYMBOL

We learned from the Gnostics that Wisdom is that divine spark hidden in the material world. But to make this idea more personal, we can think of that spark within each of us that comes alive when we are living our unique truth and purpose. In other words, Sophia's redemption in the world takes place at the centre of each of our lives.

Synchronicity is the spontaneous act of Sophia's revelation to us, but we can also actively court her presence. In the next chapter, we'll discuss a variety of methods to build on our expanding definition of dreamwork, including ritual, somatic movement, divination, and active imagination. But more than any technique, it is our *intent* that is most essential for laying bare the web of meaning connecting the world.

Sometimes meaning is revealed by accident. We may go through a traumatic experience like war, stress, extreme illness, or deprivation, and it causes a reorientation of our worldview. We may also be altered by love and loss, or through visionary states such as journeying with psychedelics. In each of these experiences, we may emerge a different person as a result of events shifting our patterns of meaning and perception. But we often forget how powerful our own intent can also be in changing how we see the world—and how it responds to us in return. Instead of defaulting to habitual consciousness, intent is a choice to see and move through the world focusing on the living connection between oneself and all sentient beings. I call this *dreamwalking*: like becoming lucid in a dream, except you are awake and the dream is reality. In this way, dreamwork becomes the spiritual practice of "giving transparency to the foregrounds of the world" that we may see their animism.*

To make yourself receptive to other ways of knowing, the first step is to shift your perceptual boundaries beyond the human scope into the animate landscape around and within you. All of nature lives in a kinship of mutuality; whether it's the pairing of trees with fungi, flowers with pollinating animals, or seed dispersal relationships, mutualistic interactions are the essence of the earth's ecosystem. Though we generally think of synchronicity as those events of undeniable magic that interrupt ordinary reality, I believe it's helpful to expand our conception of that magic to include the ways in which nature is *always* speaking to us and each other.

One form of dreamwalking I love most is to attune to the metaphors in nature. As I walk in the forest, I might see a tree that's bending over backwards that conveys a lesson on surrender. The fusion of two trunks reminds me how deeply we need each other for our mutual well-being. Maybe a sun sets at the same time a moon rises and I see how I, too, am standing on a threshold of one thing ending while another begins. A still lake reflecting a mirror image of the trees and sky above reminds me of the symmetry between my small life and the world at large. A bird alighting on my garden-Buddha's head reassures me that the thing I was considering is a good idea.

---

* This beautiful phrase appears in Erich Neumann's essay Mystical Man (1948), in which he draws on the parables of Hasidism to illustrate how it is incumbent upon every individual to redeem the divine sparks of meaning out of one's life.

You can also practise dreamwalking in the human world. Before you go to a gathering, you can set the intention to get lucid in the waking dream. Like turning on your second attention, you feel the shroud of mundanity fall away as you consider everyone in your midst as emissaries in the Imaginal World. How might your choices be different? What might you say or do, knowing your words and actions are a living dream? How unexpectedly might the world respond?

When I was first setting out on my path as a dreamworker, I faced a lot of inner and outer invalidations that made me question whether I could ever survive in normal society. One day, I went out dreamwalking in the city with the intent to discover if my life was on the right path or not. I got onto a packed streetcar at evening rush hour and settled into my seat among the exhausted, dispirited commuters. I was craving connection, but nobody would even make eye contact with me. The group was silent, and clad in the unspoken city uniform of grey and black. When an old woman boarded the next stop, dressed in a wild array of colours and textures, she stood out. Breaking the silent agreement, she began to orate a spontaneous transmission of lyrics and thoughts and nonsense. I delighted in how she dared to be different, breaking the spell of monotony and resignation. I could tell that she was making the crowd uncomfortable, but rather than acknowledge her everyone doubled down on disregarding her, and each other. When it was her stop, she made a show of carting her stuff loudly to the front of the streetcar, but before getting off she turned and looked directly at me with a glint in her eyes, and said, "Never stop dreaming!" I took this as a direct affirmation from my holy helpers, and couldn't stop giggling about it for days.

Like sitting in meditation, it takes some practice staying present for any length of time. It can also be disorienting as you move between your habitual consciousness and dreamwalking, so give yourself achievable time limits for these experiments. If you lose focus, gently remind yourself of your intent, and simply try again another time. It's also important to stay grounded, and not lose touch with real world limitations and consequences. No matter how exhilarating it is to awaken to the dreaming dimension, we all still have to "chop wood and carry water." As the Buddhist proverb suggests, we become enlightened when we can do even the most mundane things with love and presence.

As both Jung and Pauli were attempting to do in their own lives, it is possible to find a third way that is attentive to the value of both worlds at once. It was Erich Neumann who wrote, "This level synthesizes two attitudes which at first seem mutually exclusive: one which takes seriously the concrete situation in the actual, given world, and another which looks on its encounter with the numinous substratum as the only authentic reality. Their synthesis constitutes 'symbolic life.'"[10]

RECONCILING PARADOX

This "third way" brings to mind our earlier discussion on *The Thunder, Perfect Mind*, where Sophia declared herself as the embodiment of opposites. One of the central skills we develop in dreamwork is the ability to endure and reconcile paradox; to discover the creative relationship between things that, on the surface, seem contrary or opposed.

Throughout this book we've been exploring paradoxical pairs such as soul and body, wave and particle, light and dark, feminine and masculine, individual and collective, dreaming and waking, order and chaos, medicine and poison, earthly and divine. While it's the nature of rationality to habitually pick a side and stick to it, real creativity lives in the friction and reconciliation of opposites. In the exchange between polarities, a new perspective is born.

This is why dreams provide us with compensatory images, to balance out our one-sided biases. For example, a coldly intellectual person might dream of colourful and expressive characters, while someone prone to reclusion might dream of being surrounded by friends. These dreams are the soulbody's way of helping us break out of diametrical thinking. Though it takes enormous internal strength to sustain paradoxes, integrating the opposites is the beginning of all creative transformation.

In the old alchemical texts, the culmination of the chemical opus of transformation was called *coniunctio*, literally meaning conjunction or marriage of opposites. As we touched on with *Aurora Consurgens*, coniunctio was often represented as a two-headed figure, half male and half female joined at the centre, or sometimes a couple making love, symbolizing the joining of polarities in a single image. Paradoxically, this union is not one, and not two, but a third way that is *two-in-one*.

Jung called this worldview the *unus mundus* or "one world," which he believed was the unified reality from which both physical and psychic phenomena stem. In his final book, *Mysterium Coniunctionis: An Inquiry into the Separation and Synthesis of Psychic Opposites in Alchemy*, he wrote, "It is the Western equivalent of the fundamental principle of classic Chinese philosophy, namely the union of Yang and Yin in Tao."[11]

As the ancient Taoist sages taught, opposition is a precondition for union. The tension or restriction one feels in conflict evokes the energy necessary for growth. While one-sided thinking leads to stagnation, wisdom is the fruit of relating opposites. We can see this in how metaphor works by bringing unrelated contexts together to reveal their kinship. Dreams also do this in the broader sense by "physicalizing" our energetic experiences into forms—into dream images. So when we see our subtle body's experiences cast out into "physical" dream scenarios, suddenly an ephemeral thing becomes substantiated, allowing us to approach it consciously. The reverse is also true of the material world, which behaves in a dream-like fashion through synchronicity, which I am using as an umbrella term for all the ways in which energy and matter correlate. Like foes meeting in a narrow passageway, opposition forces individuals to face the ways in which they are distinct from one another, but it also reveals their affinities. I believe it is the great work of our epoch to explore the correspondence between psyche and matter—not to erase the distinction between the two, nor to render either superior, but to live in such a way that tends to their equivalence.

There is a huge movement being made in human consciousness toward a capacity for holding paradox. On the brave edges of culture, we are now seeing cooperative thinking between divergent fields and ideologies. For example, there's a nascent tolerance and appreciation in the medical world for alternative therapies, like energy work and herbal medicine. In psychology, we are beginning to see a growing ecological sensibility—taking the environment into account when evaluating an individual's mental health. People are sharing more information at the grassroots level, leading to the questioning of political and corporate systems of exploitation. In the subculture, there is a growing respect for Indigenous ways of knowing, systems thinking, emerging values of cooperation, and mutual aid. I think this next growth period in human history will be about learning to see complementarity instead of an antagonistic duality. We need a new model of consciousness that can reconcile paradox, co-liberating our psycho-physical nature as the hybrid beings we are.

As we grow our capacity to hold paradox, we have to be careful not to collapse binaries into non-existence. True paradox is the ability to contain both within a third way. It's important not to homogenize opposites into a simple perspective that erases the distinctness of both. For instance, when two nations are at war, there are always rationales on both sides for the fight. But if we say, "We are all one people, and everyone should just be at peace," it erases the unique validity of each side. As the great physicist Niels Bohr once said, "It is the hallmark of any deep truth that its negation is also a deep truth."[12] Though two things may seem at odds, they are codependent; it is across their reciprocal seam that ideas can be exchanged. True creativity comes out of consciously held conflict. What's really being asked of us in any conflict is to hold the complexity and individuality of both sides until a third way emerges. Only when opposites are unified *and* retain their distinctness can paradox be allowed to exist.

BODY AND DESIRE

While the fields of physics and psychology offer us rich conceptual frameworks and language to navigate these waters, they can also restrain us in the endless hallways of the intellect. Ultimately, dreaming is a biological process.

Consider your body, the devoted consort who bears so much, whose service to you is boundless and unwavering. Whether it communicates to you in symptoms or sensations, intuitions, emotions, or instincts, your body is the ground from which dreaming springs. Dreams are literally a biological necessity. Psyche can never be separated from soma so it's critical to restore their union in our conceptual framework, language, and approach to dreamwork. Wisdom expresses itself physically in our dreams and synchronistically in the outer world, but also in the longing and desires of our own bodies.

Many religious traditions teach that physical longing and desire are lowly or base impulses. At best, we are told that these feelings cause suffering and that we should rise above them. At worst, they are framed as sinful and punishable. But in the Sufi tradition, the longing we feel in our bodies is the natural response to being separated from divinity. When we incarnate, the soul is exiled from the Beloved like a reed plucked from the reedbed—and longing is our yearning to be reunited. It is also the sound of our being called homeward. Sophia knows the pattern of your fate and is calling you toward the life you long for, and that life is also longing for you. Resonance is that overlap between your longing and being longed for.

In the same way that difficult dreams support us to change

deeply unconscious behaviour, sometimes wisdom expresses itself in the body to move us out of old patterns. One of the ways it does this is through "eros" or sexual desire. Eros is another way to express the acausal connecting principle, or what can be more simply understood as that mystical pull that draws us into relationship with others. You can probably look back on the day you met certain people who became lasting friends or lovers to see how instantly you felt a connection with them. Over time, those connections can bear life-altering fruits.

In the case of a lover, you may find yourself compulsively drawn to someone out of the blue. Sometimes these attractions are symbiotic and result in mutually generative growth. But other times, desire can lead us into destructive situations. Even as you're being drawn to the other, you may know that doing so could blow up your life—but it is near impossible to deny your attraction to them. Occasionally, following those impulses may indeed be destructive but in a way that is necessary for your next becoming.

I worked with a gifted artist named Sonja whose initial dream featured a luminous, nude woman who was being caged by police. As she tuned into the dream feeling of being trapped and held captive, Sonja related to a difficulty expressing herself, especially with men of authority. She shared how she held back and felt tongue-tied in their company, a pattern that began with her father, an intimidating man who made her feel inadequate.

During the course of our first few months working together, she met a man named Daniel, who Sonja was powerfully attracted to. He was ambiguous about his feelings toward her, so she tried to keep her emotions in check until she knew where he stood. But Daniel was evasive and unreliable and the months went on without her gaining any clarity. Wanting to be closer to this magnetic man, she spent more and more time with him, going on spontaneous dates, spending weekends away together in the country, attending cultural events. But he would often leave their plans open-ended, or cancel at the last minute, leaving her in the lurch.

Deep down, she knew he would never make a good partner, but that eros was so strong that she had to see it through.

During that time, she dreamed of a fire that was out of control. She was patient with Daniel, forgiving of his unreliability, accommodating to his needs. But underneath that she simmered with an unexpressed anger that the dream warned might get out of control. This went on for a year, never advancing into a full relationship nor setting friendship boundaries. Then one night on the phone, Sonja exploded at Daniel. She yelled at him for his poor behaviour but her anger was so unexpected and unfamiliar that Daniel felt threatened and called the cops, telling them he feared she was unstable.

We can't help but return to that very first dream in which a nude woman was caged by police. Sonja's associations to that initial dream were about her inability to express herself in relationships with men. And she was certainly holding herself back from telling Daniel how she felt, until that fire got out of control. But after this episode and their breakup, Sonja felt a newfound sense of power and freedom. She began to have some remarkable dreams that showed where that energy was coming from.

I Won't Sweeten the Brew: Sonja's Dream

I am waiting on a determination from authorities about whether a woman I know will be restricted or allowed to move freely. While I am waiting, I wander into a forest. I begin brewing a cauldron of medicinal ingredients gathered from nature as a healing remedy. I am surrounded by forest creatures and beings. At one point I notice that dirt is getting into the cauldron but decide this is okay. When some women want to sweeten the brew, I refuse, knowing it would dilute the medicine.

As we worked with this powerful dream, it emerged that the determination from authorities on the woman's freedom was symbolic of the part of Sonja that still questioned whether she did the right thing with Daniel. Though part of her regretted how angry she became, she was also aware of how restricted she felt when she was holding those feelings back. The brewing of medicine (over a fire) was symbolic of an inner alchemy taking place as she gathered all the elements of her experience in the cauldron of her attention, to create a medicine for a healthy outcome. All of her holy helpers and instincts gathered around in support of the process.

Sonja felt the addition of dirt was an extremely important detail in this dream, along with her refusal to dilute or sweeten the brew. The dark earth is that primordial stuff of true embodiment. It is the grounding element and the death aspect of the feminine. It is the natural humus of past events without which new life would not be possible. Sonja realised she needed to include this dirty, grounding, difficult stuff in her brew in order for it to be a true medicine. The refusal to sweeten herself, as she'd done with Daniel, was the emerging surety that she was no longer willing to be diluted.

In the weeks that followed, Sonja dreamed that fragments of herself held in Daniel's possession were being returned to her across space. She absorbed them like vitamins that contained nutritious energy. Then one night she dreamed of building a new firebox with an extremely successful friend of hers, a crone she described as a battleaxe who never minced words nor held herself back. The firebox was symbolic of Sonja's new ability to conduct heat efficiently, to use anger wisely for boundaries, passion, and alchemical transformation.

As we reflected on the events of that year, it became clear that wisdom had expressed itself throughout the experience. There, in that very first dream, was a call to free the feminine. And when Sonja needed an embodied experience of that, wisdom then appeared as desire. Sonja knew intellectually that Daniel wasn't going to be the partner she wanted. But the pull of eros was too powerful so she entered into what would prove to be a transformative year. When Sonja was at last pushed to the point of being unable to restrain her anger, she finally expressed that held-back part of herself. Though she regretted losing her cool, wisdom appeared again in the powerful synchronicity of Daniel calling the cops on her like an echo of that initial dream. But the true fruit of the whole experience were those nutritious fragments of her energy being returned, the refusal of a diluting sweetness, and the archetype of the crone brandishing her sparkling new firebox.

Taken in this context, we can begin to think of our longing not as something to be eradicated or even fulfilled but as connective tissue to a greater intelligence—an artery across which we transmit and receive wisdom. When we value longing, we are more likely to let it express itself or allow it to take shape to become a new image or pattern. Instead of being overwhelmed by diffuse feeling, we can learn to venerate our longing in small or big ways, asking and answering what we long for in any given day or season. We can also centre longing in our dreamwork practice. Ask not, "What does it mean for me?" and instead ask what the dream longs for from us. When we honour and follow the longing we have for our lives, it leads us deeper into the state of resonance.

CHAPTER 12

Rituals and Enactments

IN A POETIC TRANSLATION by Coleman Barks, Rumi writes, "As you start on the way, the way appears."[1] This paradox encapsulates how it is to live a life of meaning. We can not sit back and expect fruits to grow from arid soil. We must plant a seed, water the earth, tend the ground where new life grows. We feel a sense of purpose when we are living Sophia's pattern for our lives, but discovering that purpose is far from passive. It requires our participatory involvement. Wisdom must be sought out, engaged, and elicited through ritual acts of devotion. While we cannot predict or force synchronicity, I think we can excite a *quickening* between the realms through various practices such as prayer, ritual, divination, and active imagination.

In Proverbs 8:17 Sophia says, "I love those that love me; and those that seek me earnestly shall find me." There is a sense of immediacy in this statement that implies there is an invisible link of entanglement between us and the divine. The very act of loving Sophia is to also be loved by her, and seeking is the act of being found.

In the biblical Hebrew, the word "seek" has two meanings. The first word is darash (דָּרַשׁ), which means to inquire, study or search carefully for something. The second is baqash (בָּקַשׁ), and means to beseech, request, or petition the holy in nature. In dreamwork, we begin with the first form of seeking, as we contemplate the layers of meaning that our symbols carry. Other examples of *darash* include contemplation of scriptures, prayer, or even dreamwalking. *Baqash* has at its root the power of touching or facing the holy directly. As the entanglement of Sophia's statement suggest, baquash is a kind of entering into our shared middle realm to participate directly with the archetypes and angels. This meeting and tending to the many relations in the imaginal world—including the spirits and energies of a place—is the central practice of all animistic cultures. I believe Sophia is just another way of naming the wondrous intelligence in which animism is rooted. She is the Wisdom at work both within psyche and the material world, that is calling us into cohesion with each other.

While every culture has its own language and rituals around it, animism is the most commonly held belief system of Indigenous people around the world. It is the underlying worldview that the living spirit exists in all matter—in the rivers, mountains, trees, wind, and even in shadows—and we are all in a relational web of connectedness. There's a wonderful, short poem by Gary Snyder that describes this living web:

As the crickets' soft, autumn hum
is to us
so are we to the trees
as are they
to the rocks and the hills.[2]

The word "animism" comes from the Latin root *anima*, meaning "a current of air, the vital principle, life, soul." As a worldview, animism doesn't recognize a division between wind and soul, or matter and spirit. It allows for multiple layers of knowing and describing the world. The word was popularised by anthropology to describe, often derogatively, the most common spiritual underpinning of Indigenous cultures. But it is so intrinsic to their way of life that most Indigenous peoples don't have a word for it. Just as the dream speaks in wisdom, so does the physical world. I believe the ability to perceive synchronicity, and our living web of relations, is a capacity that can be reclaimed. It is a way of seeing, a way of knowing, that grows in strength and vocabulary when practised.

Animism recognizes the life force in all matter, including places, creatures, weather, and even objects. It also recognizes beings who don't have physical bodies, like ancestors, spirits, and the animals and symbols in our dreams. Because all of life is connected, those beings are also in relationship with each other, not just in the physical biosphere, but in the ecopsyche.

I call myself an aspiring animist. Maybe this is true of anyone who wasn't raised with this layered way of seeing, because it takes practice to learn how to appreciate the world in this way. We are healing thousands of years of an enculturated severance between matter and spirit. As a result of this dualism, the mind and body have been treated by psychology as separate entities and, like most Western ontologies, serve to uphold a hierarchy between divinity, humanity, and nature.

The damaging effects of this split cannot be understated. Imagine for a moment how, without any spiritual component, secular psychology would be inherently limited, and even traumatic, for an animist. So long as an individual is treated as separate from nature and the world soul, then we alone are responsible for our happiness, or complicit in our suffering and alienation.

Psychology continues to reflect the colonial thinking of Europeans by largely denigrating animistic cultures as "primitive." In his influential studies of child development, Swiss psychologist Jean Piaget identified animism as an immature stage of cognitive development, a "magical thinking" that inhibits logic.[3] To this day, the American Psychological Association defines animism by

Piaget's terms, suggesting animists are unable to make the distinction between make-believe and reality, and are therefore childish or less evolved.[4]

But we are seeing a revival of animism in modern times, as people begin to question this limiting framework and grow curious about the unseen world behind this one. When we follow the Dreaming Way, we learn that Sophia is another name for the animating intelligence behind nature, and when we consciously participate with her—through dreamwork and divination, imaginal play, ritual, and somatic practices—we experience her coherence more frequently. No longer caught in the flat, rational existence we were accustomed to upholding, we begin to attune to the larger relational field that contains and runs through all of existence. We are able to hear languages that are not tied to words alone, but are felt in swells of energy, inner and outer symbols, gestures of nature, patterns and rhythms that temper us from within, and confirmations from the (so-called) physical world.

To stay in rhythm with the Dreaming Way, we must tend to our everyday relationship with the imaginal. Just as there are many paths up a mountain, there are a thousand ways to keep the eye of the heart open. Especially in times of chaos, disconnection, or dreamlessness, it's important to have other devotions we can turn to. Here are a few ideas to get you started.

RITUAL

As a simple ritual, I begin every day in solitude with my journal, so I can write down my dreams and reflect on their images and feelings. It creates balance in my life to give the value of my time to this practice. But you can create any ritual that resonates for you, like sitting in meditation, walking in nature, or writing a list of beautiful things you noticed in your day.

Ritual should always have a physical component. So if you have already spent time courting a dream, you will have discovered its secret longing. The next step in bringing that potential into actuality is to enact ritual in the waking world. In the Synthesis Key, I wrote about the value of keeping symbolic objects or making offerings on a dream altar, which is a powerful way to bring your dreaming into your physical space. When a dream has nourished us with wisdom, enacting ritual around that wisdom is the equivalent to reciprocating a conversation with Sophia. It doesn't need to be elaborate—in fact, it's better if it is something small and achievable. It is simply a way of saying: I acknowledge what you've given me, and I take it seriously enough to walk the wisdom of the dream.

Walking the wisdom may also look like trying out a new behaviour from a dream's prompting. For instance, let's say you dream of an elderly woman isolated in a cabin. You realize from your dreamwork that the archetype is speaking to how you've been isolating yourself from the world. Walking the wisdom may look like taking a few social risks so you can experience more connection. Or if you dreamed of an overcrowded house you were unable to escape, and your dreamwork synthesized around your need for unstructured time and space, you may enact a ritual boundary around a certain time of day devoted to imagination or spontaneity. Or for Sonja, who is slowly coming to terms with the fiery side of her nature, walking the wisdom might look like inviting her disagreements into the open instead of suppressing her anger until it burns out of control. You can treat these experiments as conscious efforts to change your habitual behaviour to see if you can manifest different outcomes in your life. You can set a time limit to focus your practice—say a month, week, or even a day—and then watch how your dreams respond. Is there a sense of growth or support for the new behaviour? Does it feel liberating or energizing? After doing a ritual, always turn back to your dreams, and your own body, to listen for a response.

Another way to enact ritual is through creativity. When you take the essence of a dream's wisdom and allow it to move you into making a painting, song, poem, sculpture, movement, or any other creative endeavour, it has a way of substantiating what might otherwise be lost in the ephemeral. We've all had those moments of learning a big lesson and then later not remembering what it was or why it was so important. Creativity is a way of keeping wisdom alive by giving the symbolic life physical substance. You certainly don't need to be an artist to do any of these things. The goal shouldn't be aesthetic beauty (though that may be a bonus) but rather a satisfying expression of your inner life—something to hold the energy of that wisdom.

MOVING YOUR SYMBOL

If you're still stuck with a dream, or you feel like it has depths that you don't yet understand, try this somatic exercise that I call Moving Your Symbol. Start by choosing a symbol, character, animal, or image from your dream to work with—something with potency that still eludes your understanding. Then find a place to sit or stand where your feet are flat on the ground and you have an arms width of space around you.

Feel the connection between the floor and your feet. Greet your old friend Gravity. Shift your weight from left to right, noticing how the entire orientation of your body changes with every small shift. Let your muscles relax as you feel and listen to the communications of your body. When we're tight and restrained, we can't hear what's being said. When we are relaxed, we have an open channel to the Dreaming Way. Take several deep breaths into your lungs, exhaling any tension you might be holding. Lend your presence to this moment.

Call to mind your chosen symbol and notice where in your body it lives. Is it in your chest or belly? Does it lay on your shoulders? Is there a sensation that goes with it? If you find yourself trapped in your thoughts, wandering off into analysis, or thinking about the future or past, lengthen up in your neck and allow your breath to connect your head with your heart.

There is no praise, no blame in this exercise, just noticing what is there. Instead of labelling any sensation that the symbol evokes as good or bad, try simply making an encounter with it, even amplifying or exaggerating that sensation. Like the Taoists teach, follow the Way of Nature as it conveys itself in your own body.

Start small and invite the symbol to show you what it needs and wants. Use the space you need and allow your symbol to guide the movement. Listen for inner and outer sounds or voices and if you want to make sounds yourself, let them come.

Try becoming your symbol. Is there a way your body wants to move to express your new shape? Follow the natural energy contained in the image. Don't try to force the feeling into something agreeable if that's not its inclination. If you feel a stuckness, heaviness, stillness, or resistance, just let that remain. If your elbow wants to move, or your body wants to lumber on all fours, or if you feel the urge to flap and fly, give that expression. Look for ebbs and swells in the movement, and respect the changing stream of energy.

Are there any unexpected or unintentional movements, like a tick, jerk, or trip? Notice this, and accept it as the body's communication. You can even try repeating those gestures, allowing them to enhance your movement. If your image begins to change, or new awarenesses arise, or if feelings swell up during your experience, allow it all to be part of your process.

When you feel ready to return to ordinary awareness, bring together everything that arose from the experience and come into a standing or seated place of stillness again. Take a moment to feel your feet touching the earth, the weight of your arms at your side. Notice in what ways you feel different.

Has your body changed since you began? Notice how you're feeling—did it create an opening, are you relieved in some way, or did it bring up grief or resistance?

Allow it to be how it is without judgement and welcome it into inclusion. Then ask yourself, what does this feeling remind you of? Is there a new awareness appearing for you? What insights are arising?

Give thanks to your body for its genius, its communications, and its ability to lead you and show what it needs. If you feel in some way disappointed, allow that to also belong. More might unfold throughout your day or in your next dream, so pay attention to the dreams that arise in the coming days. As always, honour the wisdom through complementary actions like journaling, making an offering, or taking a step in the direction of change.

DIVINATION

Whether through astrology, tarot, runes, or using bone oracles, humans have always sought to relieve our anxiety about the future through the ritual art of divination. Divination comes from the fourteenth-century word *divinacioun*, meaning the act of foretelling the future by supernatural or magical means, or discovering what is hidden or obscure.

Many divination tools were developed by sages and philosophers who studied the congruences between our internal and external realities. They would then depict those relational bonds as metaphors or symbols, like planets, court figures, branches of a tree, or even alphabets. It is believed that we can use these tools to gain insight into the archetypal patterns underwriting ordinary life through a ritualized process of interacting with divine forces. Divinatory systems rarely predict how your future will look when you get there but they can help you to navigate the obstacles along the way. There is one ancient system of divination so powerful that few can deny its accuracy.

At an estimated 5,000 years old, the Chinese *Book of Changes*, the *I Ching*, is one of the oldest books in the world. It is said to contain the wisdom of millennia for understanding the natural order of the universe. It is believed to have been developed from an ancient meditation technique to cultivate inner stillness. Once the sages slowed all activity, they noticed a flux inside that stillness. It was this movement inside the calm they called the Tao.

As we touched on, the Tao is that transient energy in matter, moving according to its own internal timing and sense of order. One who follows the Tao comes into deeper sync with, and acceptance of, that changing stream. Tao is always in a state of flux as a result of the interaction between Yin and Yang, dark and light, psyche and nature. Rooted in the fundamental idea that the universe is governed by this complementary pair, Taoism is a powerful representation of the wisdom in matter that we've been exploring.

To speak about this ineffable thing, the Chinese developed a kind of binary code, made up of broken and unbroken lines representing degrees of Yin and Yang. They identified eight core principles in nature, which they represented as trigrams (three stacked lines). When these trigrams bond in pairs, they interact in a new way, creating sixty-four unique situations represented by hexagrams (six stacked lines). It's compelling to note that this is an eerie analogy for human DNA, which is also made up of sixty-four codons, a structure that was only discovered in the early 1950s.

The way the *I Ching* works remains a mystery, but even the most rational critics are astounded by its accuracy. You start with a question for your life, and then in a process of throwing coins or yarrow sticks, you discover a hexagram answer to your question. The corresponding text for that hexagram is written in a metaphoric language of figures from ancient Chinese culture and images of nature. Translations also include commentary and interpretation for those unfamiliar with ancient Chinese customs and images. Interpretation is quite similar to dreamwork in that you are discovering relational links between worlds facilitated by metaphors.

When you contemplate the *I Ching*, you are looking for the

intersections between your temporal life and the eternal cycles of nature. Different from other divinatory systems, the *I Ching* isn't mechanistic. Like an archetypal map, it shows probabilities based on the wave-like patterns of nature. When you receive a hexagram, it says, "When you do *this*, something analogous to *this* is likely to happen."

As the great American ethnobotanist and mystic Terence McKenna explained, the *I Ching* is an ancient system of temporal mechanics. "The Chinese looked not at the world of matter, energy, and space, but the world of time .... Much in the way that science believes you can explain all nature with 108 elements, the Chinese took the position that time itself was made of elements."[5]

The hexagrams are symbolic ideograms of the archetypes at work in any given moment in time. When contemplated carefully, a reading can help you locate yourself in relation to that map. Since the archetypes are themselves patterns, they have an innate direction that can be roughly predicted. But like a wave, they are always in motion. And no wave acts alone in the sea—so the hexagrams interact with and change one another. As Bohm is credited with having said, "We are all linked by a fabric of unseen connections. This fabric is constantly changing and evolving. This field is directly structured and influenced by our behaviour and by our understanding." So if we make even a small adjustment in our attitude, it can change the outcome of our direction, or at least temper any resistance we have to unfolding events.

More than any other system of belief, the *I Ching* had a huge influence on Jung's thinking about synchronicity. He first received a German translation of this sacred text in the 1920s from sinologist and theologian Richard Wilhelm. After reading the book, Jung sat for hours under a pear tree practising the *I Ching*. He was astounded by the meaningful coincidences between his inner thoughts and the readings he received. Being introduced to the riches of Chinese heritage and Taoist philosophy via Wilhelm's translations was, as Jung put it, "one of the most significant events of my life."[6] In 1950, the text was translated into English by Cary Baynes and today this version is still regarded as the finest translation of the *I Ching*.

So while synchronicity can spontaneously occur in waking-life, it can also be summoned through this and other forms of divination. Throwing the *I Ching* is a way to participate with synchronicity in an intentional way. When you are feeling disconnected or disoriented, the ritual act of preparing a question and throwing the sticks/coins is a way of clearing your psychic field to get at the heart of your query. Contemplating the reading serves to put you back into conversation with those elemental forces of nature that are running below the surface of your life.

ACTIVE IMAGINATION

Another powerful way to engage with our symbols is through a technique developed by Jung called Active Imagination. Even when we've completed our dreamwork, we may find that certain characters or images remain elusive to us. Or a dream may end in an unsatisfactory way that we'd like to re-dream. As the name implies, we can use our imagination to consciously activate and engage with our symbols. Active imagination is a powerful and creative method for opening a dialogue between our personal and archetypal worlds.

Unlike daydreaming or fantasy, active imagination requires us to remain as lucid throughout the process as we would be in meditation. Instead of contemplating emptiness, however, we are calling an image to mind. We aren't getting swept up in that imagery, as we would in a dream, but holding fast to the intent to dialogue with the imaginal Other. At the same time, we are relaxing our ego enough to release control over how the conversation unfolds. This allows the Other enough autonomy to respond as they wish. The exchange of ideas that follows is often surprising and insightful and it can help us give form and substance to the raw, unfocused moods we experience. It can also bring about synthesis between our often contradictory outlooks.

In his book *Inner Work*, Jungian analyst Robert Johnson transcribes a brief active imagination session as recorded by one of his patients.[7] Rather than calling to mind a dream image, this woman chose to ask about a feeling of irritation she was experiencing. An image of a Japanese artist spontaneously appeared and immediately declared that she was afraid. When the dreamer asked why she was afraid, it emerged that she'd been locked up for a long time and rarely given a chance to express herself. She was afraid she'd soon be locked up again. The dreamer acknowledged the figure, and confessed that she barely knew the artist existed within her. She shared that she could now see how she rarely provided outlets for the artist to appreciate and create beauty. As brief as their conversation was, the woman realized that her irritation was concealing a deeper fear of being creatively locked away. She began to speak to the Japanese artist regularly and made room in her life for artistic pursuits.

To try this yourself, find a quiet and private room where you won't be disturbed. Keep a journal and pen nearby so you can jot down what you remember, or even write as you go. Take a moment to consider your intent, whether it is to ask a question about something brewing in your emotions or about a specific dream image. With your eyes closed, start by clearing your mind and opening a receptive place in your heart for the encounter ahead. Some people like to conjure a setting in their mind's eye that makes them feel safe and comfortable before engaging with their symbol. Then you can either summon a specific symbol to mind or let one spontaneously appear. Be patient with yourself if it doesn't appear immediately. If you feel moved to do so, you can verbalize the invitation by calling the figure forward. When an image appears in your mind's eye, try not to judge or dismiss it. Just hold it in your attention. Notice what it looks like, what energy surrounds it, whether there are any sensations or resonances with the figure in your body. Allow yourself to feel that somatic connection, even if it's uncomfortable. If your mind wanders, gently bring it back to the symbol. Keep a close eye to see if the image changes or unfolds in any way without trying to alter it yourself. The goal here is to let the image lead.

When you're ready, you can begin to interact with the Other. Jung suggested the first question be, "Who or what has come alive?" or "Who or what has entered my psychic life ... and wants to be heard?"[8] If you're working with a mysterious emotion, you can ask, "Who is the one behind this mood?" If you're calling forth an existing image from a dream, you can start by asking, "Who are you and what have you come to say?" Then let it speak.

There is a sweet spot between allowing the encounter to unfold without controlling it while also maintaining your agency in the exchange. Without criticizing what it has to say, listen carefully for your figure's response, and try not to influence the conversation in a direction you might prefer. But be sure to allow yourself to have a genuine reaction in the dialogue or interaction. It's important that you aren't just an observer or follower. If you feel you're being taken in the wrong direction, you can and should refuse to follow your inner Other. Any disagreement that ensues between you has the potential to be productive, but they are in no way the final arbiter of your life. It's important to maintain your ethical boundaries in the imagination just as you would in life. If the encounter feels antagonistic or stressful for you, it's best to end the experiment or consider trying again with supervised support.

One of the most frequent blocks people have with active imagination and dreamwork in general is the fear that they are making things up. But dreams and associations come out of the same imaginal field, so it's impossible to trick ourselves with active imagination. It's all made of the same material, spontaneously arising in the imaginal field. You can trust that what emerges in active imagination is exactly what needs to be seen or heard. If you have any lingering questions from the process, you can always put them to your dreams the next night in a dream incubation.

You can ask your inner Other any follow up questions as they arise, and keep noticing if and how the symbol changes its form. Take note of any emotional fluctuations you or they might have during your exchange. When the conversation feels complete, write down everything you saw, heard, and felt in your journal. Or if you prefer, you can use a voice recorder and transcribe it later.

For those who have difficulty visualizing imagery, Active Imagination can be done entirely on the page through automatic writing. With your image in mind, repeat the same process but allow your pen to record what spontaneously emerges in the conversation between you and the Other. Give yourself and the Other a name for clarity on what is said by whom in the dialogue. Active Imagination may also take the form of spontaneously occurring ideas and feelings that are less conversational in nature, but no less insightful.

Dreamwork is really a multi-sensorial practice, so it can feel limiting to approach dreams with language alone. Active Imagination allows us to stay in a tactile, visual relationship with the dreamscape. We see the figure, hear its voice, and we meet it in imaginal space. Jung also encouraged us to paint and draw what comes out of these sessions. Though he wrote very little about the topic, his *Red Book* was a shining example of how these imaginative explorations can be brought to life.[9] You might choose to render your experience in a sculpture, or dance it, write a poem, song, or prayer from it. Whatever form of expression you prefer, the important thing is to keep the conversation alive by doing something to honour the wisdom you received.

REALIZING WISDOM

We know that Wisdom is found in the archetypal patterns that unfold in our dreams. Intrinsic to each of us is this organizing intelligence that holds the instructions for our potential. But its ultimate actualization requires extrinsic factors—it needs enactment of some kind in the physical world. An acorn can just as soon decay if it isn't planted, watered, and given the right sunlight and nutrition. So too must we tend to and nurture the great oak within.

Realizing wisdom is a participatory act. There are many who remain stuck and embittered by an event or problem because they've given up engaging with it, either by succumbing to a cynicism about the immutability of life or turning away from the issue out of discomfort or neglect. But it is our earnest attentiveness to the question in our hearts that excites a response from the world. Whether courting a dream, doing active imagination and somatic play, or enacting a ritual and divination to dream an idea forward, magic is made by tending to our everyday relationship with it.

We must drop the armour of disbelief or even cynicism that may have been insulating us from magic. We must be willing to trust life again, to be porous enough to be in conversation with the mystery. The participatory act requires openness and vulnerability. This can be hard when terrible things have happened in your life. If you believe the world is meaningful and responsive to you, then how do we make sense of tragedy and loss?

We make the mistake of thinking that finding meaning must be positive. Meaning often comes out of adversity. We might never have the sensitivity, perspective, and purpose we do without hardship. Post-traumatic growth only becomes possible with an acceptance of this fact. Though it's rarely possible to recognize it during the acute pain of such events, sometimes we need things to fall apart. The disenchantment and loss of meaning is precisely what gives rise to new images. They are the precursors to a new world. If things always remained as they were, we would never reach for new ideas or stretch to change our shape. Think of how often the world has been remade: how empires have fallen and been rebuilt on the ruins; how species going extinct gives rise to new genetic variations; how when an animal dies, a tiny ecosystem comes to life on its carcass. There is a danger in believing the death phase of the cycle might be perpetual—that we may never feel alive again. Grieving and railing against our losses is necessary, but when we are ready, we must actively turn toward that questing field and actively imagine a new way forward.

There is a proportional relationship between the magic you believe in and the magic you experience. There is a wonderful teaching in the *I Ching* for Hexagram 50 known as *Ting* (Cauldron). It represents the container in which personal transformation takes place. For witches, the cauldron is where magic is brewed. In Alchemy, its equivalent is the hermetic vessel. It represents the commitment and attentiveness you bring to your as-yet unmanifest future.

The quality of ingredients you add to your recipe is your offering of intent and it determines the quality of assistance you receive from the holy in nature. But once your petition has been made, you must also allow those ingredients to simmer and combine into a new form. You may experience this period of "being cooked" as a depression that feels endless, an abysmal loneliness, or even a wound that seems incurable. You may be tempted to force your way through or attempt to control the situation. But the cauldron reminds us that if you remain humble and benevolent toward yourself, the quality of your intent is all you need to contribute while the world shapes itself. When we are making soup in our house, there is always a moment when we need to step back and "let the ingredients speak to each other."

How do you forge a connection with magic when you are feeling dull, disconnected, depressed, alienated, or bitter? On the one hand, it is essential to allow for periods of grief, disconnection, and despondency in personal transformation. This is a natural response to any death process while the former self (the old life) decomposes. On the other hand, we must be conscious not to linger there too long. There is a danger of getting stuck in the cynicism of disappointment. When the demons of doubt and despair are at their worst, this is when we should stay attentive for signs of Sophia. She often appears in times of anguish to show us that the path doesn't end here. All of this is leading into our next becoming.

This is why the images in our dreams are so important. They show us what progress we are making, even if it's slow, so we can endure the hardship a little longer. We can centre these images in the cauldron of our attention, elevating their importance until they grow or multiply. Life may appear to be pushing you back, but it's likely in service to a course correction. We stay in depression for as long as is necessary to cook the ingredients of our situation until we are able to integrate them as the nourishment they are. It may not seem like it now, but whatever hardship you are enduring is forging you. And if you want clues about what you are becoming, look for the surprising elements in your dreams. Maybe it is the appearance of a new archetype, an oddly different viewpoint, or a small token of hope amidst the rubble. This is the flicker of light in an otherwise complete darkness that you must venerate and protect.

After years of mysterious and debilitating pain, I was finally diagnosed with Rheumatoid Disease in 2016. In the three years that followed, my doctors experimented with several drugs used to treat autoimmune disease. By 2019, I found myself in the depths of despair after a round of chemo that incapacitated me with such profound fatigue that I was unable to get off the couch for more than a few minutes at a time. I was in an extraordinary amount of pain that rendered me disabled on every front. I couldn't walk or lift a glass of water and needed help dressing and feeding myself— but I was also incapable of forming thoughts or sentences. On top of it all, I was experiencing chronic insomnia and was often awake all night with the anxiety of being on a speeding train heading toward my own destruction. As my husband and I dragged ourselves through this wasteland together, most of our friends disappeared from our lives. With the exception of my sweetheart, I felt excruciatingly alone. Death was so close that sometimes I swear I could feel it breathing down my neck.

One night I dreamed of arriving to a secret garden I'd frequently visited. It belonged to an elder who'd curated a luscious sanctuary in her backyard. Filled with mystical objects and thriving plants, it was a place where all the animals and creative people felt like they belonged. But when I opened the gate, I found it had been decimated. The crone had left, and the garden had been dismantled, leaving nothing but debris behind. I wandered around the remains, grieving and disoriented. Then I looked down in the rubble and found a small stone icon, upon which was painted the Minoan serpent goddess who holds a snake in each hand raised above her head. Though I didn't know it at the time, this was a dream that led me into the heart of Sophia.*

This dream began a powerful string of synchronicities that would unfold over the next two years. They kept me alive with their small but mighty promise of life on the other side of death. Serpents are often associated with the renewal of life because they shed their skin, but I also found a similar figure in depictions of the Asclepion temples—priestesses who kept snakes as "familiars" because they were understood to travel between the worlds seen and unseen, to retrieve medicines to cure the ill.

Without knowing anything about this dream, a few months later a friend of mine gave me a framed print by the photographer Holly Wilmeth of a woman wearing a boa constrictor, called "Transformation." Though it seemed impossible to believe, I took this dream and synchronicity as reassurance that there would be life after the tremendous losses I was enduring. As acts of ritual, I put Holly's photograph in a prominent place on my dream altar so

* Years later, as I was in the final stages of writing this book, I learned that the Goddess Ashera of ancient Israel, (Wisdom consort of Yaweh) was also known as *dāt batni*, "Lady of the Serpent." She is often associated with the Egyptian Goddess Qetesh who is frequently depicted holding serpents.

I could be reminded every day of this promise. And I found a painting of the Minoan goddess to cover my dream journal.

Several months later, I gathered with my dream community for our annual retreat. I asked everyone to bring an object symbolizing the longing they have for their lives and I brought Holly's photograph with me. When it came time to share, I explained that I hadn't been sure I'd be able to make it to this year's retreat because of my illness but I was given this dream of the snake goddess to hold as a promise that there would be life on the other side of so much loss and pain. I placed the photograph with the many other talismans on our shared altar that we kept alive with offerings and prayer over the following days.

On the final night of our retreat, we gathered around the bonfire under a clear and starry night as the moon rose over the orchard. We made our prayers to Sophia and told the Inuit story of the Skeleton Woman, a haunting tale about the life/death/life cycle. And as we were saying our final prayers a miracle happened. Under the full moon, a snake appeared in our circle. Thirty women gasped with amazement and silently watched the creature slither around the fire until it reached me! For a moment, it snuggled up on my left boot in the grass, where it rested. Tears sprang to my eyes as if Sophia herself had comforted me. When it was ready, the snake left through my legs out into the dark behind me.

This is a moment that years later we still recount to one another because while many of us have experienced synchronicity before, it was never in a group of that size. And never had anyone ever seen a snake appear in their circle around a fire before. A few weeks later my firekeeper, a wonderful woman named Miriam, came home one day to find a snake had left its skin on her stoop. She said she knew it was meant for me, so she bundled it up in some sacred cloth and sent it to me. It was right around that time that my doctor finally found a treatment that helped slow the progression of my disease.

You could say that Sophia provided me with a pattern to follow by offering me the image of the Serpent Goddess. Yet it would have been far easier to focus on the dismantled garden that had become my world. Once a sanctuary of vitality and belonging, my body and mind had become an inhospitable pile of rubble. The wise old woman, a supportive inner figure as well as an outer identity, was downsizing. Like her, I was no longer able to provide a place for others to gather in belonging. With my limited energy and resources, I needed to move into a less demanding way of life that wasn't as costly to my health. But I also experienced a kind of exile from the garden of my own imagination as I became unable to sleep or dream or even write. I felt I was staggering across this bleak hardship without any clear sense of being guided.

The dream mirrored all of this for me, but it also showed me that something was left behind. Something ancient and powerful was becoming available to me, and I continue to grapple with what that means in my life going forward. But it's as if I have earned something from that dismantling: a power that can only be contacted by meeting death squarely and finding something left to live for. Or at the very least, a fierceness that out of necessity cuts away anything that detracts from my sense of purpose and well-being.

There are times when it's impossible to make meaning out of what's happening to you. The crisis itself is not *for* anything and doesn't have inherent meaning. But we have a choice of what to put in our cauldron. We can stew on the disappointment, pain, loss, and levelling. Or we can choose to participate in the making of our lives, and create meaning from the rubble.

Sophia handed me an image of redemption, but I could have easily discarded it. I could have called the synchronicities surrounding it a coincidence. But instead I entered into the conversation with the Imaginal World by choosing to put the Serpent Priestess in my cauldron. The very act of putting my attention on the symbol invited it to express itself in increasingly miraculous ways. Different from "positive thinking," which is

often in denial of the excruciating truths of loss and grief, participating with Sophia can be done in disconnection, in concert with
grieving, while fumbling in the dark.

We are often taught that if we don't feel connected or guided
by something greater than ourselves, or even by our own intuition,
that something is wrong with us—that disconnection is inherently
bad. Yet everyone periodically (and even protractedly) goes
through periods of disconnection from Sophia. I think there's
enormous value in these fallow times, though it's rarely obvious as
we're going through them. Sometimes we are being stripped of
unnecessary armour. Sometimes we are hibernating and replen-
ishing depleted resources. Sometimes we haven't understood a
lesson we need to learn. Sometimes we are incubating something
deep below the surface of our consciousness and the stasis and
lack of light is a necessary condition for it to fully gestate. Maybe
it's a kindness—a period of inactivity meant to prepare you for a
demanding odyssey to follow. Or maybe you are being trained by
your own suffering to possess extraordinary compassion that may
comfort someone also trapped in the underworld.

Dreaming as a Village

NOT ONLY DOES Wisdom guide our individual lives, she works through our relationships like a mycelial network of combined intelligence. We can call this network the *ecopsyche*, which I define as the shared psyche of all beings that is indivisible from our physical world. When we share our dreams in sacred togetherness, we recognize how necessary and essential every one of us is to the creation of our shared culture. Like each having a piece of one giant puzzle, we need each other to get the complete picture of the world we're collectively creating (and holding back).

Indigenous cultures have been coming together to share and interpret their dreams for the fulfilment of self and community throughout history and on every continent. Though dreaming traditions vary widely from culture to culture, the power and potency of these circles is clearly evident, even in small dreaming groups that aren't embedded in tradition. For the sake of our future on earth, we need to bring dreaming back to the people.

When we neglect the reciprocity between the worlds, life begins to feel two-dimensional and flat. We've all been there. You may be there now. You may feel that sense of disconnection, numbness, or growing disappointment toward life. These are the symptoms of living in a materialist cul-de-sac. We have forgotten (or never been taught) how to have a conversation with the holy in nature.

Humans have never been separate from the natural world, though we have constructed elaborate and insular systems to convince us otherwise. We've gone so far with this effort that we believe our highest achievements are the places we have dominion over nature: we dam rivers for power, cut down old-growth trees for our constructions, even deprive our own bodies of basic needs to extend our productivity. Meanwhile, we are completely dependent on nature's generosity to function at the most basic levels—to breathe, drink, be nourished, shelter ourselves, etc.

In the most intimate way imaginable, nature is thriving within you through dreams, intuitions, instincts, creativity, longing, and resonance. Like all beings in the ecopsyche, the invisible intelligence of Sophia is animating your life. Though you may feel like you're in the dark, she is working tirelessly to bring you into congruence with the rest of nature. At any given time, we are either turning toward this kinship or away from it. Those who choose to follow the Dreaming Way feel a deep thrum of connection and purpose, even in times of solitude.

THE MAGIC OF DREAMSHARING

If we understand the Imaginal World as a place of wisdom transmission, ancestral knowledge, and emergent creativity, then sharing dreams in a group is like cross-pollination. Hearing what dreams others are receiving, allowing those images to also work on us, automatically diversifies and enriches our imagination.

One of the ways dreamsharing can be cultivated is at the breakfast table in your own family. The earlier a child is encouraged to remember and share their dreams, the more likely they will grow to value them throughout their lives. This will give them access to a treasure trove of resources that will not only enrich them spiritually and psychologically but will help strengthen their imaginal capacity. They need this, above all else, to create a better world for future generations.

Dreamsharing with children shouldn't be overly complicated. When you wake up together, simply start by sharing your own dream. It always helps a little one feel safe in sharing if you share first. Then you can ask, "Did you dream last night?" The Temiar people of the Malay Peninsula encourage children to share their dreams informally every morning. They have a wonderful greeting, *"Maloo' ha-ciib 'a-tee',"* meaning, "Where have you been to?" which serves as an invitation to share those dream adventures.[1]

All that's required to nurture dreaming in a young person is simply listening, maybe sharing some of your wonder with them, like, "Wow, that sounds amazing!" or "What a special dream!" You might even say, "Oh, that must have been scary!" but only if they've given you some indication that it was frightening for them. It's important, regardless of age, to not put our own feelings onto another person's dream unless we've agreed in advance to play together in that way.

It is wise to avoid interpreting or asking invasive questions to a young person regarding their dream. It's best to consider that the dream they've had is an experience unto itself and it should be treated as real. If your little one is having nightmares and feeling overwhelmed by scary dreams, you can create a talisman for them, like an animal helper or a doll with special powers who you introduce as a dream helper. Give the talisman a name and put it under their pillow before bed. Tell the child to call on them anytime they are feeling afraid in a dream and the helper will be by their side.

There was an amazing group of dreamers in Israel who came together weekly to share their dreams with each other. But rather than talking about those dreams, they painted them. One dreamer would recount a dream to the group, and then each participant in the circle would paint the image that most resonated for them. Afterwards, they would share why they chose that symbol and how it touched them personally. When everyone is done sharing, the original dreamer would tear off the parts of those paintings that felt meaningful to him or her and reassemble them in a collage. The result was a colourful collaboration that brought new perspectives together and always resulted in a layered understanding of the dream for all involved.

In the Talmud, Rabbi Bana'ah says, "There were twenty-four interpreters of dreams in Jerusalem. Once I dreamt a dream and I went round to all of them and they all gave different interpretations, and all were fulfilled."[2] It's possible that many layers are valid simultaneously: it's only when we see through different sets of eyes that we gain a complete picture.

I know of no other practice as bonding as sharing dreams. Because of the subtle nature of the experiences we have in the dreaming dimension, sharing them cuts through the superficial to reveal the most intimate concerns of the soul, often unexpectedly, to the dreamer themselves. But what we don't always anticipate is how it deepens our friendships to share at this level of intimacy. Not only do your secret pieces receive the healing balm of presence, but in some quantum, mycelial way the listener is also being worked upon by the dream's eloquence. Dreamwork is relational and the practice itself engenders closeness between us. Together, we weave the symbols into our shared lexicon, like cosmic inside jokes, as we learn to live into their teachings. Our shared metaphors are touchstones of wisdom that generate power when invoked, transporting us instantly back into that eternal dimension of our lives.

The emergence of shared themes feels miraculous because we are so often under the impression that we alone are struggling with certain blocks. But this is the real power of a dream circle—it restores the lived experience of being in an ecosystem. Not as a metaphor, but an actual ecology attempting to become conscious together. When we share our dreams in a group, not only are we pooling our resources and insights creating a broader leverage upon which to shoulder difficulty and sustain triumph, but we are a microcosm for the culture. It is much easier to make a shift in consciousness when doing it with others, and its resonance is more far-reaching. When we witness another overcoming a hindering pattern, we see how it can be done so it makes it easier for us. But also, we model different ways of overcoming so it's as if we create a power shared among ourselves that extends beyond our personal capacity.

Many people frame power as the opposite of love, as if one were the shadow of the other, and that when we are consumed with power, we are lacking in love. But Martin Luther King Jr. understood power in a very different way. He said, "Power at its best is love implementing the demands of justice, and justice at its best is power correcting everything that stands against love."[3] Different from the "power over" seen in hierarchical institutions like government, academia, and corporations, which is attained through the retention of resources and decision-making control, "power among" is a horizontal distribution of influence. It recognizes all members as necessary to the group's success, and power flows in all directions, making leadership flexible and more complex. Like a forest is an intricate network of reciprocal relationships, we too can thrive in cooperative power.

As intimacy grows between members, the circle begins to move as an ecosystem does, sharing symbols like nutrients for the group, working out toxins together, and reaching into space and light for all to thrive. The result is a more powerful shared psyche. In combined capacity, a committed dream group has broader leverage to overcome collective hindrances and envision new ways forward. I know another amazing group of dreamers, made up of

Arabs and Jews, who meet in the West Bank of Israel-Palestine to envision a future of peace between their states. They erect a tipi as a temporary dream lodge and incubate dreams together on how to achieve that vision of peace.

When people dream together, it becomes more common to experience synchronicity as a group like the experience I shared regarding the fire snake. This is because of the synergistic psychic strength of the collective. It's much harder to maintain reciprocity between the inner and outer worlds by ourselves. Just having a regular place and time to meet ritually to discuss dreams is like a heartbeat keeping the practice refreshed and alive.

In my work, I facilitate many temporary dream groups and always encourage participants to keep working together once we are done, if they are willing and able. A number of those groups have gone on for years and continue to thrive independently. Much of the dreamsharing is done virtually but some groups go on to meet at in-person retreats together. I love hearing back from these groups about the lasting friendships that have formed as a result, and the stories of magic that emerge from the shared language of resonant symbols.

Just like the rest of nature works in networks and associations, dreams are transmissions for us all. Since we are not just isolated individuals, our dreams sometimes have wisdom for others in our community or they may be predictive of something the group needs to know as a whole about its environment. It often happens in my dream groups that when one person works with and under-stands a dream, the others present feel its gifts as their own.

In some Indigenous cultures, when dreams are shared between people who live and hunt together, certain dreams are interpreted as coming from the land itself. These dreams may speak of a shared concern like oncoming weather, the migrational patterns of animals they hunt (or who hunt them), or the visionary purpose of an individual within the community. This overlap of concerns between self, others, and the earth is a worldview common to many First Nations cultures. Jeanette Armstrong, Professor of Indigenous Studies for the University of British Columbia, writes, "When we say the Okanagan word for [human beings], we are actually saying, 'the ones who are dream and land together.'" She goes on to explain that the first part of a word refers to the physical realm and the second part of the word refers to the dream or unseen world. "The third part of the word," Armstrong continues, "means that if you take a number of strands of hair or twine ... and then rub your hands and bind them together, they become one strand."[4]

This threefold way of viewing the world is found on every continent. In his book *African Psychology: The Emergence of a Tradition*, Dr. Augustine Nwoye synthesized what he found to be the shared values of diverse African cultures' perspectives on dreams. Nwoye writes, "Dreaming in Africa is taken as another way of knowing or gaining access to the truth, that is more specific and precise than is true of ordinary intuition and insight."[5] He says the fundamental aspect of African psychology is the worldview of "interpenetrating realms of existence." He describes this as an "interconnectedness that exists between humans and spirit and the individual and the community, including that of the self and the 'other.'"[6] Some dreams, he explains, are known to originate from a source other than the dreamer's personal psychology. These dreams may contain wisdom or healing advice for someone other than the dreamer, such as a neighbour, relative, or friend. I often hear similar reports of dreams that focus on a loved one's concerns, especially in more intimate relationships.

Dreamsharing in groups is also a powerful way to heal the separation between the worlds of matter and spirit in collective consciousness. It is a way of tending to their equivalence, reuniting the opposites as two perspectives on reality. We can learn from peoples throughout the world who have preserved this embedded way of thinking in their cultures.

The Ese Eja are an Indigenous group of people, dispersed along the southwestern Amazon basin of Peru and Bolivia, who have a sophisticated relationship with their dreams. In her essay "That Which I Dream Is True," anthropologist Dr. Daniela Peluso shares how the Ese Eja people observe dreaming as a place of multiple overlapping realities.

Central to Esa Eja's way of life is *Eshawa*, which roughly translates as "soul" or "spirit." But unlike our understanding of the word "soul" as belonging to the individual, Eshawa is a "concept of personhood that connects the self with all species and the spirit world." In other words, Eshawa is a "spiritual unity and corporeal diversity."[7] Personhood is a multiplicity shared with all humans, animals, and plants, as well as a shared psyche. Dreaming is understood as a way of seeing, learning, and knowing through all these perspectives. As Peluso writes, "Dreams are sources of knowledge and channels of communication between multiple worlds that feedback dynamic information unhindered by physical or ontological distances."[8] The Ese Eja also gain access to Eshawa through the use of ayahuasca, ceremony and storytelling, solo forest experiences, and some states of illness. Dreams are central to the culture because they provide literal, metaphoric, prophetic, and ancestral wisdom. They provide insight into the healing properties of plants, warnings of the dangers or opportunities in hunting and fishing, and guide the naming of children through ancestral kinship systems with animals.

The Yukaghirs are Indigenous hunters living in the basin of the upper Kolyma River in Siberia who experience no duality between waking and dreaming. As anthropologist Rane Willerslev writes, "the world of dreams and waking-life are two sides of the same reality, which together constitute one world, and neither is therefore amenable to prioritization."[9] In Willerslev's book *Soul Hunters*, he goes on to contrast how the Yukaghirs view dreaming not as an escape from conscious restraints, as Freud famously viewed it, but quite the opposite. He explains that the dreaming self "sets out in search of meanings that will help it accomplish concrete objectives in waking-life." As Willerslev puts it, "the dreaming self is as phenomenally aware as when the person is awake."[10] So while the hunter's body is asleep, his soul descends below the surface of things into "the shadow world" where he seeks "the invisible counterparts of the animals, their master-spirits, and seduces them into supplying him with prey."[11] For the Yukaghirs, whether dreaming or waking, one is always engaged in both the imaginal and the physical world, inseparable from the web of relations in their environment.

HOW TO START A DREAMSHARING GROUP

If you are interested in starting your own dreamsharing group, two things are absolutely necessary to create a community over the long term: someone willing to take the lead in calling others to gather and someone willing to answer that call. Being a dream-circle leader means shouldering considerable responsibility but responding to the invitation is also a kind of generosity. It is a way of giving relevance to the efforts and intent to forge closeness. It says that no matter how busy or tired I might be, dreamsharing with you is important to me. Ideally it's best to alternate the leadership role so that everyone can participate equally. At different times we all need to be held and dream circles work best when there is no hierarchical structure. Real intimacy is forged when everyone is willing to explore their vulnerability with the group. With enough calls made and enough answers to those calls, the fabric of community is eventually woven.

When starting a dream circle together, it's important to write some guidelines for how the process will work, what commitment is expected of your participants and, because of the sensitive nature of dreams, what ethics you vow to uphold together. Whether you're using the Courting the Dream process I've shared in this book, or some other method for working with dreams, make sure that everyone has read the instructive material before participating.

Then consider writing out your group's ethics together, or simply adapt the text that follows. Everyone should have their own copy of this text so they can review it at any time. If someone new joins the group, have them read and agree to the guidelines before joining the circle. Alternatively, a group leader can read them aloud as needed. These aren't set in stone, so if you discover a need for elaboration, or if a conflict comes up that isn't addressed in the ethics, you can democratically adapt the text. You might also decide to create a short form version of this document distilled into a few simple vows like "I will not try to fix you," "I will keep what you share confidential," "I will own my projections," and "I respect you as the expert of your own dream." Here are some suggestions to get you thinking about your own ethical guidelines for group dreamwork:

The Dreamer is the Expert: No one understands the significance of a dream better than the dreamer. Sharing your dreams in the open is a wildly intimate undertaking that places you in a position of vulnerability. As a result, anyone who claims authority over, or assigns meaning to another's dream, can bring harmful, misleading, and even dangerous consequences.

Ethical dreamwork follows the dream and the dreamer's own associations and feelings. The Courtship Method is designed to follow the dreamer's lead, giving them the ultimate authority over the depth and pace of the process. The facilitator of the session should be monitoring the process to keep the group on track, and be aware of any discomfort arising for the dreamer. It is their job to preserve the integrity of the group's ethics. At any given time, they can ask how the dreamer is feeling and if they consent to each stage in the process. If the dreamer chooses to stop sharing at any point, this decision should be treated with the utmost respect. It is always within their right to refuse to share, to say what doesn't resonate, to correct any misapprehensions, or to end the process completely, even if that's disappointing to the group.

Creating a Safe Space: Confidentiality is essential within your dreamsharing circle. Both the dreams and the life stories of all group members should remain within the group. If members have a history together, it's important that they obtain permission from one another before sharing any details from each other's lives that haven't emerged organically in the dreamwork process.

It's common for unexpected emotions to arise during dream-work and it's best if the whole range of responses are explicitly welcomed at the outset of any dream session. But dreamwork is not a substitute for psychotherapy. When it comes to dreams that replay traumatic events, the dreamer should consider working on that material with a mental health professional. There's always a danger that sharing a traumatic dream in an inexperienced environment can be re-traumatizing.

If someone decides to share a dream that has potentially triggering or graphic content, such as sexual abuse, racism, violence, or self-harm, it's best to offer a content warning to the group and ask for everyone's consent to proceed. By the same token, if the facilitator is feeling triggered or out of their depth during the session, it's important that they vocalize that feeling in a non-judgemental way to the group. In the rare case that somebody is feeling too overwhelmed to proceed, they can ask for a volunteer to take over the facilitation process.

Another way to create safety in your circle is to promise not to try to fix each other. People find this vow remarkably difficult to uphold, because when we see another person suffering, we automatically want to help them. But advice giving rarely has the power that holding presence does. When we carry the perspective that the dreamer knows best, then our energy goes into recognizing the dream's authority, insights, and unique beauty. In this way, everyone receives wisdom.

Allow for natural periods of silence within all stages of the

Courtship process. Sometimes reluctant truths and introverted speakers only emerge in the sacred pauses. Like prayer, sharing quiet moments together is a way of inviting the sacred to come through.

Diversity is Power: The real power of a dreamsharing circle is that together we bring a tapestry of perspectives and insights to bear on a single dream. As we learn to move and thrive as an ecosystem, we become increasingly skilled at being inclusive both toward the figures within our dreams and to the viewpoints of others in our circle. We also acknowledge that there may be multiple layers of meaning in a single dream, so it's best if everyone remains open to many interpretations being true at once.

There are many different dreamwork traditions around the world and the more we expose ourselves to different practices, the richer we become. While talking is a deeply effective way to work with dreams, you may want to experiment with somatic exploration, dream re-enactment, or creative play. You could also try painting your dreams or incubating solutions to community problems together. There is no single valid method for working with dreams. Along these lines, it's important to be sensitive toward the different cultural traditions, religious perspectives, sexual and gender identities, and varying abilities in your group. Vow to avoid imposing your biases and opinions on each other in all circumstances. Everyone's contribution is necessary, and our work as an ecosystem is to value all members as essential.

Own Your Projections: One of the toughest things to overcome in group dreamwork is our habit of assigning meaning to each other's symbols. It happens frequently that someone is sure they know what another member's dream is about, so they make statements to that effect or ask leading questions prompting the dreamer to the desired answer. Because they are in a vulnerable state, the dreamer is susceptible to going along with others' projections. So it is the responsibility of the facilitator and the group to make sure everyone is asking open-ended questions or framing their projections as their own using first person language.

Alternatively, you can use the projective method developed by Dr. Montague Ullman called Dream Appreciation. In his method of working with dreams, he suggests everyone in the circle pretend as if the dream were their own. Not addressing the dreamer directly, each member can offer their perspective and insight freely using the starting phrase "If this were my dream ..."[12] It's important to remember that what comes after the ellipsis must be framed using "I" language to describe one's own feelings and experiences of the dream (which may or may not be true for the dreamer).

Shares of this nature can be followed up with a question to the dreamer, such as, "What was your experience of that scene/character/situation?" This gives the dreamer the opportunity to disagree, contradict, and correct. It's important to remember that the dreamer has the final authority to discern and voice what resonates and what doesn't.

Let it Be Awkward: People carry a lot of fear of groups, sharing, and of wanting to connect to each other. There is also a lot of awkwardness around observing the sacred in a way that isn't attached to religious dogma, which invariably means we may feel like we're faking it at first. This is completely normal—we've been estranged from this way of life for so many generations. And while we long for it at the deepest level, we may also fear it. But consider that all rituals were first invented by someone often following the guidance of their dreams. Your longing to create and be held in ritual is the same longing your ancestors felt—under the same stars, the same moon, and emergent from the same wellspring of dreams. So let yourselves be awkward together. Begin to weave a new history from scratch.

To start a dream circle, all you need is the commitment to keep showing up and slowly, imperceptibly, it will begin to feel more natural. I recommend starting small. Maybe there is only one person you want to share dreams with or maybe there are four. Whatever your number, let it be more than enough. You may also want to cap your membership at six or eight. Each dreamwork session takes 60–90 minutes, so if you tend to two dreams per gathering, it could take a month for every participant to get a turn in the hot seat. It's also important to create a solid foundation with core participants before growing too large. You may decide to close your circle for a time as you build this foundation or you may feel stable enough to add new members. It's best to choose people who you feel are a good fit for your circle based on your intuition and the agreement of the group.

Decide on the intervals of your gatherings and commit to those dates. I love to gather on the new moon or the Sunday closest to that date. But you may decide you'd like to see each other more often, so you can mark new and full moons as dream circle dates. You may even decide to meet weekly! It's always a good idea to send out an email reminder a few days before a gathering with any organizational details you might need to share.

If you don't have a community hub where you can gather, you can meet in each other's homes, if it's convenient. It's preferable to rotate the location, so one person isn't always hosting the gathering for others. The more volunteers willing to host and lead the circle, the lighter the responsibility is for everyone. Mornings tend to be the best time to share dreams because they are still fresh in our minds, but any time of day works. It's best to keep the session focused and simple, maybe just bringing tea and light snacks for socializing before or after your circle. This will maximize the time you have for sharing dreams. If you're meeting virtually, consider organizing physical gatherings once a year at a destination that suits everyone to enjoy being in each other's physical company. While it's wonderful that we have online options, there's nothing quite like breaking bread together and holding hands.

Facilitation is essential in any group endeavour but when it comes to dreamsharing among peers a reciprocal leadership model tends to work best. We normally think of leadership as one person in charge. But reciprocal leadership means that everyone in the group, at one time or another, assumes the role of facilitator. Rather than one individual being expected to know everything while everyone else follows passively, every member of the group is expected to learn and hold the process for each other. The real leader in the Dreaming Way is the dream itself. So every aspect of facilitation should be in support of allowing Wisdom to reveal itself.

You may decide to designate one facilitator at each gathering to make sure everything is going as intended or you can choose to split this role between two or even three people. You may have a host taking care of the physical space, a timekeeper in charge of flow of process, and a facilitator running the ceremonial and care aspects of the circle. But logistics, ceremony, and holding the integrity of the group can also be managed by one person. It is the facilitator's job to send out the email reminders, choose whose dream will be tended to, ensure things start and end on time, and build in bathroom and snack breaks. They will also guide the process, keeping the group on track with each phase, so the group can complete the Courtship process. The facilitator will also keep an ear out for any breach of ethics if someone is interrupting, side-tracking, giving unwanted advice, or interpreting another's dream. Because you've already agreed on what the group ethics are, this should be a straightforward process for everyone involved. Ideally, you keep each other from these habits but occasionally it is necessary for the facilitator to step in and remind the group when they've strayed from the guidelines.

The facilitator should lead the opening of the circle, keep track of the dreamwork process, as detailed below, remind everyone what steps are next, and also close the circle when the gathering is complete. This may seem like a lot of responsibility, but it's important to see the group process as collaboration. If at any point you're feeling stuck or unsure of how to handle something, I encourage you to be transparent about this. The circle is there to support you. Eventually, it will become a natural process for everyone.

Before you begin, it's important to decide on how to organize your time. I recommend at least two hours per gathering, which should be plenty of time for two dreams. Any more than three hours and people will grow tired, but any less than two might not be quite enough time to go in depth. That said, it occasionally happens that a dreamer feels complete in a shorter amount of time, in which case you can ask the group if they are open to working on an additional dream, or if everyone would like to wrap up early. Here's a sample agenda followed by more in-depth sample of the process:

Opening (5–10 mins): This is when everyone gets settled, a dreamer is chosen to share, and the ceremonial prayer or intent is spoken.

Dreamsharing (10–20 minutes): If the dreamer reads the dream, ask them to tell it a second time from memory (without sharing associations). Depending on the length and detail of the dream, the amount of time it takes to share will vary but 20 minutes is usually enough time for a single dream.

Questions (30-45 minutes): In this phase, the group uses the Wonder Key to ask about the symbols in the sequence they appear in the dream and the dreamer is free to share their feelings and associations.

Reflect and Relate (5–10 minutes): This phase is for making connections from the dream back to waking-life. Once you get comfortable with the Courtship process you can combine these two Keys instead of breaking them into separate processes.

Synthesis (10–15 minutes): With an eye toward discovering the "secret longing" of the dream, the facilitator should work directly with the dreamer in this phase to synthesize the important insights that emerged from the dreamwork. When that feels complete, let the dreamer decide what symbol was most meaningful for them and allow the group to contribute ideas for how to ritualize or enact the energy of the dream.

Closing (1 mins): Take a moment to give thanks to the dreamer and the group for each dreamwork session.

Break (5 minutes): Before starting the next dream, the facilitator can suggest a bathroom break.

SAMPLE DREAMWORK PROCESS

Facilitating group dreamwork takes some practice, and your group will find its own rhythm and flow, but here are some simple steps to give you a sense of how the process might unfold. Be sure to refer back to the Courtship Keys for a more nuanced approach.

If you are gathering in person, you can designate a sacred area in your space for dreamsharing by creating a comfortable, peaceful circle of chairs or pillows. Always make sure there is tea and water nearby and provide cozy blankets in case anyone gets cold. Create a simple altar in the centre by laying down a pretty scarf or fabric, any symbolic or power objects that you've chosen together, and a candle with some matches. In my invitations to the group, I ask everyone to bring a symbolic object or living decorations, like flowers or leaves from the land, that they'd like to contribute to the altar.

I light the candle or ring a bell to signal the opening of the circle. I like to begin with a non-denominational prayer giving thanks to the group for sharing their precious time with the circle and to the holy in nature for guiding us through our dreams. I ask that we be receptive enough to hear and follow Wisdom's guidance. You might choose to add a few words about the seasonal threshold, cycle of the moon, or any natural elements at work in the world. When we acknowledge the collectively felt energies of the time, it helps to remind us of our connectedness. Sometimes I like to add an intention for our work together, such as the hope that any benefits we derive from our time together are meaningful for everyone present and everyone we come into contact with. Then I often offer the following: "May the wisdom we discover ripple out through the ecopsyche to those who need it most. Now we're ready to begin!"

1. After the circle is opened, ask if anyone would like to share a dream. It's understood that priority goes to anyone who hasn't recently shared a dream in the group. Alternatively, you could do a quick round of dreamsharing, where everyone shares something brief (under 3 minutes) about their dreams without feedback. This creates an atmosphere of intimacy since everyone gets a glimpse into each other's inner life. This may also serve to make obvious which dreamer should go first.

2. The chosen dreamer tells the dream (without associations) in its entirety. Remind them to share the dream in present tense if possible. The facilitator can then ask them to tell the story a second time if they were reading from a journal since many more details emerge when being told from the heart/memory.

3. The group listens with Embodied Presence—notice any feelings you have as the dream unfolds. Get comfortable—even excited—about not knowing where the dream or the process will lead. Listen for any communications from the unconscious (yours and theirs) in signals from the body, hits of intuition, instinctual reactions, emotions, and even synchronicities in the environment or in your own dream life.

4. The facilitator can now use the Reflection Key to recapitulate the dream to the dreamer and ask for any clarifications along the way. If they get lost or don't remember something from the dream, they can ask the dreamer, "Is there anything I missed?" or "What happens next?" Alternatively, the group can do this together, taking turns to reflect each scene or interaction from the dream in the order they unfold and combine it with the next step.

5. Each individual can now begin to follow their curiosity with the Wonder Key. The group takes turns asking questions, but it's essential to follow the sequence of the dream to support the

natural unfolding of insight. The previous step can also be combined here where a part of the dream is retold and then a question is formed from that content. For instance, "In the next scene, you are moving into a new building you described as beautiful and ancient. Can you say more about that space, and how it may have been used in the past?"

Throughout the dreamwork process, the dreamer should be explicitly invited to share any strong associations or feelings that spontaneously arise in response to the dream's images. But if the dreamer begins to stray too far from the dream material, the facilitator can gently nudge them by saying, "Let's come back to the dream," and pick up from the last scene they worked on. If the dream is overwhelmingly long, you can refer to the dramatic structure of a dream to identify the key turning points. This structure can help move you from each broad stage of the dream to the next. Alternatively, you can ask the dreamer to pick three or four significant moments in the dream that hold the most intensity or curiosity, and letting some of the extraneous detail go. focus on those core symbols.

If the circle is stuck for questions, ask the dreamer where the spirit of inquiry is leading them. The facilitator should keep an ear out for any "leading questions." These are questions that are framed to get a specific answer. For instance, "You said you were moving into an old building and found a giant open furnace, do you think you might need to express the fire of your anger?" If the dreamer hasn't made this explicit association from furnace→fire→anger, then this is a leading question derived from the group member's projection on the dream. The facilitator can point this out and ask the member to reframe it as an open-ended question. If you have a hypothesis about the dream's meaning, you can turn it into an open-ended question, like, "You said you were moving into an old building and found a giant open furnace. What do you think that furnace was used for?" You may be surprised by how the direction of your hypothesis changes when following the dreamer's lead. Though the dreamer can and will have sponta-neous associations relating to waking-life throughout the process, it's best at this stage to only ask questions about the objective dream reality.

6. The group should now have a robust description of the dream and, using the three R's of the Relating Key (relate, recog-nize, remind), can begin asking for the dreamer's associations to its symbols. For example, "You said the furnaces in the historic building were likely used for practising women's magic. Can you relate to moving into a new but ancient practice of women's magic in your life?" At this point in the process, the group should be framing their questions to find correlations between the dream dynamics and the dreamer's life.

More often than not, an entryway into the dream's significance will have already appeared spontaneously in the process. For instance, a dreamer will hear themselves say something out loud that gives them a flood of recognition in a metaphor. The facili-tator should keep an eye out for these moments in the dreamer's body language and encourage them to share their experience with the group. Such aha! moments can be an anchor in the Relating Key, giving context for future questions. For instance, let's imagine the dreamer recognizes the "move into practising natural magic" as relating to her physical move out of the city into a forest cabin where she feels more free to play with art and ritual. Now the group can look at the other symbols in the context of this magical part of her life coming alive. For instance, if a scene follows in which a family member is dismissive toward her, now we know that this creative aliveness is provoking a dismissive inner response. If an entryway into meaning hasn't become obvious yet, ask the dreamer if they have a sense of what their dream is about.

7. When the core metaphors have been bridged back to the dreamer's waking-life, the facilitator can begin the Synthesis process. I recommend taking a few moments of silence before beginning to synthesize. This allows the dream to settle, the group

to reflect on all that's been shared, and the facilitator to consider what they want to say next.

The task of this Key is to retell the dream as a coalescence of insights revealed by the Courtship process. For instance, "The dream seems to say you are moving into a new-but-ancient way of life, discovering women's magic. Having left the city and moved into the forest, you are awakening a passion for natural magic and art-making. This change is transformative for you, but it is also provoking an internal dismissiveness. What I love about this dream is that you shrug off that critical voice and turn back toward your exploration." Synthesizing a dream like this is an artform that takes time to master. When you're starting out it can help to take notes during the dreamwork process. Your notes don't need to be overly detailed, they should just help you remember the most resonant and insightful moments in the session so you can mirror them back to the dreamer.

After the facilitator has offered a synthesizing statement, the dreamer can share how they feel about the process or if they have anything to add. The group can then be invited to have a more open discussion, to share how it felt to watch the process unfold, ask any lingering questions, or point out something that may have gotten missed. Here, members can also share their projections on the dream so long as they frame their comments using first-person language. For instance, "I related so much to that moment of dismissal from the family member in the dream. I often have blocks in my own creative process where an inner critic tells me what I'm doing doesn't matter or isn't magical. I was inspired by how you shrugged it off and I could use a little of that confidence." Or, "I was struck by the furnaces in this dream and they made me think of my own anger. I've been thinking lately how helpful my anger can be in reminding me to set boundaries." The facilitator should be mindful of anyone attempting to direct any unasked-for advice toward the dreamer in this phase of the work. They can gently remind the individual that the group's role is not to give advice but support the dreamer's own knowing.

8. You will know it's time to close the session when a natural quiet comes over the group or the dreamer has expressed a resonance and gratitude for what has been revealed. Some dreams leave us with more questions than answers. So to close a dreaming process, the facilitator can ask the dreamer, "What would you say is the secret longing of this dream?" or "Which way do you think the energy of the dream wants to go?" As a final exercise, you can play together as a group with ideas for a ritual that might honour that longing and give thanks for what's been received. Finally, check in with the dreamer to make sure they feel well and complete.

As you bring your circle to a close, make an offering of your combined thanks. You can either do this "popcorn style" by asking if anyone wants to contribute their gratitude in closing or the facilitator can speak on behalf of the group. Here's an example of what I might say to close a circle:

I give thanks to [name of the dreamer] for sharing this powerful dream with us, and to everyone in our circle for sharing your presence with us today. I am grateful for the opportunity to share at this depth with you, and to be woven deeper into friendship through our shared love of dreaming. I give thanks to our families and circumstances for making room in our lives that we may be here together. I acknowledge all those who long for a place of community like this, and pray that what ripples of kindness we create in our togetherness reach their shores that they too may know belonging. I give thanks to the holy invisible helpers in our lives, be they our intuitions, instincts, feelings, or symbols for guiding our lives with Wisdom. Know that we remember you, remembering us, and may we be ever more receptive to your guidance.

With that, you may choose to blow out a candle, ring a bell, or bow to each other. When you're done and before you break the circle for socializing you can bring up logistical organizing tidbits and schedule the next session.

I thank you for taking the brave steps you are taking to create community around dreamsharing. Though it may not seem like much, you are contributing to a new culture of people who venerate their dreams and practise at belonging so the young souls who are growing up around us will feel more at home in the world.

CHAPTER 14

The Ocean in the Drop

AS I NEAR the end of writing this book, I am gifted with a special dream that I want to share with you because I think it is as much for you, as it was for me.

She's Alive

In the dream, I am midwifing the birth of a child. The labour has been touch-and-go for both mother and daughter. There were times when I thought neither would make it. But suddenly here she is, in my hands! As I cradle the tiny newborn, still covered in fluids from the womb, I notice in amazement that she has not-one-but-two umbilical cords emerging from the centre of her belly. As I watch her small chest rise and fall with breath, I feel my worries begin to ebb. She is alive and healthy. She opens her eyes for the first time and looks directly into mine. In this holy moment, we are each seeing and being seen. I carry her squirming little body to a basin of warm water and begin to bathe her feet first. As I dunk her deeper into the water, I intend to immerse myself with her.

The Jungian analyst James Hollis wrote that the Self is the

"archetype of order within us." He didn't mean order in the sense of a static arrangement of quirks and qualities, but the purposeful development unfolding in our psyche. "One might say that the Self *selves*, or that we experience it *selving* through our somatic, affective and imaginal experiences. (...) Psyche or soul, then, is simply our word for the mysterious process through which we experience the movement toward meaning."[1]

In the process of writing this book, I too have been *selving*. It was touch and go as I laboured to put language to the ineffable dimensions of Wisdom in the Dreaming Way, especially in a time of global unrest. But in so doing, my connection to Wisdom has solidified within me—as I hope she has for you. Perhaps this is why the baby has a "two-in-one" umbilical cord. She was born of two mothers, seen and unseen, both sources of essential nourishment. It is astounding to look back on that dream I received so many years ago, that first led me to follow Sophia, when I excavated the Serpent Goddess from the rubble of a dismantled garden. I never could have predicted that she would lure me into the ancient history of religion and mysticism, down into the very syntax of metaphor, even into the mind-boggling world of quantum mechanics. As I gaze into the eyes of this newborn life, and she looks back at me, I realise that in conceiving this book, I too have been made anew.

We are continuously giving birth to new versions of ourselves. Just as all life reproduces in the material world, so too is it in psyche. In the paradoxical way of wisdom, we are both creator and creation, parent and child. Fractals are perhaps the best way to visualise this marvel of nature.

The term "fractals" was coined by the mathematician Benoit Mandelbrot in 1975. It describes geometric shapes that repeat their pattern on every scale. In other words, the whole shape can be found within each small part—like how the blade of a fern is made up of tinier ferns. This phenomenon, where each scale is embedded within the next like Russian nesting dolls, is called "self-similarity" and it can be found throughout nature, including in psyche.

Commonly visualized as the Mandelbrot Set, fractals are mathematical patterns that repeat infinitely, no matter how micro or macro the scale. Though we normally think of parts making up the whole, in fractal geometry the whole makes up each part. For example, a tree has a central trunk from which branches grow, out of which twigs then sprout, from which leaves emerge—but they all have the same set of ratios and characteristics. So each twig and every branch—even the veins on each leaf—replicate or approximate the shape of the whole tree. Amazingly, the distribution of branch sizes on a single tree fractally replicates the distribution of sizes of trees in its native forest.

Another great example of a natural fractal is Romanesco broccoli which as a whole has the same spiralling shape as can be found in each of its buds. Those buds are then covered in smaller buds that reiterate the same pattern. Under a microscope, the crystals within a snowflake replicate the shape of the flake itself. You can find fractals in blood vessels, lungs, neurons, shorelines, electricity, branching rivers, and even our own heartbeats and sleep cycles. Fractals are so ubiquitous as nature's design solution to growth, resilience, distribution, and even decay, that we could call them the algorithms of the universe.

It's astounding to consider that dreams are also fractally organized. While fractals are easy to spot in the physical universe, they are much harder to measure in consciousness because they take symbolic form. But when you've worked with enough dreams, you begin to discover how one fragment of a dream can contain the pattern of the whole dream. One dream can express the core routines running in an individual's psyche. One person's psyche can echo the central dynamics of their culture. One culture's myth reiterates the elemental structure of myths everywhere. It's turtles all the way down.*

In dreams, fractals don't appear as geometric shapes but as recursive symbols, patterns, and motifs. We see this manifest in how multiple dreams in a night revolve around a single topic. Or how our earliest childhood dreams foretell the core patterns we'll be working with in our lifetime. Similarly, the first dream brought into analysis is often predictive of the central issue that will focus the course of therapy. Dreams are also fractal in how they never really have a definite beginning or ending. We always come away from a dream feeling as if there were more we can't remember. But when we bring our attention to the fragment we do have, we discover it has infinite depths. Like a fractal zoom generated on a computer, the deeper we look, the more there is to discover. The patterns that we experience in our individual dreams can also be found on larger and larger scales. As explored in Chapter 5: Patterns in the Unknown, archetypes are those symbolic fractals that transcend culture and historical epoch to echo in individual dreams everywhere.

One of the key features of fractals is that while they are self-similar, they can also have unique variations. We normally think of recurring dreams as all the same but it's more accurate to call them recursive, because while the core pattern of feelings, actions, or strategies may be the same, each dream is slightly different. The setting may have changed, the threat may be new, or you may have a different strategy in response to the situation. These variations are enormously important because they show the evolution in your fractal pattern. Think back to my dream of the monk

---

* There's an old parable of unknown origin about a young student who asks his teacher what is supporting the earth. His teacher replies, "Why the world sits on the back of a giant turtle." The student thinks about this for a moment and then asks, "But Master, what does that turtle stand on?" The Master answers, "That turtle rests on the back of an even larger turtle." "Oh," breathes the student in amazement, until a quizzical look reappears on his face. "But Master..." The Master raises his hand to stop him mid-sentence, and says, "I know where you're going with this, and you're very clever, but it's turtles all the ways down."

working on the growing edge of a spiral garden. Though he may keep arriving at the same point as he comes around the spiral, it is also new because he's gained distance from the centre. This is a potent metaphor for how we adapt to our complexes. We can't alter their basic shape in us but we can gain distance from them as we learn to regulate and broaden our perspective.

If you look at any fractal structure, you'll find its centre remains solid and stable. But as you move further toward its living edge, it grows more complex and variable, like a natural shoreline. There is a similar dynamism in our own psychological development as we alternate between periods of stability and novelty. When we stay too long in our established patterns, we eventually grow bored, rigid, and may even begin to deteriorate mentally and physically. In *A Fractal Epistemology for a Scientific Psychology*, psychologist Terry Marks-Tarlow writes, "It is a characteristic of pathological systems that they are unduly rigid and over-regular in their functioning, which makes them incapable of developing and/or adapting to changing situations."[2] When we move outwards to those edge places of newness and complexity in life, we experience growth, connectedness, and synchronicity. But we also can't give ourselves too freely over to chaos. Stability is necessary for any healthy psyche but we also need flexibility to keep growing and developing. Dreamwork is a middle way between the extremes.

It's one of the great mysteries of the universe that life emerges and decays in this way but dreamwork allows us a glimpse into the matrix of our own perceptions. While science uses microscopes and telescopes to find the patterns of the universe, we look to our recurring symbols to see how we conceive of and experience the world. In dreamwork, we are stepping into the imaginal borderlands to consciously participate with those images that shape us instead of allowing them to replicate autonomously. As we engage with our metaphors, we change the way we see the world. Like doubling the number of colours we can paint with, we develop a subtler and more complex palette for viewing and interacting with the world. When we understand a metaphor, we are becoming aware of how we perceive the issue at hand and meet it with some degree of agency. We take a step outside the habitual pattern to see the patterning field itself. This act of seeing interrupts the replication and can even reorient our perspective completely.

There are endless variations of images generated in our dreams, but, as we've discovered, they are far from random. Like a meta-consciousness, Sophia is the patterning of patterns in nature and psyche. She knows who we are meant to become, and is pulling us toward that potential. She holds an image of wholeness and refracts it back to us in every dream. When we experience that "arc of release" in discovering the correspondence between a metaphor and our waking-life, what we're feeling is the resonance of the part with the whole. Wisdom is this ability to see the totality in the splinter, to feel the pieces coming into correspondence. It soothes our anxiety because it reminds us that we aren't in charge. There is a pre-potent process at work. Whether in replication, expansion, or even collapse, these movements are in equilibrium with the Dreaming Way.

We can't ever know Sophia directly, because the deeper we look the more complex she becomes. We can follow fractals all the way down and never get to the seed algorithm, the whole that originated all the parts. In the *Tao Te Ching*, Lao Tsu wrote:

The Tao begot one.
One begot two.
Two begot three.
And three begot the ten thousand things.[3]

But if we follow the idea that the whole can be found in every small part, then we don't need to look any further than our own lives to find a universe of dynamics. We can draw a proverbial circle around ourselves and look into the micro-worlds of our

THE OCEAN IN THE DROP

dreams to see the entirety of existence. Like the sunflower, the nautilus shell, and the spiral galaxy, we came into life with an inborn pattern to fulfil. But the paradox is that we are also living in a participatory universe. We have the power to dissolve and restructure our perceptions, which in turn shapes life around us. Whether in the course of dreamwork, making art, or through somatic practices, ritual, and psychedelics, we can step into the intermediate dimension between patterns to find novel ideas coalescing. Here, in these borderlands of plasticity, we can generate new order from the chaos.

When I was writing the book *Belonging*, I was determined to follow the creativity of my dreams. Like a years-long dream incubation, I wanted to unlearn my limited beliefs on the subject that plagued my life. One of the first dreams I received was of a deck that had been freshly built onto the back of a house. The builders had cut a hole where a tree was to be planted, as if it could be wedged into place. But naturally, after some time, the tree was restricted from growing any larger and a harrowing scene followed. The deck began to rapidly decay like a time-lapse film until it dissolved into a heap of organic black ash. I understood this was my old image of belonging. Belonging wasn't a static place of attainment. Anyone wedged into a predesigned place will eventually outgrow it. Unlike fitting in, belonging had to be dynamic. This meant that exile and loneliness were equally vital on the path of true belonging. This became a core idea in the book. My old pattern of belonging had to dissolve and decay for a new, more sophisticated paradox to emerge. It utterly changed the way I conceived of belonging and it resonated for so many of my readers who recognized this truth in their own experiences.

You may think of dreamwork as a personal undertaking but in a fractal ecology, your efforts can have global implications. This is the basis of all magic and shamanism: Since the whole can be found in the fragment, any changes we make at the smallest level disperses into the ecopsyche. The implications of this are huge. It means that what is originating in the edge-places of your psyche echoes with emergent phenomena in the larger ecopsyche. This is a two-way phenomenon in that your unique discoveries also contribute to the greater unfolding of collective consciousness.

At the base of every dream there is a statement of balance. We can learn about it by asking questions: What polarities are at odds? Is one gaining traction over others? Is anyone in your inner ecosystem suffering with neglect or overcrowding? Can an effort be made to tend to their equivalence? Like other ecosystems in nature, there are many things that can lead to disequilibrium or even breakdown. For example, parasitism is when one species preys incrementally on another and causes it harm. Extinction, when a species dies out due to environmental stressors, also has cascading effects on biodiversity. Another danger is the abandonment of mutualism to live autonomously. These same dangers exist for the soul. We must learn how to tend to our inner and outer worlds, that we may keep them in harmony.

In shamanic cultures, it is the role of the medicine person to act as an intermediary for this delicate kinship; to keep the community's relations with spirits and the rest of nature in balance.[4] But it is the responsibility of *all* people to tend to that reciprocity. Whether through prayer, dreaming, eloquence, or ritual, offerings made to the unseen world are an important part of daily life. If this continuous engagement is neglected, it can result in drought, scarcity of resources, or conflict in communities. It can also manifest in illness and other human disorders like anxiety, depression, greed, and even violence. When these impulses are left unchecked, there can be a cascade of consequences for other species in our larger community.

In modern Western civilisation, we don't have such individuals designated to tend to the larger community of relations. Government generally caters to the interests of the ruling classes, doctors strictly care for the physical body, and psychoanalysts attend to the mental health of individuals privileged enough to afford them.

Most of our helpers are siloed in their specialties, vastly inconsiderate of diverse cultural and ecological contexts. The older cultures understood nature's web of relations as intimately linked to our well-being. Nothing exists in isolation from all other things and, fundamental to that worldview, dreaming is cherished for its literal, prophetic, spiritual, and metaphoric powers.

One of the essential tasks of individuation is learning to differentiate between your personal truth and the inherited beliefs of traditional society. It's from this knowing that you begin to live with real purpose, offering your unique piece into the creation of a new culture. Your soul is embedded in a diverse world of living and mutually evolving psyches, so while your dreaming is concerned with how you get along with your inner community, for better and worse, your soulbody is fractally embedded in a larger body.

When we widen our perspective to think of purpose not as personal but mutual, it becomes a practice of living in symbiosis with a larger way. Purpose is found by perceiving the needs of our ecosystem—that of the earth and our own bodies, our family systems, communities, and in consciousness itself. Purpose is the undertaking to fulfil those needs in our soul's particular way with frequency and constancy. Yes, it is about discovering your unique contribution to the world but when you strip away the context of capitalism, it is simply about living in harmony with your intrinsic pattern of truth. And that small pattern will, by its nature, fit into the larger pattern of nature's fractal ecology. It's the resonance between the two that gives you a feeling of living your purpose.

So if you are assailed by inner and outer critics who say that doing dreamwork is navel-gazing in a time of world crisis when what we really need is action—consider this: These two things are not mutually exclusive, but symbiotic. If we move into action from the same anxieties that got us into this trouble in the first place, we'll never fix the brokenness of the world. We will only replicate the conflicts we hope to solve. First we must locate ourselves in our own mythic story and in the longer, ancestral momentum of our people. Only then will we know which way to go.

As Rumi writes, "Let the drop of water that is you become a hundred mighty seas. But do not think that the drop alone becomes the Ocean—the Ocean, too, becomes the drop!"[5] Eventually, we will return to the great source from which we all came, but in the meantime, that source is animating each of our lives. To fix the world, we only have to each start with our own mighty sphere. There is a story coming through your life, which has behind it the legacy of generations. I believe the greatest work you can do is to come into knowing that story, and to nurture the emergent story in others. Not only because it connects you to a sense of meaning that will galvanize your life but because that meaning also fits into a larger pattern wanting to constellate; the story of our mutually flourishing future.

In the microcosm of your life, the entire universe is nested. When you resolve your inner conflicts, a key for peace is made available to others. When you innovate beauty, those seeds are dispersed into the great dream. While the world sows discord and ugliness, you can choose not to clone those memes. You can strive instead to propagate harmony. You always have some say in what occupies your thoughts and dreams. Beginning with yourself, you can aspire to create an atmosphere of compassion and acceptance. You can turn your intent toward the life-giving cusp of novelty.

Remember that the Imaginal World is a real place unto which you are umbilically connected. It is, and always has been, as much a source of life to you as the material world. But like the alchemical cauldron, the quality of ingredients you place there determines how well you are fed and, in turn, how well you feed the world.

Aspire to dream kinder dreams. Dream of the ancient love that is driving your destiny. Dream of rooms you've not yet discovered, and worlds you didn't know existed. Dream of eternal flames, mysterious springs, and entryways through roots of trees. Know that the earth's creativity in you is fathomless. Give your novel ideas form in the world. Honour them with eloquence in poetry, render them in bright colours on canvas, and let them move you into living your life differently.

Let your fears come close enough so you may see their true face. Know that in the heart of every poisonous and fearsome foe lies a longing to be loved, and power to be claimed. There is a medicine in your willingness to face them that will heal the world. Even your most dangerous stalkers want to be dis*spelled* in the light of your courage.

Conjure and fill your imaginal well with fresh images and forms. Be curious about the unusual, weird, and impossible creatures emerging in your dreams. Know them as living beings, who evoke responses in your body, whose wellness is interdependent with your own. Seek to understand them not just with your thoughts, but in the chambers of your resonance. Let the correlations between the worlds show themselves on their own time. All that is required of you is to make room to remember that you are a hybrid being, born of two worlds and beholden to both. What you dream matters. Not only because it's how you find the meaning of your life, but it is an essential piece of the great dream we are dreaming together.

Notes

PREFACE

1. John O'Donohue, *Anam Cara: Wisdom from the Celtic World,* Audio Version, Sounds True (1996)

1. THE IMAGINAL WORLD

1. The Gospel of Philip, *The Nag Hammadi Scriptures,* edited by Marvin Meyer, HarperOne (May 26, 2009)
2. Henry Corbin, "Mundus Imaginalis or "The Imaginary and the Imaginal," delivered at the Colloquium on Symbolism in Paris in June 1964, and appeared in *Cahiers internationaux de symbolisme 6,* Brussels 1964, p 3–26
3. Dr. Bettany Hughes, author and historian, in an interview for *English Heritage* (2016)
4. Clarissa Pinkola Estes, *Women Who Run with the Wolves: Myths and Stories of the Wild Woman Archetype,* Ballantine Books (1995)
5. Madeline Miller wrote *The Song of Achilles,* Ecco (2012) and *Circe,* Back Bay Books (2020)
6. John Keats, *On Negative Capability: Letter to George and Tom Keats,* Hampstead, Sunday, (22 December 1818)
7. This quote is from a collection on nature compiled by the Sufi Inayati Order in New Zealand: https://sufinz.com/nature/
8. Carlos Castaneda, *The Teachings of Don Juan: A Yaqui Way of Knowledge,* University of California Press, (1968)
9. Interview with Marc Ian Barasch in *The Sun Magazine* (Issue 248, 2011)

2. WISDOM OF SOPHIA

1. Translated by Nathaniel Campbell, from the Latin text of Hildegard of Bingen, *Liber Divinorum Operum,* ed. A. Derolez and P. Dronke, in CCCM 92 (Turnhout: Brepols, 1996)
2. J. Gary Sparks, private audio seminar on Marie Louise Von Franz's book, *Aurora Consurgens*
3. For a deeper exploration of the relationship between feminist theory and Jungian studies: Susan Rowland, *Jung: A Feminist Revision* Polity, (2002)
4. Bernard Anderson, *Understanding the Old Testament,* Pearson (1975), *p 568*
5. Sharon Ryan (2007), *Nicomachean Ethics,* VI, (1141b)

6. Valerie Tiberius, *The Reflective Life: Living Wisely with Our Limits*, Oxford University Press, (2008)
7. Anderson, *Understanding the Old Testament*, (p 577)
8. Marie Louise Von Franz, *Number and Time: Reflections Leading Toward a Unification of Depth Psychology and Physics*, Northwestern University Press (1986), p. 214
9. Definition of "ḥokhmah" from Encyclopedia.com
10. Prov. 8:21–31, New Revised Standard Version Updated Edition
11. 1 Corinthians 1:30
12. Margaret Barker, *The Secret Tradition, Journal of Higher Criticism*, (1995)
13. Wisdom of Solomon 7:22–8:1, New Oxford RSV
14. Anne Baring, "A Crucial Time of Choice," article in *Paradigm Explorer*, (2021)
15. Anne Baring, *The Dream of the Cosmos: A Quest for the Soul*, Chapter 4: The Great Mother, Archive Publishing, (2019)
16. Baring, "A Crucial Time of Choice"
17. Eric Neumann, *The Great Mother* (1955), p 331
18. Jerusalem Bible, Sirach-Ecclesiasticus, (6:26)
19. Anderson, *Understanding the Old Testament*
20. von Franz, *Number and Time*, (p 35)
21. Ibid.
22. Translated by James M. Robinson, *The Thunder, Perfect Mind*, The Nag Hammadi Library, HarperCollins, (1990)
23. Carl Gustav Jung, Collected Works (CW) 13 § 163
24. Marie-Louise von Franz, *Aurora Consurgens: On the Problem of Opposites in Alchemy*, a companion volume to C.G. Jung's *Mysterium coniunctionis*, Inner City Books, (2000) Originally published (1966)
25. Ibid.
26. Ibid., forward ix
27. Hildegard of Bingen, "Antiphon for the Angels" from *Symphonia: A Critical Edition of the "Symphonia Armonie Celestium Revelationum,"* translated by Barbara Newman, Cornell University Press (1988, 1998)
28. Sparks, Aurora audio seminar
29. Viktor E. Frankl, *Man's Search for Meaning*, Beacon Press, (2006), originally published (1946)
30. Toni Morrison "No Place for Self-Pity, No Room for Fear," The Nation magazine, (2015)
31. Marija Gimbutas, *The Language of the Goddess*, Thames and Hudson (2006)
32. Marija Gimbutas, *The Living Goddesses*, University of California Press (2001)
33. Lucius Apuleius, translated by Robert Graves, *The Golden Ass: The Transformations of Lucius*, Farrar, Straus and Giroux (1951)
34. Susan Cole, Marian Ronan, Hal Taussig, *Wisdom's Feast: Sophia in Study and Celebration*, Sheed & Ward (1996) p 60
35. Sparks, Aurora audio seminar
36. C. G. Jung, *CW 20: Mysterium Coniunctionis*, Princeton University Press (1970)
37. Ibid.

3. ORIENTATION IN THE OTHERWORLD

1. Terence McKenna, *Empowering Hope in Dark Times*, lecture at the Wilshire Ebell Theater (June 2, 1991)
2. Graham Harvey, *Animism: Respecting the Living World*, Columbia University Press (2005)
3. "μυώ" (mystikos) WordReference English-Greek Dictionary, WordReference.com. Archived from the original on November 4, 2016.
4. Robinson, *The Thunder, Perfect Mind*
5. Henry Corbin, *The Voyage and the Messenger: Iran and Philosophy*, North Atlantic Books (1998)
6. Sparks, Aurora audio seminar
7. The term "mother tree" is from *Finding the Mother Tree* by ecologist Suzanne Simard, Allen Lane (2021)
8. Richard Tarnas, *Cosmos and Psyche: Intimations of a New World View*, Plume/Penguin Group, 2006
9. For more on the history of Lucid Dreaming see S.A. Mota-Rolim, K. Bulkeley, S. Campanelli, B. Lobão-Soares, S. de Araujo DB, Ribeiro, "The Dream of God: How Do Religion and Science See Lucid Dreaming and Other Conscious States During Sleep?" *Front Psychol.* 2020 Oct 6;11:555731. doi: 10.3389/fpsyg.2020.555731

4. TYPES OF DREAMS

1. C. G. Jung, *Memories, Dreams, Reflections*, Vintage (1965) p 175-176
2. For more reading on this topic, see *Real Magic: Ancient Wisdom, Modern Science, and a Guide to the Secret Power of the Universe* by Dean Radin PhD, Harmony (2018), or *Morphic Resonance: The Nature of Formative Causation* by Rupert Sheldrake, Park Street Press (2009)
3. H. Loewald, "On the therapeutic action of psychoanalysis. *International Journal of Psychoanalysis*," 41 (1960), p 29
4. https://adaa.org/understanding-anxiety/facts-statistics
5. "... the cause of neurosis is the discrepancy between the conscious attitude and the trend of the unconscious." C.G. Jung, *CW 16*, §26
6. The Tavistock Lectures, *CW 18*, §389
7. James Hollis, *Tracking the Gods: The Place of Myth in Modern Life*, Inner City Books, (1995)
8. Erin J. Wamsley, "Dreaming and Offline Memory Consolidation," *Curr Neurol Neurosci Rep.* 2014 Mar; 14(3): 433
9. J. O'Neill, B. Pleydell-Bouverie, J. Dupret D, Csicsvari, "Play it again: reactivation of waking experience and memory," *Trends Neurosci.* 2010;33:220–9
10. L. De Gennaro, C. Cipolli, A. Cherubini, et al., "Amygdala and hippocampus volumetry and diffusivity in relation to dreaming," *Hum Brain Mapp.* 2011;32(9):1458–70. doi:10.1002/hbm.21120
11. C.G. Jung, *CW 8*, §342

12. C.G. Jung, "The Psychology of the Child Archetype," *CW 9i*, §267
13. *The Book of Symbols: Reflections on Archetypal Images,* Taschen; Illustrated edition (2010)
14. Marc Ian Barasch, *Healing Dreams,* Riverhead (2002)
15. Stephen LaBerge PhD and Howard Rheingold, *Exploring the World of Lucid Dreaming,* Ballantine Books (1991)
16. Collins English Dictionary, 7th ed. (2005)
17. "Numinous." Merriam-Webster.com Dictionary, Merriam-Webster (2024)
18. Ryan Hurd, *Sleep Paralysis: A Guide to Hypnagogic Visions and Visitors of the Night,* Hyena Press (2010) is a good resource for anyone struggling with these kinds of dreams.

5. METAPHOR: LANGUAGE OF KINSHIP

1. Oxford Learner's Dictionary, s.v. "metaphor, n., (July 2023)
2. M. Davis, *Aristotle's Poetics: The Poetry of Philosophy,* Rowman & Littlefield Publishers, (1992)
3. Kristen C. Elmore and Myra Luna-Lucero, "Light Bulbs or Seeds? How Metaphors for Ideas Influence Judgments about Genius," *Social Psychological and Personality Science,* Volume 8, Issue 2 (DOI 10.1177/1948550616667611), 2016
4. Ibid.
5. Paul H. Thibodeau, Leah Boroditsky, *Metaphors We Think With: The Role of Metaphor in Reasoning,* (2011)
6. Jan Zwicky, *Wisdom & Metaphor,* Brush Education; Revised edition (2014), p 16
7. Louise Glück, *The Best American Poetry,* Collier Books (1993)
8. "Sleep and sensorimotor integration during early vocal learning in a songbird," by Sylvan S. Shank and Daniel Margoliash, *Nature* (2009). doi: 10.1038/nature07615
9. A. Pophale, K. Shimizu, T. Mano, et al., "Wake-like skin patterning and neural activity during octopus sleep. "*Nature* 619, 129–134 (2023). https://doi.org/10.1038/s41586-023-06203-4
10. Zwicky, Wisdom & Metaphor, p 11
11. Edward F. Edinger, *Archetype of the Apocalypse: Divine Vengeance, Terrorism, and the End of the World,* Open Court, (1999) p 1–7

6. PATTERNS IN THE UNKNOWN

1. Christopher Alexander, et al., *A Pattern Language: Towns, Buildings, Construction,* Oxford University Press; Illustrated edition (1977)
2. Paraphrasing Carl Jung. Ann Belford Ulanov, *The Feminine in Jungian Psychology and in Christian Theology,* Northwestern University Press, (1971) p 48

3. Arthur Darby Nock, *Sallustius: Concerning the Gods and the Universe*, Cambridge University Press; Illustrated edition (2013)
4. James Hillman, "Why Study Greek Mythology," lecture at Pacifica Graduate Institute for Myth program, (December 13, 1994)
5. Ibid.
6. Hans Christian Andersen, *The Ugly Duckling, New Fairy Tales*. First Volume. First Collection, Nye Eventyr. Første Bind. Første Samling, (1843)
7. Toko-pa Turner, *Belonging: Remembering Ourselves Home*, Her Own Room Press (2018)
8. Anderson, (1843)
9. C. G. Jung, *Mysterium Coniunctionis*, p 545
10. Mizuta Masahide, *Zen Poetry: Let the Spring Breeze Enter*, Translated by Lucien Stryk, Takashi Ikemoto, Grove Press; First edition (1995)
11. Anderson, (1843)
12. Translated by Nathanial M. Campbell, from the Latin text of Hildegard of Bingen, *Liber Divinorum Operum*, The Catholic University of America Press, (2018), p 47–49
13. Joseph Campbell, *Myths to Live By*, Penguin Books (1993), p 14
14. C.G. Jung, CW: Volume 8: Structure & Dynamics of the Psyche,(1970), § 561–564

7. UNIVERSAL DREAM ELEMENTS

1. Long since out of print, this influential book by Hall/Van de Castle, *The Content Analysis of Dreams*, was published by Appleton-Century-Crofts (1966).
2. *Castle and Hall's original ten categories were* Characters, Social Interactions, Activities, Striving: Success and Failure, Misfortunes and Good Fortunes, Emotions, Physical Surroundings: Settings and Objects, Descriptive Elements, Food and Eating, and Elements from the Past.
3. James Hollis, *Finding Meaning in the Second Half of Life: How to Finally, Really Grow Up*, Gotham Books (2005), p 153–54
4. C.G. Jung, "A Review of the Complex Theory," *CW, Vol 8*, p 92
5. Rollo May, "Freedom and Responsibility Re-Examined," *Behavioral Science and Guidance: Proposals and Perspectives, (1963)*
6. Sean Kane, *Wisdom of the Mythtellers*, Broadview Press, (1998) p 113
7. James Hillman, Margot McClean, *Dream Animals*, San Francisco: *Chronicle* (1997)
8. James Hillman, "The Animal Kingdom in the Human Dream," Eranos lecture, (1982)
9. Andy Fisher, *Radical Ecopsychology*, State University of New York Press, (2013) p 95
10. C.G. Jung, "Psychological Aspects of the Mother Archetype," 1938/1954, *CW 9i*, § 184

8. FORGETTING AND REMEMBERING

1. Carlos Castaneda, *The Teachings of Don Juan: A Yaqui Way of Knowledge*, University of California Press, (1968)
2. C.G. Jung, *The Red Book: A Reader's Edition*, WW Norton; Illustrated edition (2012)

9. COURTING THE DREAM

1. *My Octopus Teacher is a documentary* directed by Pippa Ehrlich and James Reed, starring Craig Foster, (2020).
2. "wonder." *The Oxford Pocket Dictionary of Current English*. Encyclopedia.com, (18 Oct. 2023)
3. David Whyte in his interview for "On Being with Krista Tippett," (2016)
4. Zwicky, *Wisdom & Metaphor*, (§ 60)
5. Charles Simic, "Notes on Poetry and Philosophy," *Wonderful Words, Silent Truth*, University of Michigan Press (1990) p 64
6. Zwicky, *Wisdom & Metaphor*, p 11
7. David Whyte, "Sometimes," *David Whyte Essentials*, Many Rivers Press (2019)

10. POISON IS THE MEDICINE

1. Turner, *Belonging: Remembering Ourselves Home*
2. Robert Louis Stevenson, *The Strange Case of Dr. Jekyll and Mr. Hyde*, Longmans, Green & Co. (1886)
3. Robert Bly, *A Little Book on the Human Shadow*, Harper One (1988)
4. The source of this paraphrase in unknown, but refers to Rule 6 of Turkish author Elif Shafak's *Forty Rules of Love*, a novel about the thirteenth-century Sufi poet Jalāl al-Dīn Muḥammad Rumi (Persian: جلال‌الدین مُحمّد رُومی) and his teacher Shams-i-Tabrīzī (Persian: شمس تبریزی) (1185–1248), Penguin Books (2011)
5. Marie Louise von Franz, *Projection and Re-Collection in Jungian Psychology*, Open Court (1999) p 51–52
6. *Dancing in the Flames* is a documentary about Marion Woodman directed by Adam Greydon Reid (2009)
7. Von Franz, *Projection and Re-Collection in Jungian Psychology* (1999)
8. Ibid.
9. C.G. Jung, *CW 13: Alchemical Studies*, § 335 (1945)

11. WISDOM IN MATTER

1. This quote is from the video "Wholeness & Fragmentation," a short excerpt from David Bohm's presentation in Amsterdam, in 1990, as featured in the documentary Art Meets Science & Spirituality in a Changing Economy.

2. Lloyd Khan, *Builders of the Pacific Coast*, Shelter Publications; Illustrated edition (2008)
3. Annie Dillard, *Pilgrim at Tinker Creek*, Harper Perennial Modern Classics (2013)
4. C.G. Jung, Wolfgang Pauli, *Atom and Archetype: The Pauli/Jung Letters*, Princeton University Press; Revised edition (2014)
5. Ibid.
6. Ibid.
7. Ibid.
8. Derrick Jensen, *Dreams*, Seven Stories Press (2011) p 236
9. Jung/Pauli, *Atom and Archetype*
10. Erich Neumann, "Mystical Man," (1948), *The Mystic Vision; Papers from the Eranos Yearbooks*, edited by Joseph Campbell, Bollingen Series XXX, Princeton University Press (1968)
11. C. G. Jung, *CW: Vol 14, Mysterium Coniunctionis: An Inquiry into the Separation and Synthesis of Psychic Opposites in Alchemy*, Routledge & Kegan Paul, (1963)
12. Max Delbruck quoting Niels Bohr, "Mind from Matter: An Essay on Evolutionary Epistemology" Blackwell Scientific Publications; First Edition (January 1, 1986)

12. RITUALS AND ENACTMENTS

1. Jalal ad-Din Muhammad Rumi, from the poem "The Way That Moves as You Move," *A Year with Rumi: Daily Readings by Coleman Barks*, Harper San Francisco, (2006) p 137
2. Gary Snyder, *Axe Handles: Poems*, Counterpoint LLC; Reprint edition (2005)
3. J. Piaget, *Language and Thought of the Child*, Routledge (1923)
4. "animism." APA Dictionary of Psychology, (2023)
5. Terence McKenna, interview in Hawaii, October 1998 (https://youtu.be/IkAVnG-Jya8?t=945) Transcript: https://www.asktmk.com/talks/Time+and+the+I+Ching
6. C.G. Jung, *CW 15*, §74
7. Robert A. Johnson, *Inner Work: Using Dreams and Active Imagination for Personal Growth*, HarperOne; Revised ed. edition (2009)
8. C.G. Jung, *Letters Vol. 1*, p 28–29
9. C.G. Jung, *The Red Book*, WW Norton; Illustrated edition (2009)

13. DREAMING AS A VILLAGE

1. Sarvananda Bluestone PhD, *The World Dream Book*, Destiny Books (2002) p 219
2. Babylonian Talmud: Tractate Berakhot 55b
3. Martin Luther King Jr., *The Autobiography of Martin Luther King, Jr.*, Grand Central Publishing; Illustrated edition (2001)
4. Jeanette Armstrong, "Sharing One Skin," *Cultural Survival*, (2010)

5. Dr. Augustine Nwoye, *African Psychology: The Emergence of a Tradition*, Oxford University Press, (2022) p 182–185
6. Ibid.
7. Daniela M. Peluso, "That Which I Dream Is True: Dream Narratives in an Amazonian Community," *Dreaming: Journal of the Association for the Study of Dreams*, Vol 14 (2004)
8. Ibid.
9. Rane Willerslev, *Soul Hunters: Hunting, Animism, and Personhood Among the Siberian Yukaghirs*, University of California Press; 1st edition (2007) p 176
10. Ibid., p 175
11. Ibid.
12. Montague Ullman, *Appreciating Dreams: A Group Approach*, Cosimo Publications (2006) p 34

14. THE OCEAN IN THE DROP

1. James Hollis, *Swamplands of the Soul: New Life in Dismal Places*, Inner City Books (1996) p12
2. Terry Marks-Tarlow et al., *Fractal Epistemology for a Scientific Psychology*, Cambridge Scholars Publishing (2020)
3. Lao Tsu, *Tao Te Ching*, translated by Feng & English, (1972), chapter 42
4. For further reading on Shamanism: *Archaic Techniques of Ecstasy* by Mircea Eliade, Princeton University Press (2020), *The Woman in the Shaman's Body: Reclaiming the Feminine in Religion and Medicine* by Barbara Tedlock, Bantam (2005), *Food of the Gods: The Search for the Original Tree of Knowledge A Radical History of Plants, Drugs, and Human Evolution* by Terence McKenna, Bantam (1993), *The Way of the Shaman* by Michael Harner, HarperOne (1990)
5. Rumi, *A Garden Beyond Paradise*, trans, by Jonathan Star, Bantam Books (1992), p 148–149

Acknowledgments

It's a wonder this book came to life during what turned out to be a period of tremendous upheaval in history, both in my personal life and in the world. But one global pandemic, multiple social uprisings, two *sellovictions*, chronic illness, and one move across the country later, she is alive thanks to a handful of amazing allies.

I am especially grateful to my beloved friend and editor Terri Kempton. I can't imagine writing any books without the clarifying wisdom of our friendship. Terri's formidable partner Connor Cochran has also been an essential part of my publishing journey, supporting me with everything from contracts to book design, and even shipping. I am lucky to call these people family, and aspire to their living example of generosity.

This book would not have been possible without the contributions of my old friend Gary Sparks, who first introduced me to Sophia, and offered me his expertise on wisdom in hours of recorded lectures.

To my closest friend, Peter DeLeeuw, I offer thanks for lovingly pushing me further into my daring with his brilliant and poetic marginalia. Sue Ann Gleason, for her fantastic feedback and meticulous edits. Lucy H. Pearce for encouraging me to share more of my story, J.K. Fowler for stepping in at a crucial moment to let me know I was further along than I realised, and Marie Eve Noel, who offered me her lakeside cottage in Quebec to finish this writing.

Finally, I owe my deepest debt of gratitude to Craig Paterson, my astounding partner and best friend in life. You keep me going in both practical and figurative ways every single day. Thank you for being your patient, wise, and delightfully weird self—and for buying me emergency bagels when I needed them.

Toko-pa was named after a Maori deity—the *Parent of the Mist*. Her maternal grandparents survived the Holocaust and emigrated from Warsaw to Canada, with the resilience and strength of their ancestors. Toko-pa's rich cultural heritage as an Ashkenazi Jew born on a farm in Devon, then raised in Montreal as a Sufi in the Ināyati Order, shaped her distinctive path.

A musician and arts journalist, Toko-pa's journey took a profound turn when she returned to Sufism and the study of dreams in her late twenties. She founded the Dream School in 2001, teaching a unique blend of Sufism with Jungian dreamwork, and has since nurtured a global community of dreamers.

She released her first book *Belonging: Remembering Ourselves Home (2018)*, about the human longing for connection. It won several awards including the 2018 Gold Nautilus and the 2018 Gold Readers' Favourite, and has been translated into 10 different languages.

Toko-pa currently resides in a historic Ottawa Valley village with her husband Craig, under the wisdom of a centuries-old oak tree, continuing to inspire and guide others on their own path to belonging.

Made in the USA
Las Vegas, NV
20 September 2024

95562491R00215